Sandra K. Roe, MS
Alan R. Thomas, MA, FLA
Editors

The Thesaurus: Review, Renaissance, and Revision

The Thesaurus: Review, Renaissance, and Revision has been co-published simultaneously as *Cataloging & Classification Quarterly*, Volume 37, Numbers 3/4 2004.

Pre-publication
REVIEWS,
COMMENTARIES,
EVALUATIONS...

"**A** GREAT COLLECTION that explains what was, what is, and gives just a glimpse of what could be. It will become a resource on any shelf.... Brings together authors who have experience in all facets of the thesaurus world–creating, managing, teaching, leveraging, evaluating, consulting, selecting software, and speculating on future designs to support the use and exchange of thesauri."

Vivian Bliss, MSLIS, JD
Taxonomist
MSX User Assistance
Microsoft Corporation

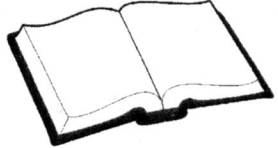

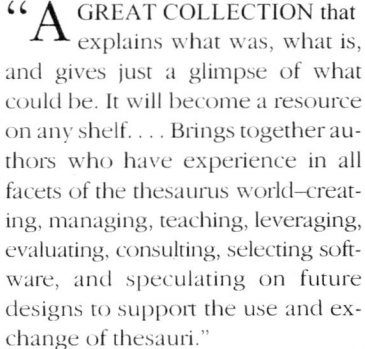

More pre-publication
REVIEWS, COMMENTARIES, EVALUATIONS

"THIS BOOK IS THE MISSING LINK that connects 50 years of experience in traditional thesaurus construction to the age of the Internet. By uniting the substantial knowledge base about thesauri that resides within the field of library and information science with fresh insights into the use of controlled vocabularies on the World Wide Web, the editors have succeeded in assembling A TRULY VALUABLE TEXT. Whether you're an aspiring information architect or an experienced library professional, this book is REQUIRED READING. . . . PUTS HTML, XML, TOPIC MAPS, AND THE SEMANTIC WEB INTO CONTEXT."

Peter Morville
President
Semantic Studios
Co-author of Information Architecture for the World Wide Web

"VERY VALUABLE for students and others who are building their first thesaurus. The chapter on the history of the thesaurus and relevant standards is excellent. The book provides a good overview of the methods used to evaluate a thesaurus. It also contains an inspiring chapter that gives a lot of new insights into how thesauri can be used to improve subject access in networks and the Internet, discussing the proposed Thesauro-Web, a network of thesaurus access and navigation services based on XML."

Gerhard J. A. Riesthuis, PhD
Docent
University of Amsterdam
Department of Archive
and Information Sciences

The Haworth Information Press
An Imprint of The Haworth Press, Inc.

The Thesaurus: Review, Renaissance, and Revision

The Thesaurus: Review, Renaissance, and Revision has been co-published simultaneously as *Cataloging & Classification Quarterly*, Volume 37, Numbers 3/4 2004.

Cataloging & Classification Quarterly™ Monographic "Separates"

Below is a list of "separates," which in serials librarianship means a special issue simultaneously published as a special journal issue or double-issue *and* as a "separate" hardbound monograph. (This is a format which we also call a "DocuSerial.")

"Separates" are published because specialized libraries or professionals may wish to purchase a specific thematic issue by itself in a format which can be separately cataloged and shelved, as opposed to purchasing the journal on an on-going basis. Faculty members may also more easily consider a "separate" for classroom adoption.

"Separates" are carefully classified separately with the major book jobbers so that the journal tie-in can be noted on new book order slips to avoid duplicate purchasing.

You may wish to visit Haworth's Website at . . .

> http://www.HaworthPress.com

. . . to search our online catalog for complete tables of contents of these separates and related publications.

You may also call 1-800-HAWORTH (outside US/Canada: 607-722-5857), or Fax 1-800-895-0582 (outside US/Canada: 607-771-0012), or e-mail at:

> docdelivery@haworthpress.com

- ***The Thesaurus: Review, Renaissance, and Revision,*** edited by Sandra K. Roe, MS, and Alan R. Thomas, MA, FLA (Vol. 37, No. 3/4, 2004). *Examines the historical development of the thesaurus, and the standards employed for thesaurus construction, use, and evaluation.*

- ***Knowledge Organization and Classification in International Information Retrieval,*** edited by Nancy J. Williamson, PhD, and Clare Beghtol, PhD (Vol. 37, No. 1/2, 2003). *Examines the issues of information retrieval in relation to increased globalization of information and knowledge.*

- ***Electronic Cataloging: AACR2 and Metadata for Serials and Monographs,*** edited by Sheila S. Intner, DLS, MLS, BA, Sally C. Tseng, MLS, BA, and Mary Lynette Larsgaard, MA, BA (Vol. 36, No. 3/4, 2003). *"The twelve contributing authors represent some of the most important thinkers and practitioners in cataloging." (Peggy Johnson, MBA, MA, Associate University Librarian, University of Minnesota Libraries)*

- ***Historical Aspects of Cataloging and Classification,*** edited by Martin D. Joachim, MA (classical languages and literatures), MA (library science) (Vol. 35, No. 1/2, 2002 and Vol. 35, No. 3/4, 2003). *Traces the development of cataloging and classification in countries and institutions around the world.*

- ***Education for Cataloging and the Organization of Information: Pitfalls and the Pendulum,*** edited by Janet Swan Hill, BA, MA (Vol. 34, No. 1/2/3, 2002). *Examines the history, context, present, and future of education for cataloging and bibliographic control.*

- ***Works as Entities for Information Retrieval,*** edited by Richard P. Smiraglia, PhD (Vol. 33, No. 3/4, 2002). *Examines domain-specific research about works and the problems inherent in their representation for information storage and retrieval.*

- ***The Audiovisual Cataloging Current,*** edited by Sandra K. Roe, MS (Vol. 31, No. 2/3/4, 2001). *"All the great writers, teachers, and lecturers are here: Olson, Fox, Intner, Weihs, Weitz, and Yee. This eclectic collection is sure to find a permanent place on many catalogers' bookshelves. . . . Something for everyone. . . . Explicit cataloging guidelines and AACR2R interpretations galore." (Verna Urbanski, MA, MLS, Chief Media Cataloger, University of North Florida, Jacksonville)*

- ***Managing Cataloging and the Organization of Information: Philosophies, Practices and Challenges at the Onset of the 21st Century,*** edited by Ruth C. Carter, PhD, MS, MA (Vol. 30, No. 1/2/3, 2000). *"A fascinating series of practical, forthright accounts of national, academic, and special library cataloging operations in action. . . . Yields an abundance of practical solutions for shared problems, now and for the future. Highly recommended." (Laurel Jizba, Head Cataloger, Portland State University Library, Oregon)*

The LCSH Century: One Hundred Years with the Library of Congress Subject Headings System, edited by Alva T. Stone, MLS (Vol. 29, No. 1/2, 2000). *Traces the 100-year history of the Library of Congress Subject Headings, from its beginning with the implementation of a dictionary catalog in 1898 to the present day, exploring the most significant changes in LCSH policies and practices, including a summary of other contributions celebrating the centennial of the world's most popular library subject heading language.*

Maps and Related Cartographic Materials: Cataloging, Classification, and Bibliographic Control, edited by Paige G. Andrew, MLS, and Mary Lynette Larsgaard, MA, BA (Vol. 27, No. 1/2/3/4, 1999). *Discover how to catalog the major formats of cartographic materials, including sheet maps, early and contemporary atlases, remote-sensed images (i.e., aerial photographs and satellite images), globes, geologic sections, digital material, and items on CD-ROM.*

Portraits in Cataloging and Classification: Theorists, Educators, and Practitioners of the Late Twentieth Century, edited by Carolynne Myall, MS, CAS, and Ruth C. Carter, PhD (Vol. 25, No. 2/3/4, 1998). *"This delightful tome introduces us to a side of our profession that we rarely see: the human beings behind the philosophy, rules, and interpretations that have guided our professional lives over the past half century. No collection on cataloging would be complete without a copy of this work." (Walter M. High, PhD, Automation Librarian, North Carolina Supreme Court Library; Assistant Law Librarian for Technical Services, North Carolina University, Chapel Hill)*

Cataloging and Classification: Trends, Transformations, Teaching, and Training, edited by James R. Shearer, MA, ALA, and Alan R. Thomas, MA, FLA (Vol. 24, No. 1/2, 1997). *"Offers a comprehensive retrospective and innovative projection for the future." (The Catholic Library Association)*

Electronic Resources: Selection and Bibliographic Control, edited by Ling-yuh W. (Miko) Pattie, MSLS, and Bonnie Jean Cox, MSLS (Vol. 22, No. 3/4, 1996). *"Recommended for any reader who is searching for a thorough, well-rounded, inclusive compendium on the subject." (The Journal of Academic Librarianship)*

Cataloging and Classification Standards and Rules, edited by John J. Riemer, MLS (Vol. 21, No. 3/4, 1996). *"Includes chapters by a number of experts on many of our best loved library standards.... Recommended to those who want to understand the history and development of our library standards and to understand the issues at play in the development of new standards." (LASIE)*

Classification: Options and Opportunities, edited by Alan R. Thomas, MA, FLA (Vol. 19, No. 3/4, 1995). *"There is much new and valuable insight to be found in all the chapters.... Timely in refreshing our confidence in the value of well-designed and applied classification in providing the best of service to the end-users." (Catalogue and Index)*

Cataloging Government Publications Online, edited by Carolyn C. Sherayko, MLS (Vol. 18, No. 3/4, 1994). *"Presents a wealth of detailed information in a clear and digestible form, and reveals many of the practicalities involved in getting government publications collections onto online cataloging systems." (The Law Librarian)*

Cooperative Cataloging: Past, Present and Future, edited by Barry B. Baker, MLS (Vol. 17, No. 3/4, 1994). *"The value of this collection lies in its historical perspective and analysis of past and present approaches to shared cataloging.... Recommended to library schools and large general collections needing materials on the history of library and information science." (Library Journal)*

Languages of the World: Cataloging Issues and Problems, edited by Martin D. Joachim (Vol. 17, No. 1/2, 1993). *"An excellent introduction to the problems libraries must face when cataloging materials not written in English.... should be read by every cataloger having to work with international materials, and it is recommended for all library schools. Nicely indexed." (Academic Library Book Review)*

Retrospective Conversion Now in Paperback: History, Approaches, Considerations, edited by Brian Schottlaender, MLS (Vol. 14, No. 3/4, 1992). *"Fascinating insight into the ways and means of converting and updating manual catalogs to machine-readable format." (Library Association Record)*

Enhancing Access to Information: Designing Catalogs for the 21st Century, edited by David A. Tyckoson (Vol. 13, No. 3/4, 1992). *"Its down-to-earth, nontechnical orientation should appeal to practitioners including administrators and public service librarians." (Library Resources & Technical Services)*

Describing Archival Materials: The Use of the MARC AMC Format, edited by Richard P. Smiraglia, MLS (Vol. 11, No. 3/4, 1991). *"A valuable introduction to the use of the MARC AMC format and the principles of archival cataloging itself." (Library Resources & Technical Services)*

Subject Control in Online Catalogs, edited by Robert P. Holley, PhD, MLS (Vol. 10, No. 1/2, 1990). *"The authors demonstrate the reasons underlying some of the problems and how solutions may be sought. . . . Also included are some fine research studies where the researchers have sought to test the interaction of users with the catalogue, as well as looking at use by library practitioners." (Library Association Record)*

Library of Congress Subject Headings: Philosophy, Practice, and Prospects, by William E. Studwell, MSLS (Supp. #2, 1990). *"Plays an important role in any debate on subject cataloging and succeeds in focusing the reader on the possibilities and problems of using Library of Congress Subject Headings and of subject cataloging in the future." (Australian Academic & Research Libraries)*

Authority Control in the Online Environment: Considerations and Practices, edited by Barbara B. Tillett, PhD (Vol. 9, No. 3, 1989). *"Marks an excellent addition to the field. . . . [It] is intended, as stated in the introduction, to 'offer background and inspiration for future thinking.' In achieving this goal, it has certainly succeeded." (Information Technology & Libraries)*

National and International Bibliographic Databases: Trends and Prospects, edited by Michael Carpenter, PhD, MBA, MLS (Vol. 8, No. 3/4, 1988). *"A fascinating work, containing much of concern both to the general cataloger and to the language or area specialist as well. It is also highly recommended reading for all those interested in bibliographic databases, their development, or their history." (Library Resources & Technical Services)*

Cataloging Sound Recordings: A Manual with Examples, by Deanne Holzberlein, PhD, MLS (Supp. #1, 1988). *"A valuable, easy to read working tool which should be part of the standard equipment of all catalogers who handle sound recordings." (ALR)*

Education and Training for Catalogers and Classifiers, edited by Ruth C. Carter, PhD (Vol. 7, No. 4, 1987). *"Recommended for all students and members of the profession who possess an interest in cataloging." (RQ-Reference and Adult Services Division)*

The United States Newspaper Program: Cataloging Aspects, edited by Ruth C. Carter, PhD (Vol. 6, No. 4, 1986). *"Required reading for all who use newspapers for research (historians and librarians in particular), newspaper cataloguers, administrators of newspaper collections, and–most important–those who control the preservation pursestrings." (Australian Academic & Research Libraries)*

Computer Software Cataloging: Techniques and Examples, edited by Deanne Holzberlein, PhD, MLS (Vol. 6, No. 2, 1986). *"Detailed explanations of each of the essential fields in a cataloging record. Will help any librarian who is grappling with the complicated responsibility of cataloging computer software." (Public Libraries)*

AACR2 and Serials: The American View, edited by Neal L. Edgar (Vol. 3, No. 2/3, 1983). *"This book will help any librarian or serials user concerned with the pitfalls and accomplishments of modern serials cataloging." (American Reference Books Annual)*

The Future of the Union Catalogue: Proceedings of the International Symposium on the Future of the Union Catalogue, edited by C. Donald Cook (Vol. 2, No. 1/2, 1982). *Experts explore the current concepts and future prospects of the union catalogue.*

The Thesaurus: Review, Renaissance, and Revision

Sandra K. Roe, MS
Alan R. Thomas, MA, FLA
Editors

The Thesaurus: Review, Renaissance, and Revision has been co-published simultaneously as *Cataloging & Classification Quarterly,* Volume 37, Numbers 3/4 2004.

The Haworth Information Press®
An Imprint of The Haworth Press, Inc.

Published by

The Haworth Information Press®, 10 Alice Street, Binghamton, NY 13904-1580 USA

The Haworth Information Press® is an imprint of The Haworth Press, Inc., 10 Alice Street, Binghamton, NY 13904-1580 USA.

The Thesaurus: Review, Renaissance, and Revision has been co-published simultaneously as *Cataloging & Classification Quarterly*™, Volume 37, Numbers 3/4 2004.

© 2004 by The Haworth Press, Inc. All rights reserved. No part of this work may be reproduced or utilized in any form or by any means, electronic or mechanical, including photocopying, microfilm and recording, or by any information storage and retrieval system, without permission in writing from the publisher. Printed in the United States of America.

The development, preparation, and publication of this work has been undertaken with great care. However, the publisher, employees, editors, and agents of The Haworth Press and all imprints of The Haworth Press, Inc., including The Haworth Medical Press® and Pharmaceutical Products Press®, are not responsible for any errors contained herein or for consequences that may ensue from use of materials or information contained in this work. Opinions expressed by the author(s) are not necessarily those of The Haworth Press, Inc. With regard to case studies, identities and circumstances of individuals discussed herein have been changed to protect confidentiality. Any resemblance to actual persons, living or dead, is entirely coincidental.

Cover design by Marylouise E. Doyle.

Library of Congress Cataloging-in-Publication Data

The thesaurus : review, renaissance, and revision / Sandra K. Roe, Alan R. Thomas, editors.
    p. cm.
    "Co-published simultaneously as Cataloging & classification quarterly, v. 37, nos. 3/4, 2004."
    Includes bibliographical references and index.
    ISBN 0-7890-1978-7 (alk. paper) – ISBN 0-7890-1979-5 (pbk. : alk. paper)
    1. Subject headings. 2. Information retrieval. 3. Electronic information resource searching. I. Roe, Sandra K. II. Thomas, Alan R. III. Cataloging & classification quarterly.
Z695.T495 2004
025.4'9–dc22

2003027318

Indexing, Abstracting & Website/Internet Coverage

Cataloging & Classification Quarterly

This section provides you with a list of major indexing & abstracting services. That is to say, each service began covering this periodical during the year noted in the right column. Most Websites which are listed below have indicated that they will either post, disseminate, compile, archive, cite or alert their own Website users with research-based content from this work. (This list is as current as the copyright date of this publication.)

Abstracting, Website/Indexing Coverage . . . . Year When Coverage Began

- *CNPIEC Reference Guide: Chinese National Directory of Foreign Periodicals* 1995
- *Current Cites [Digital Libraries] [Electronic Publishing] [Multimedia & Hypermedia] [Networks & Networking] [General]* 2000
- *Current Index to Journals in Education* . . . . *
- *FRANCIS. INIST/CNRS <http://www.inist.fr>* 1999
- *IBZ International Bibliography of Periodical Literature <http://www.saur.de>* 1995
- *Index Guide to College Journals (core list compiled by integrating 48 indexes frequently used to support undergraduate programs in small to medium sized libraries)* 1999
- *Index to Periodical Articles Related to Law* 1989
- *Information Science Abstracts, published 9 times a year, with over 249,000 records, is an exceptional information science source for librarians, information scientists & information professionals <http://www.infotoday.com>* 1992
- *Informed Librarian, The <http://www.infosourcespub.com>* 1993
- *INSPEC is the leading English-language bibliographic information service providing access to the world's scientific & technical literature in physics, electrical engineering, electronics, communications, control engineering, computers & computing and information technology <http://www.iee.org.uk/publish/>* 1983

(continued)

- *Journal of Academic Librarianship: Guide to Professional Literature, The* 1997
- *Konyvtari Figyelo (Library Review)*. 1995
- *Library & Information Science Abstracts (LISA)* <http://www.csa.com> 1989
- *Library & Information Science Annual (LISCA)* <http://www.lu.com> 1998
- *Library Literature & Information Science* <http://hwwilson.com> 1989
- *OCLC ArticleFirst* <http://www.oclc.org/services/databases/> .... *
- *OCLC ContentsFirst* <http://www.oclc.org/services/databases/> .... *
- *PASCAL, c/o Institut de l'Information Scientifique et Technique, Cross-disciplinary electronic database covering the fields of science, technology, & medicine. Also available on CD-ROM, and can generate customized retrospective searches* <http://www.inist.fr> 1999
- *Periodica Islamica* 1994
- *Referativnyi Zhurnal (Abstracts Journal of the All-Russian Institute of Scientific and Technical Information– in Russian)* 1992
- *SwetsNet* <http://www.swetsnet.com> 2001

*Exact start date to come.

Special Bibliographic Notes related to special journal issues (separates) and indexing/abstracting:
- indexing/abstracting services in this list will also cover material in any "separate" that is co-published simultaneously with Haworth's special thematic journal issue or DocuSerial. Indexing/abstracting usually covers material at the article/chapter level.
- monographic co-editions are intended for either non-subscribers or libraries which intend to purchase a second copy for their circulating collections.
- monographic co-editions are reported to all jobbers/wholesalers/approval plans. The source journal is listed as the "series" to assist the prevention of duplicate purchasing in the same manner utilized for books-in-series.
- to facilitate user/access services all indexing/abstracting services are encouraged to utilize the co-indexing entry note indicated at the bottom of the first page of each article/chapter/contribution.
- this is intended to assist a library user of any reference tool (whether print, electronic, online, or CD-ROM) to locate the monographic version if the library has purchased this version but not a subscription to the source journal.
- individual articles/chapters in any Haworth publication are also available through the Haworth Document Delivery Service (HDDS).

The Thesaurus: Review, Renaissance, and Revision

CONTENTS

Introduction
    Sandra K. Roe
    Alan R. Thomas
	1

The Thesaurus: A Historical Viewpoint, with a Look to the Future
    Jean Aitchison
    Stella Dextre Clarke
	5

Teach Yourself Thesaurus: Exercises, Readings, Resources *Alan R. Thomas*	23
A Practical Exercise in Building a Thesaurus *James R. Shearer*	35
Thesaurus Construction: Key Issues and Selected Readings *Marianne Lykke Nielsen*	57
Thesaurus Consultancy *Leonard Will*	75

Thesaurus Evaluation
    Leslie Ann Owens
    Pauline Atherton Cochrane
	87

User Comprehension and Searching with Information Retrieval Thesauri *Jane Greenberg*	103
Distributed Thesaurus Web Services *Eric H. Johnson*	121

Tools of the Trade: Vocabulary Management Software 155
    Melissa A. Riesland

Multilingual Subject Access: The Linking Approach of MACS 177
    Patrice Landry

An Interview with Dr. Amy J. Warner (June 2003) 193
    Alan R. Thomas
    Sandra K. Roe

Index 199

ABOUT THE EDITORS

Sandra (Sandy) K. Roe, MS, earned a master's degree in Library and Information Science from the University of Illinois at Urbana-Champaign and a second master's in Anthropology from Minnesota State University, Mankato. She is Serials Librarian at Illinois State University. Ms. Roe is also News Editor for *Cataloging & Classification Quarterly* and cataloger of the OCLC WorldCat Collection Set of bibliographic records for the eHRAF Collection of Ethnography. From 1999-2003 she was Nonprint Cataloger at Minnesota State University, Mankato.

Alan R. Thomas, MA, FLA, is Visiting Associate Professor at Pratt Institute, New York. He has taught at several British and American schools of library and information science, published many articles and book reviews, and edited collections in the field of knowledge organization. Mr. Thomas has served on the committees of four controlled vocabularies and is a member of the editorial board of *Cataloging & Classification Quarterly*.

ALL HAWORTH INFORMATION PRESS
BOOKS AND JOURNALS ARE PRINTED
ON CERTIFIED ACID-FREE PAPER

Introduction

The thesaurus within the context of information retrieval was developed approximately 50 years ago in an environment quite different from the one we find ourselves in today. While paper-based formats like printed books and printed serials remain, new formats continue not only to emerge but to proliferate. A recent OCLC report tells us that annual production projections for digital materials by the year 2007 are too large to estimate.[1] Beyond the challenge of new formats and the quantities and interrelationships of those formats, additional layers of complexity are added as national libraries, bibliographic utilities, and other private and governmental entities work toward bilingual and multilingual subject access within and across online collections and catalogs. Despite all that distances us from 50 years ago, there is this commonality: an interest in thesauri. There is an unprecedented interest in thesauri and related types of vocabulary switching tools not just within the library community but also from the business community, information architects, and linguists. For instance, Rosenfeld and Morville in *Information Architecture for the World Wide Web* predict that "thesauri [will] become a key tool for dealing with the growing size and importance of web sites and intranets."[2]

In this time of renewed interest in thesauri, this collection of papers is designed to serve three purposes. The first purpose is to acquaint or remind the Library and Information Science (LIS) community of the history of the development of the thesaurus and the standards for thesaurus construction. Aitchison and Dextre Clarke, both active in standards development, provide a rich historical piece that takes the reader from the first use of the word "thesaurus" in the context of information retrieval to the present day challenges of interoperability and end-user usability.

The second purpose of this collection is to provide bibliographies and tutorials from which any reader can become more grounded in her or his understanding of thesaurus construction, use, and evaluation. In "Teach Yourself Thesaurus," Thomas outlines the skills one needs to create a thesaurus and supplies the reader with sources of additional readings for each. To provide an opportunity to practice these skills, Shearer presents a series of exercises intended to teach the process of building a thesaurus from an alphabetical list of terms. In contrast to Thomas' paper, Nielsen's presentation of readings is organized by the technical processes involved in thesaurus construction and the particular problems related to each, including methodologies to gain knowledge about an information environment through the study of information-seeking behavior. Do you want to hire a thesaurus consultant or become one yourself? Will's article, "Thesaurus Consultancy," outlines the steps in a thesaurus project and reviews the roles and functions of both the consultant and the client. Owens and Cochrane describe evaluation methods which can be applied to a thesaurus as it is being created or used to evaluate an existing one.

The third purpose is to address topics related to thesauri but that are unique to the current digital environment, or network of networks. Greenberg presents the results of a query-expansion study that explores user comprehension and application of the thesaurus in the ABI/Inform database. Johnson proposes a distributed thesaurus Web service, while Riesland presents criteria for evaluating vocabulary management software packages. In "Multilingual Subject Access," Landry describes the MACS project which links equivalent headings in English, French, and German subject heading lists so that users can access online catalogs in the language of their choice. To close, Dr. Amy J. Warner describes NISO's current initiative[3] to revise Z39.19 *Guidelines for the Construction, Format, and Management of Monolingual Thesauri* in an interview with the editors.

Taken together, these papers are intended to inform the reader about thesaurus construction, its history and development, and to speculate on its future. While it seems clear that the skills involved in thesaurus construction will continue to serve us well, it is less certain whether the thesaurus will be our next generation vocabulary switching tool of choice. That function may be carried out by some form of taxonomy, ontology, mind map, or something as yet unnamed and undefined. Among developments to monitor in this rapidly changing information environment will be the work of various standards-making bodies and the new audiences and applications for their work.

Sandra K. Roe
Alan R. Thomas

ACKNOWLEDGEMENT

The editors would like to express their appreciation to Jeff A. Jenson for his assistance in verifying the citations throughout this collection of articles.

NOTES

1. Five-Year Information Format Trends (Dublin: OCLC Library and Information Center, 2003) p. 1. Available online at URL: http://www.oclc.org/info/trends/.

2. Rosenfeld, L. and P. Morville. 2002. *Information Architecture for the World Wide Web*. 2nd ed. Sebastopol, CA: O'Reilly, p. 188.

3. National Information Standards Organization. "Developing the Next Generation of Standards for Controlled Vocabularies and Thesauri" (Bethesda: NISO, 2003). Available online at URL: http://www.niso.org/committees/MT-info.html.

The Thesaurus: A Historical Viewpoint, with a Look to the Future

Jean Aitchison
Stella Dextre Clarke

SUMMARY. After a period of experiment and evolution in the 1950s and 1960s, a fairly standard format for thesauri was established with the publication of the influential *Thesaurus of Engineering and Scientific Terms (TEST)* in 1967. This and other early thesauri relied primarily on the presentation of terms in alphabetical order. The value of a classified presentation was subsequently realised, and in particular, the technique of facet analysis has profoundly influenced thesaurus evolution. *Thesaurofacet* and the *Art & Architecture Thesaurus* have acted as models for two distinct breeds of thesaurus using faceted displays of terms. As of the 1990s, the expansion of

---

Jean Aitchison is an independent consultant specializing in thesaurus design and construction. She compiled the pioneering *Thesaurofacet* in 1969, and later compiled many faceted thesauri, including the *International Thesaurus of Refugee Terminology*. She was advisor on the design of the *BSI ROOT Thesaurus*, and is joint author of the practical manual *Thesaurus Construction and Use*, now in its 4th edition. Stella Dextre Clarke is Convenor of a Working Group of the British Standards Institution, which is currently revising and extending the British Standards for monolingual and multilingual thesauri. Also an independent consultant specializing in the design and implementation of knowledge structures such as thesauri and taxonomies, she runs workshops and courses on construction of these tools.

[Haworth co-indexing entry note]: "The Thesaurus: A Historical Viewpoint, with a Look to the Future." Aitchison, Jean, and Stella Dextre Clarke. Co-published simultaneously in *Cataloging & Classification Quarterly* (The Haworth Information Press, an imprint of The Haworth Press, Inc.) Vol. 37, No. 3/4, 2004, pp. 5-21; and: *The Thesaurus: Review, Renaissance, and Revision* (ed: Sandra K. Roe, and Alan R. Thomas) The Haworth Information Press, an imprint of The Haworth Press, Inc., 2004, pp. 5-21. Single or multiple copies of this article are available for a fee from The Haworth Document Delivery Service [1-800-HAWORTH, 9:00 a.m. - 5:00 p.m. (EST). E-mail address: docdelivery@haworthpress.com].

http://www.haworthpress.com/web/CCQ
© 2004 by The Haworth Press, Inc. All rights reserved.
Digital Object Identifier: 10.1300/J104v37n03_02

end-user access to vast networked resources is imposing further requirements on the style and structure of controlled vocabularies. The international standards for thesauri, first conceived in a print-based era, are badly in need of updating. Work is in hand in the UK and the USA to revise and develop standards in support of electronic thesauri. *[Article copies available for a fee from The Haworth Document Delivery Service: 1-800-HAWORTH. E-mail address: <docdelivery@haworthpress.com> Website: <http://www.HaworthPress.com> © 2004 by The Haworth Press, Inc. All rights reserved.]*

KEYWORDS. Thesauri–history, thesauri–standards, thesauri–format, facet analysis, classification

EARLY HISTORY

An early account of the history of the thesaurus occurs in Alan Gilchrist's *Thesaurus in Retrieval*, published in 1971.[1] The author points out that the word comes from the Greek, and according to the *Shorter Oxford Dictionary*, first appeared in English in 1736. It then had the meaning 'a treasury or storehouse of knowledge, as a dictionary, encyclopedia and the like.' The most famous thesaurus is the one devised by Peter Mark Roget in 1852, entitled the *Thesaurus of English Words and Phrases*. This was arranged not in alphabetical order, but systematically, according to the concepts that the words express; the object being to find the word or words that most aptly convey an idea. It was not until about a century later that the term was applied to vocabulary lists used in information retrieval.

A thesaurus, in the information retrieval sense, is defined in the current international standard, ISO 2788, as 'the vocabulary of a controlled indexing language, formally organized so that the *a priori* relationships between concepts (for example as "broader" and "narrower") are made explicit.'[2] Its aim is to match the vocabulary used by the indexer with the language of the searcher, and thus improve the retrieval of relevant documents. Initially, the thesaurus was designed to be applied in indexing and searching using coordinate indexing, a manual postcoordinate system developed by Batten,[3] Calvin Mooers,[4] and others. In a postcoordinate system, index terms may be assigned to a document without regard to syntax, contrasting with a precoordinate system, where the terms are combined into a fixed string by the indexer. On retrieval, in a postcoordinate system, the searcher may use any combination of terms to find relevant items.

The origins of the information retrieval thesaurus have been well documented, not only by Gilchrist but also by Vickery,[5] Lancaster,[6] and Roberts.[7] There is agreement that in the context of information retrieval the word 'thesaurus' was first used in 1957 by Peter Luhn of IBM.[8] The first thesaurus actually used for controlling the vocabulary of an information retrieval system was developed by the Du Pont organisation in 1959, and the first widely available thesauri were the *Thesaurus of ASTIA Descriptors*, published by the Department of Defense, 1960,[9] and the *Chemical Engineering Thesaurus* published by the American Institute of Chemical Engineers.[10]

The thesaurus evolved through the 1950s in various forms, including the Uniterm System, devised by Taube.[11] This used uncontrolled, single words extracted from the text of a document. Difficulties inevitably arose in a situation where only single-word terms were available to deal with synonyms, homonyms, generic searches, and other problems. Uniterms frequently have different meanings depending on context, application, or viewpoint. Lacking qualifiers, they are unable to express these specific differences. For example, the concept of 'thermal insulation' is very different from that of 'electrical insulation' and the single-word term 'insulation' is inadequate to distinguish between them. The system in its pure form did not last long, as the Uniterms were inadequate for specific indexing and difficult and ineffective in searching. It was eventually superseded by vocabularies containing significant numbers of 'bound' or compound terms. These early thesauri began to control synonyms and homographs, and to display hierarchical and associative relationships between terms.

It was possible to note the difference between the developing thesaurus and the conventional subject heading list of that time, with its headings and subheadings, and rules for combining these into index strings. Although subject heading lists had 'see' and 'see also' references to link terms, they mostly lacked precise rules for vocabulary control and term relationships.

Throughout this period, all the thesauri listed terms in alphabetical order. A standard format emerged in 1967 when the *Thesaurus of Engineering and Scientific Terms* (*TEST*)[12] was published, superseding the earlier *Thesaurus of Engineering Terms* of the Engineers Joint Council (EJC).[13]

In *TEST* the alphabetical thesaurus already had most of the features present in the 'standard thesaurus' of the next 30 years, including the equivalence, hierarchical, and associative relationship types still used today.[14] Rules of thesaurus construction and use, now so familiar, were already well developed, and are set out in *Appendix 1: Thesaurus rules and conventions*. There is an explanation of the difference between preferred terms, or descriptors, to be used in indexing, and the corresponding non-descriptors linked by the equivalence relationship, including both synonyms and quasi-synonyms. There is guidance on the form of the descriptors: for instance, noun form, singular *v.* plural, abbreviations, punctuation, and the word order of compound terms. Term definitions, the problem of homographs, and the use of qualifiers are also considered. The description of the hierarchical relationship linking Broader Terms with their Narrower Terms covers polyhierarchical relationships, too. Related Terms, which are linked by the associative relationship, are described as having a close but non-hierarchical relationship. The familiar tags used in English language thesauri are listed as:

	Tag
Use	USE
Use for	UF
Broader term	BT
Narrower term	NT
Related term	RT

INTRODUCTION OF STANDARDS FOR THESAURUS CONSTRUCTION

According to Krooks and Lancaster[15] there have been standards and guidelines for thesaurus construction from very early days. They credit Eugene Wall with solving many of the problems of alphabetical thesaurus construction by 1967, and the 'Rules and conventions' in *TEST* owed much to his influence. Another influential contributor to thesaurus standards was Derek Austin, who with Dale, wrote *UNESCO's Guidelines for the Establishment and Development of Monolingual Thesauri*,[16] later incorporated into the 1986 edition of the international standard ISO 2788. This introduced into the standard the concept of the systematic thesaurus and facet analysis. Arising out of his experience in the design of the PRECIS indexing system, Austin also introduced into this standard more precise rules on the handling of compound terms.[17]

The first edition of the international standard for monolingual thesauri was published rather earlier, in 1974. The companion ISO 5964,

Guidelines for the Establishment and Development of Multilingual Thesauri, was published in 1985.[18] The international standards for thesauri have been adopted by several countries, including the UK, France and Germany, as their own national standards. Thus in the UK, for example, there are national standards BS 5723[19] and BS 6723,[20] identical to ISO 2788 and ISO 5964, respectively. The U.S. Standard on monolingual thesaurus construction is *ANSI/NISO* Z39.19, 1993.[21] It is largely compatible with ISO 2788:1986, but covers certain areas of vocabulary control in more precise detail. It was the first standard to deal with screen displays and with management control systems. There is no U.S. Standard on multilingual thesaurus construction.

EARLY PREDOMINANCE OF THE ALPHABETICAL APPROACH

A predominant feature of the early thesaurus was the alphabetical display of descriptors and non-descriptors, showing under each descriptor synonyms, broader, narrower and related terms, and scope notes where needed. A subject overview, if it existed at all, was a subordinate part of the thesaurus. In *TEST* the bulk of the 690 pages is devoted to the main alphabetical sequence of terms, a permuted index, and a hierarchical index (a separate listing of top terms showing their narrower terms at all levels). These additional types of display became a common feature in thesauri over the next thirty years.

A subject overview, or systematic display, if it existed at all, was of secondary importance in most thesauri in the early days. A detailed classified arrangement, as in an enumerative classification scheme, was considered too complex and outdated to have a role in postcoordinate information retrieval, where clear and simple terms were needed to be used in combination for optimum results. However, some thesauri had rudimentary systematic sections, consisting of broad subject categories. *TEST* had a small section presenting 22 subject categories, with subgroups to one level only, against which the descriptors were posted in alphabetical order. The many thesauri designed for international organisations by Jean Viet, best known as the compiler of *Macrothesaurus*, had more sophisticated subject groupings. *Macrothesaurus* was first published in 1972 and is now in its 5th edition.[22] An example taken from the 1985 edition is shown below. The Descriptor Group Display consists of main groups, divided into subgroups, and within the subgroups descriptors are organised into further clusters.

```
14  DEMOGRAPHY. POPULATIONS
    14.01  POPULATION DYNAMICS
    14.01.01
        CIVIL REGISTRATION
        DEMOGRAPHIC STATISTICS
        POPULATION DATA
            USE: DEMOGRAPHIC STATISTICS
        etc.
```

The systematic section in this style of thesaurus was typically subordinate to the alphabetical section rather than providing the heart and core of the thesaurus. Full details of broader, narrower and related terms are shown only in the alphabetical display.

An exception was *Medical Subject Headings*,[23] often known as *MeSH*, that from early editions in the 1960s, placed value on its tree structures. These present the descriptors in extensive hierarchies (of 10 levels or perhaps more in some places), arranged within broad categories and subcategories. The notation used in the tree structures exactly expresses the hierarchical levels and so allows the searcher to make an 'exploded' search using the notation for a descriptor to retrieve items indexed by the descriptor and all of its narrower terms. The alphabetical section does not conform to the usual thesaurus layout (for example, it does not show BTs and NTs) and serves mainly as an index to the tree structures. However, it does include scope notes, synonyms, and related terms.

THE DEVELOPMENT OF A CLASSIFIED, SYSTEMATIC APPROACH

It has come to be self-evident that a classification scheme is an indispensable tool when compiling a thesaurus. When the editor is forced to work solely within an alphabetical list of numerous descriptors, at the level of the individual term, there is a sense of working 'blind.' In contrast, where a rigorous classification is developed, providing an overall picture of the subject area, the compiler has a better chance of building accurate and meaningful relationships between the terms.

About a decade before the emergence of the thesaurus, S. R. Ranganathan in India developed an innovative classification technique known as facet analysis. His ideas spread to the United Kingdom in the late 1940s and early 1950s. The resulting classification schemes had more in common with the thesaurus that was to come than the existing enumerative classification systems. The technique analyses complex subjects into constituent categories of the same inherent type. These fundamental categories include actions, comprising processes and operations; entities, such as natural objects, products, materials; agents, including personnel and equipment; and time and place. In the field of education, for instance, there would be a teaching methods facet, arising from the operations category; an educational personnel facet from the personnel category; a teaching aids facet from the equipment category, and so on. The facets are mutually exclusive, and the terms within each facet share a common characteristic. A 'facet indicator,' or 'node label,' is often inserted to name that common characteristic. The terms so grouped tend to be short and simple, and may then be used in combination with other simple terms to express compound subjects, either postcoordinately when indexing using a thesaurus, or as precoordinated class marks in the context of a faceted classification scheme.

Enthusiasts for this new technique came together in London to set up the Classification Research Group (CRG), to exchange ideas, and to develop faceted classification schemes in various special subjects. D. J. Foskett,[24] J. Mills,[25] B. C. Vickery,[26] and Eric Coates[27] were among these pioneers. By 1955 the technique was sufficiently formulated for the CRG to issue a paper setting out the case for the use of facet analysis as the basis for successful information retrieval;[28] two years later an international conference was held at Dorking to promote faceted classification.

One of the special faceted classification systems compiled by a CRG member was for the library of English Electric Company. After the scheme had been in operation for a few years, the decision was made to update it, and to support it with the alphabetical thesaurus, then at the cutting edge of information retrieval, rather than with an index. The terms and relationships appearing in the thesaurus were derived from the classification system, and together the two parts formed an integrated whole. The resulting thesaurus, published in 1969, was the first to use facet analysis. It was appropriately named *Thesaurofacet*.[29]

Thesaurofacet was followed by of a series of faceted classifications integrated with thesauri, differing slightly in the distribution of relational data between the systematic and alphabetical sections. These included the first edition of the *UNESCO Thesaurus*,[30] the *BSI ROOT Thesaurus*,[31] and the *International Thesaurus of Refugee Terms*.[32] In this style of thesaurus, the main subdivisions are subject fields or disciplines, and within them facet analysis is used to determine the relationships between the terms within each field, and at the same time to build hierarchical and associative relationships with terms in other subject fields. The fully faceted 2nd edition of the *Bliss Bibliographic Classification* was an important inspiration for relationships and order of concepts in some of these thesauri.[33] Guidance on how to build this type of thesaurus is found in *Thesaurus Construction and Use*, 4th edition, Section J.[34]

In another style of faceted thesaurus, the area of knowledge covered by the thesaurus is divided first by fundamental categories (entities, actions, space, time, etc.), and not by subject fields or disciplines. The *Construction Industry Thesaurus*[35] was an early example of this style, but the more recent *Art & Architecture Thesaurus*[36] is an outstanding example. The terms are grouped in seven facets, including Activities, Agents, Materials, etc. Under these facets and their subfacets, 'guide terms' are used to arrange the terms further according to characteristics of division. The guide terms are labels inserted into a hierarchical display for grouping purposes, and they function rather like facet indicators. Unlike the *Thesaurofacet* style of thesaurus, the current edition is monohierarchical, and terms in each major hierarchy all belong to the same fundamental facet.

THE ADVENT OF COMPUTER-AIDED THESAURUS CONSTRUCTION

In the early days most thesauri were compiled manually. This was a slow and frustrating operation. In the case of *Thesaurofacet*, the alphabetical section was held in a series of 20 or more shoe boxes, containing cards for 16,000 descriptors and 7,000 non-descriptors. Any changes to relationships between the terms involved hand-alteration of the first term, and then a walk across the room to make reciprocal changes to the relevant term record in another box. Such an operation was greatly vulnerable to human errors, not least to mid-process interruptions. Finally, both alphabetical and systematic displays of the completed thesaurus had to be printed using a conventional printing process.

By the late 1970s computer-aided compilation of thesauri was more common. However, there was no software to maintain a systematic display of the faceted thesaurus style. The alphabetical section of the first edition of *UNESCO Thesaurus* and its hierarchical display were computerised, but the systematic display from which the alphabetical thesaurus was derived, although published, was not machine-readable. Although software was developed for subsequent thesauri of this style, notably the *BSI ROOT Thesaurus*, and the *International Thesaurus of*

Refugee Terms, it is no longer commercially available. The software of the 1980s mostly relied on minicomputers or mainframes, and so is effectively redundant if not converted for the desktop environment. This leaves a most unfortunate gap for developers of thesauri in the *Thesaurofacet* style. Fortunately, there is software available for other styles of faceted systematic displays, including the *Transportation Research Thesaurus*,[37] designed by David Batty, and faceted thesauri of the *Art & Architecture Thesaurus* style.

END-USER ACCESS

The early thesauri were developed in a paper-based era. The information retrieval systems they were applied to were sometimes automated, using punched cards, for example. But basically the search environment was limited to one workplace, where information professionals mediated in all searches. The information staff were trained in using the thesaurus, a large tome that stood by the bank of filing cards or the optical coincidence viewer.

In the '70s and '80s, when electronic databases became more widely available, either through online hosts or later CD-ROM discs, there was still the tradition of access at one terminal, with the collection of printed thesauri around it. Trained searchers became fluent in the search command languages and the controlled vocabularies at their disposal, which they applied to a finite number of well-defined databases. Trained indexers played a vital part, too. Quality control both at input and at output ensured that the power of the thesaurus was fully harnessed and searches were effective.

We face a changed environment now. In the era of the empowered end-user, a PC on almost every desk provides interactive access to an unfathomable network of networks, where an infinity of databases, portals and other electronic resources jostle for attention. Alongside the users with an expectation that they *ought* to be able to find anything out there on the Internet, their "web publisher" colleagues sit busily adding to the proliferation of information resources. There is not a mediator in sight, much less one trained in the arts of indexing or controlled vocabulary searching.

We face a paradox. Ostensibly, the need and the opportunity to apply thesauri to information retrieval are greater than ever before. On the other hand, users resist most efforts to persuade them to apply one. Several challenges need to be addressed:

- Access to information proceeds through any number of different portals, gateways, and search engines, many geared to particular audiences and subject areas. There is no universal thesaurus, but a multitude of different vocabularies for different applications.
- In the 'publish once, re-utilise many times' environment, it is hard to predict in which systems or networks a given document may eventually appear. Indexers must struggle to foresee all the needs that may arise for a given document.
- With the data entry/indexing task distributed among a vast number of authors, webmasters, system administrators, etc., quality control cannot be enforced across organizational boundaries.
- How can we train end-users to use a thesaurus properly? The experience of most information providers is that users do not want to cope with anything complicated, and the thesaurus is perceived as very complicated. Those beautifully presented systematic displays, carefully designed for selecting the right term(s) for each required concept, are often rejected as an unnecessary impediment and delay between the user and his goal.

Confronting these challenges has led to two major trends in thesaurus developments today. Firstly, the hunt is on for adaptations that will make a controlled vocabulary much quicker, easier, and more intuitive to use. Secondly, the drive for interoperability of systems means we must design our vocabularies for easy integration into downstream applications such as content management systems, indexing/meta-tagging interfaces, search engines, and portals. In some systems it is also necessary for two or more vocabularies to "interoperate," perhaps via mappings between corresponding terms.

TOWARDS MORE INTUITIVE VOCABULARIES

The popularity of *Yahoo!*[38] has proved that many untrained users are happy to browse through a simple classified directory, pointing and clicking on established headings rather than actively thinking of search terms. Many software vendors and system developers are adopting and adapting this browsing model, commonly associated with the name 'Taxonomy.'

So far there is no standard for how to build a taxonomy, nor even an agreed definition of the term in its new context. As a collection of case studies shows,[39] organizations are using the term to mean whatever they want it to mean–ranging from some pioneering innovations to putting a new title on the cover page of an existing thesaurus. Most of today's taxonomies are in the corporate sector, and hence unavailable for public viewing. But a few examples, differing widely from each other in structure and philosophy, may be accessed via the Internet. See, for example, the Northern Light taxonomy,[40] Wordmap,[41] or the Government Category List,[42] for use in the UK public sector.

Despite the lack of a standard definition, some common features may be detected. Most of them have a classification scheme as the backbone. (If they did not, how could they possibly justify the name of taxonomy, already long established in most dictionaries as roughly synonymous with classification?) Many also have some thesaural features, such as equivalence and associative relationships working behind the scenes. But the hierarchical relationships in taxonomies typically do not conform to the guidelines in the thesaurus standards; they are more loosely applied and function like the sort of hierarchy found in a conventional classification scheme.

As well as making things easier for the searcher, some taxonomies aspire to ease the job of the indexer (or rather, the cataloguer, since we are talking about classifying rather than indexing the resources). Automatic categorization is becoming increasingly popular, operating in tandem with a corporate taxonomy. The technology may be imperfect, but it is improving all the time, and it certainly cuts the cost of data preparation.

Even more intuitive than browsing with a taxonomy, another approach is to hide the search vocabulary altogether. At the simplest level, synonym sets for selected terms can be used to drive automatic expansion of free-text search queries. The result can be a significant gain in recall with very little loss of precision, provided care is taken to limit the synonyms to unambiguous ones. Although a standard thesaurus may be used as the source of synonyms,[43] a vocabulary built for this purpose does not need hierarchical or associative relationships, nor even the concept of 'preferred terms.' The basic requirement is just a collection of synonym sets, in which each member of the set has equal status.[44] Again, there is no standard format for the synonym sets; different software packages each use their own formats.

Altogether more sophisticated than query expansion via synonyms is the dream of a 'Semantic Web.'[45] Here the user addresses a software agent in his own language, and the agent responds in an apparently intelligent manner, interpreting the query and using the result to broker some transactions with other agents across the Web. For such applications we need 'ontologies' comprised of terms, relationships between the terms, and a set of inference rules.

'Ontology' is another term used quite loosely in different circles, but in the artificial intelligence (AI) community, it is often defined as 'a formal, explicit specification of a shared conceptualization.'[46] Implicit in this somewhat impenetrable definition is the requirement that concepts in the ontology, and the constraints on them, should be carefully defined. Relationships between the concepts should be specified much more precisely than is customary in thesauri. For example, whereas most thesauri use the abbreviations BT and NT to cover all hierarchical relationships, whether generic, instantial, or partitive, an ontology used for AI applications would need to discriminate between these three. Similarly, the associative (RT) relationship would need to be separated out into cause/effect, material/property, etc. As Green[47] points out, 'The intuitive understanding that humans bring to relationships is not shared by computational devices.' Provided the terms in the system are defined and the nature of their inter-relationships is specified, a computer can make inferences when communicating with another computer.

Summarizing the search for vocabularies that work more intuitively, we see that there are trends working in opposite directions. In the hugely popular taxonomies on the one hand, relationships between terms are more loosely defined than in thesauri. In the ontologies that will support computer-to-computer communications in AI applications such as the Semantic Web, we see the need for much more precisely defined term relationships.

INTEROPERABILITY

Systems interoperability is another aspect of making things easier for users. In the old days, after looking up the printed thesaurus, one proceeded to key the selected term(s) into the indexing system or the search system. Nowadays, the inefficiency and potential errors associated with rekeying are unacceptable. Terms must be copied over from the electronic thesaurus by copy-and-paste or, preferably, by clicking on them. The search system has to be capable of interacting with the thesaurus database so that users can browse it while they search, perhaps selecting a high-level term and all its narrower terms for an exploded search, and so on. Such transactions are not difficult, provided standards are applied for data exchange formats and protocols.

The interoperability requirements take on another twist when the user wants to search across several databases or websites, all using different thesauri. The same concept may be represented by different terms in different thesauri, and the same term in different thesauri may have different meanings. To enable cross-database searching, some form of mapping between the terms of different vocabularies is required. This is not so easy to achieve.

Exactly the same problem arises when the different ontologies in the Semantic Web are required to work together. Not only that, but thesauri may soon need to intercommunicate with ontologies and with taxonomies, in diverse applications still to come. Work on the solutions is still very much in progress.

THE EFFECT ON THESAURUS STANDARDS

The above concerns were amply reflected in the *Workshop on Electronic Thesauri* held in 1999 by representatives of NISO, APA, ASI and ALCTS, on planning a standard for electronic thesauri.[48] Among its recommendations were the following:

> The standard should provide for a broader group of controlled vocabularies than those that fit the standard definition of "thesaurus." This includes, for example, ontologies, classifications, taxonomies and subject headings, in addition to standard thesauri. The primary concern is with shareability (interoperability), rather than with construction or display. Therefore this new standard will probably not supersede Z39.19, but supplement it.

On the other side of the Atlantic, The British Standards Institution (BSI) has set up a small Working Group to review the standards for both monolingual and multilingual thesauri. These British Standards, BS 5723 and BS 6723 (last revised in 1987), are identical to ISO 2788 and ISO 5964, respectively. While the initiative was taken by BSI and the first tangible result should be a revised British Standard, the outcome will be offered to the international community, which will have the option of adapting and adding to it as appropriate.

The recommendations of the USA workshop cited above are a call to arms for the UK Working Group, too. Part of the Group's current thinking is that the scope of the multilingual section of the standard should be extended to cover all sorts of mapping between vocabularies. In other words, it should provide for mappings between two thesauri or classification schemes in one natural language, as well as between the different language versions of one multilingual thesaurus. This may prove to be easier said than done!

CONCLUSIONS

Four decades of experiment and development have helped us refine thesauri to the point where they are very effective tools in the environment where trained professionals use a controlled vocabulary for both indexing and searching. A check of bibliographies of thesauri available on the Web[49] reveals the names of several long-standing and venerable thesauri, among other newer titles. While it is not possible to estimate how many 'traditional' thesauri continue in operation, whether published or for in-house use, it must be a considerable number.

Today's pressures for intuitive end-user access and seamless flows of information from one system into another, however, compel new thinking on the ways of designing, implementing and presenting vocabulary search tools. Some of the changes amount to hiding the vocabularies behind the scenes; others look like simplification to the point of 'dumbing down,' and must evoke some grief among the thesaurus-using community.

The techniques developed and carefully honed over the years by thesaurus compilers will not be lost, however. Skills ranging from facet analysis of a subject field to the grouping of synonyms and the identification of relationships between concepts are still seen to be of value in new forms of retrieval aids. These will increasingly involve a synthesis of automatic indexing techniques and modified thesaurus and classification methodologies, to ensure effective web searching and navigation in the future.

NOTES

1. Alan Gilchrist, *The Thesaurus in Retrieval* (London: Aslib, 1971).
2. ISO 2788-1986. Documentation–Guidelines for the Establishment and Development of Monolingual Thesauri, 2nd ed. (Geneva: International Organization for Standardization, 1986).
3. W. E. Batten, "A Punched-Card System of Indexing to Meet Special Requirements," in *Proceedings of the 22nd Aslib Conference* (London: Aslib, 1947), 37-39.
4. Calvin N. Mooers, "The Indexing Language of an Information Retrieval System," in *Information Retrieval Today*, Wesley Simonton, ed. (Minneapolis, Minnesota: University of Minnesota, 1963), 21-36.
5. B. C. Vickery, "Thesaurus–A New Word in Documentation," *Journal of Documentation* 16, no. 4 (1960): 181-189.
6. F. W. Lancaster, *Vocabulary Control for Information Retrieval* (Arlington, Va.: Information Resources Press, 1986).
7. N. Roberts, "The Pre-history of the Information Retrieval Thesaurus," *Journal of Documentation* 40, no. 4 (1984): 271-285.

8. H. P. Luhn, "A Statistical Approach to Mechanized Encoding and Searching of Literary Information," *IBM Journal of Research and Development* 14, no. 2 (Oct. 1957): 309-317.

9. *Thesaurus of ASTIA Descriptors.* (Arlington, Va.: Armed Services Technical Information Agency, 1960).

10. *Chemical Engineering Thesaurus: A Wordbook for Use with the Concept Coordination System of Information Storage and Retrieval* (New York: American Institute of Chemical Engineers, 1961).

11. Documentation Incorporated, *Installation Manual for the Uniterm System of Coordinate Indexing* (Dayton, Ohio: ASTIA Document Service Center, 1953).

12. *Thesaurus of Engineering and Scientific Terms: A List of Engineering and Related Scientific Terms and Their Relationships for Use as a Vocabulary Reference in Indexing and Retrieving Technical Information* (New York: Engineers Joint Council and US Department of Defense, 1967).

13. *Thesaurus of Engineering Terms* (New York: Engineers Joint Council, 1964).

14. Stella G. Dextre Clarke, "Thesaural Relationships," in *Relationships in the Organization of Knowledge.* Carol A. Bean, and Rebecca Green, eds. (Dordrecht: Kluwer, 2001), 37-52.

15. D. A. Krooks and F. W. Lancaster, "The Evolution of Guidelines for Thesaurus Construction," *Libri* 43, no. 4 (1993): 326-342.

16. D. Austin and P. Dale, *Guidelines for the Establishment and Development of Monolingual Thesauri,* 2nd ed., PGI-81/WS/15 (Paris: UNESCO, 1981).

17. Derek Austin, *PRECIS: A Manual of Concept Analysis and Subject Indexing,* 2nd ed. (London: British Library Bibliographic Services Division, 1984).

18. ISO 5964-1985. *Documentation–Guidelines for the Establishment and Development of Multilingual Thesauri* (Geneva: International Organization for Standardization, 1985).

19. BS 5723:1987 *British Standard Guide to Establishment and Development of Monolingual Thesauri,* 2nd ed. (London: British Standards Institution, 1987).

20. BS 6723:1985 *British Standard Guide to Establishment and Development of Multilingual Thesauri* (London: British Standards Institution, 1985).

21. National Information Standards Organization, *Guidelines for the Construction, Format, and Management of Monolingual Thesauri,* ANSI/NISO Z39.19-1993 (Bethesda, Md.: NISO Press, 1994).

22. *Macrothesaurus for Information Processing in the Field of Economic and Social Development,* 5th ed. (Paris: OECD Development Centre, 1998). Also available online at URL: http://info.uibk.ac.at/info/oecd-macroth/.

23. *Medical Subject Headings (MeSH).* Annually updated. Bethesda, Md.: National Library of Medicine. Also available online at URL: http://www.nlm.nih.gov/mesh/MBrowser.html.

24. D. J. Foskett, *Classification and Indexing in the Social Sciences.* 2nd ed. (London: Butterworths, 1974).

25. J. Mills and V. Broughton, *Bliss Bibliographic Classification,* 2nd ed. (London: Bowker-Saur 1977-2000; K G Saur 2001-).

26. B. C. Vickery, *Faceted Classification: A Guide to Construction and Use of Special Schemes* (London: Aslib, 1960).

27. E. J. Coates, *The British Catalogue of Music Classification* (London: Council of the British National Bibliography, 1960).

28. Classification Research Group, "The Need for a Faceted Classification as the Basis of All Methods of Information Retrieval." Originally published in 1955, but reprinted in *From Classification to "Knowledge Organization": Dorking Revisited or "Past is Prelude,"* edited by Alan Gilchrist. FID Occasional Paper No. 14 (The Hague, Netherlands: International Federation for Information and Documentation, 1977), 1-9.

29. Jean Aitchison, Alan Gomersall, and Ralph Ireland, *Thesaurofacet: A Thesaurus and Faceted Classification for Engineering and Related Subjects* (Whetstone, Leicester: English Electric Company, Ltd., 1969).

30. Jean Aitchison, *UNESCO Thesaurus: A Structured List of Descriptors for Indexing and Retrieving Literature in the Fields of Education, Science, Social Science, Culture, and Communication* (Paris: UNESCO, 1977).

31. *BSI ROOT Thesaurus*, 2nd ed. (Milton Keynes, England: British Standards Institution, 1985).

32. Jean Aitchison, *International Thesaurus of Refugee Terminology*, 2nd ed. Compiled under the auspices of the International Refugee Documentation Network. (New York and Geneva: United Nations High Commissioner for Refugees, 1996).

33. Jean Aitchison, "A Classification as a Source for a Thesaurus: The Bibiliographic Classification of H. E. Bliss as a Source of Thesaurus Terms and Structure," *Journal of Documentation* 42, no. 3 (1986): 160-181.

34. Jean Aitchison, Alan Gilchrist, and David Bawden, *Thesaurus Construction and Use: A Practical Manual*, 4th ed. (London: Aslib, 2000).

35. *Construction Industry Thesaurus*, 2nd ed. Compiled by the CIT at the Polytechnic of the South Bank under the direction of Michael J. Roberts. (London: Department of the Environment, Property Services Agency, 1976).

36. *Art & Architecture Thesaurus*, 2nd ed. (Oxford and New York: Published on behalf of the Getty Art History Information Program by Oxford University Press, 1994). Also available online at URL: http://www.getty.edu/research/tools/vocabulary/aat/.

37. Information Designs Limited, "Transportation Research Thesaurus (TRT)" designed by David Batty, CDB Enterprises, Inc. for the Transportation Research Board of the U.S. National Research Council (2001-). Available online at URL: http://www.infodesigns.com/.

38. "Yahoo!" Available online at URL: http://www.yahoo.com/.

39. Alan Gilchrist and Peter Kibby, eds., *Taxonomies for Business: Access and Connectivity in a Wired World* (London: TFPL Ltd., 2000).

40. "Northern Light." Available online at URL: http://www.northernlight.com/.

41. "Wordmap." Available online at URL: http://www.wordmap.com/.

42. "Government Category List," compiled by Stella G. Dextre Clarke (2002). Download from http://www.govtalk.gov.uk/ or access directly at http://195.224.227.150/gcl/content/.

43. Jaana Kristensen, "Expanding End-users' Query Statements for Free Text Searching with a Search-aid Thesaurus," *Information Processing & Management* 29, no. 6 (1993): 733-744.

44. Stella G. Dextre Clarke, "Thesauri, Topics and Other Structures in Knowledge Management Software," in *Dynamism and Stability in Knowledge Organization. Proceedings of the Sixth ISKO Conference*, Clare Beghtol, Lynne C. Howarth, and Nancy J. Williamson, eds. (Würzburg, Germany: Ergon Verlag, 2000), 41-47.

45. Tim Berners-Lee, James Hendler, and Ora Lassila, "The Semantic Web," *Scientific American* 284, no. 5 (2001): 34-43.

46. Ying Ding, "A Review of Ontologies with the Semantic Web in View," *Journal of Information Science* 27, no. 6 (2001): 377-384.

47. Rebecca Green, "Relationships in the Organization of Knowledge: An Overview," in *Relationships in the Organization of Knowledge*, Carol A. Bean, and Rebecca Green, eds. (Dordrecht: Kluwer, 2001), 3-18.

48. Jessica Milstead, 1999. "NISO/APA/ASI/ALCTS Workshop on Electronic Thesauri: Planning for a Standard." Available online at URL: http://www.niso.org/news/events_workshops/thesau99.html. *[Editor's note: In 2003 a NISO initiative to revise Z39.19 grew out of the recommendations developed at this workshop. See "Developing the Next Generation of Standards for Controlled Vocabularies and Thesauri" for more information. Available online at URL: http://www.niso.org/committees/MT-info.html.]*

49. Leonard Will, "Publications on Thesaurus Construction and Use." Available online at URL: http://www.willpowerinfo.co.uk/thesbibl.htm.

Teach Yourself Thesaurus: Exercises, Readings, Resources

Alan R. Thomas

SUMMARY. A rationale for self-instruction in thesaurus-making is presented. Some definitions of a thesaurus are given and sources suitable to begin self-tuition indicated. A sound grasp of grammar is emphasized and appropriate readings and exercises recommended. Readings in classification, facet analysis, and subject cataloging are described. An approach for deconstruction and reconstruction of sections of classification systems and thesauri is proposed and explained. Procedures for using exercises in thesaurus construction are detailed. The means of examining individual thesauri is suggested. The availability and use of free software are described. The creation of opportunities for self-learning is considered. *[Article copies available for a fee from The Haworth Document Delivery Service: 1-800-HAWORTH. E-mail address: <docdelivery@haworthpress.com> Website: <http://www.HaworthPress.com> © 2004 by The Haworth Press, Inc. All rights reserved.]*

KEYWORDS. Thesaurus construction, classification, thesauri–analysis, thesauri–self-instruction

INTRODUCTION

This paper, intended for practitioners in and students of information and library science, seeks to describe some methods and sources which

---

Alan R. Thomas, MA, FLA, is Visiting Associate Professor, Pratt Institute, New York.

The author would like to thank James R. Shearer for reading the draft of this paper and offering constructive suggestions.

[Haworth co-indexing entry note]: "Teach Yourself Thesaurus: Exercises, Readings, Resources." Thomas, Alan R. Co-published simultaneously in *Cataloging & Classification Quarterly* (The Haworth Information Press, an imprint of The Haworth Press, Inc.) Vol. 37, No. 3/4, 2004, pp. 23-34; and: *The Thesaurus: Review, Renaissance, and Revision* (ed: Sandra K. Roe, and Alan R. Thomas) The Haworth Information Press, an imprint of The Haworth Press, Inc., 2004, pp. 23-34. Single or multiple copies of this article are available for a fee from The Haworth Document Delivery Service [1-800-HAWORTH, 9:00 a.m. - 5:00 p.m. (EST). E-mail address: docdelivery@haworthpress.com].

http://www.haworthpress.com/web/CCQ
© 2004 by The Haworth Press, Inc. All rights reserved.
Digital Object Identifier: 10.1300/J104v37n03_03

support self-instruction in thesaurus construction. Emphasis has been placed on the relatively stable intellectual processes of making an information retrieval thesaurus, with only brief attention to the faster-moving aspect of thesaurus management software. The self-instruction in construction should also contribute to appreciation of the practical benefits of using a thesaurus.

Some information professionals may have taken courses or seminars in thesaurus construction at some stage in their careers but have become rusty, yet are now confronted with a thesaurus problem and decision. By studying and working through the items presented below, it should be possible to get a purchase on the basic theories and applications of a thesaurus and other controlled vocabularies. Other information and library personnel may not have attended any prior formal educational events. For them, elementary self-instruction should provide a start, to be enhanced subsequently by further reading and by taking "live" or distance-learning courses and workshops. The paper may also prove of value to students of information and library science, helping them to connect their knowledge and skills in classification, cataloging, indexing, and searching to the related subject of thesaurus design and use.

Self-tuition can serve as prelude to more thorough studies or it may serve to remind of previous learning and rekindle interest in thesaurus creation and utilization. It may contribute to a greater confidence and competence in analyzing the need for a first or a new thesaural system, and also in assessing at what stages, in what respects, and to what degree consultants will be employed.

Texts from the professional literature that have proved or appear to be especially simple, fundamental, relevant, and lucid have been drawn upon and recommended, regardless of their date or form. Such contributions span a long period of time and cover matters theoretical and/or practical. Many of the earlier texts and exercises are notably clear and effective in inculcating the basic principles and practices of thesaurus creation, even if they may diverge somewhat in presentation respects from recommendations given in more recent standards.

WHAT IS A THESAURUS?

Definitions abound in the professional literature. The meanings vary over time, with emphases on different functions, structures, and users.

Among succinct, insightful explanations, Slamecka[1] offers that the thesaurus "prescribes the term to be assigned, and/or it suggests the concepts and terms to be considered instead of, or in addition to, terms thought of by indexers without the aid." According to Paice,[2] "A thesaurus provides a summary listing of the terms in a domain and the main relations between them." Pollard[3] understands a thesaurus as "a set of terms, a set of relationships, and a set of displays showing relationships between terms." Among Web sites, the mda (Museum Documentation Association) Archaeological Objects Thesaurus[4] and the Australian Pictorial Thesaurus "about" pages[5] are examples of good descriptions.

How a thesaurus supports the work of an indexer is well-caught by Wellisch.[6] The ways a thesaurus serves searchers is revealed in the Introductory and Tutorial texts that preface many thesauri.

WHERE TO BEGIN?

A good start may be made by reading a paper by Batty[7] which gives a clear-cut and comprehensive overview of basic steps and issues to be considered. These include users and the scope of their needs, identifying sources of the raw vocabulary, gathering it and refining it, cluster formation and arrangement, notation, the degree of precoordination, making references, and adding, deleting, and amending terms. A slightly earlier paper[8] introduces the argument for and against controlled vocabulary and the rationale for a thesaurus, adding a brief history which includes adaptation to the faceted model.

There are many Web sites that provide a good start. The American Society of Indexers (ASI) site[9] includes three useful pages. *How Do I Build a Thesaurus* briefly deals with the top-down and the bottom-up methods of construction, and how to maintain the thesaurus. *Thesaurus Management Software* begins with a very short introduction and then provides a listing of software packages. This list is in two parts–first, stand-alone packages, such as MultiTes, STRIDE, Term Tree 2000; secondly, database modules which form integral parts of larger systems. Both these pages have been prepared by Jessica Milstead. The third page, entitled *Thesauri Online*, consists of a short list of those online thesauri found most useful by visitors to the ASI web site.

An introductory tutorial by Tim Craven[10] on *Thesaurus Construction* sets out to teach the basics of making an information retrieval thesaurus. This well-presented tutorial is excellent on fundamentals, and the various quizzes worthwhile, quite exacting, and fun to work through. Sections are: What Is a Thesaurus?; Collecting Terms; Modifying and Inventing Terms; Preferred Terms and Non-preferred Terms; Semantic Relations; BT, NT, and RT References; Scope Notes; and Thesaurus

Displays. The BT, NT, and RT References section carries four quizzes, the Thesaurus Displays section has no quiz; each of the other sections includes a quiz. The module concludes with a useful Glossary of Terms.

Leonard D. Will and Sheena E. Will[11] maintain the Willpower Information site which contains much basic information, further references, and tools. The paper on *Thesaurus Principles and Practice* has twelve parts, is brightly and attractively presented with many examples and pictorial illustrations. Two helpful lists are provided: *Publications on Thesaurus Construction and Use* and *Software for Building and Editing Thesauri*.

LANGUAGE KNOWLEDGE AND SKILL

A key prerequisite to formulating the terms of a controlled vocabulary is a thorough grasp of the different syntactic patterns within multiword single concept terms (e.g., programmed textbooks) and within multiword precoordinated terms (e.g., bird migration). Another requirement is to understand the end-users' needs, their habitual vocabularies, and their likely interpretation of word orders. Because of the growth of English as a worldwide language, Iwe emphasizes the "acute need for more information on the language and how is used in different situations and by different people."[12]

What is required is that thesaurus terms are specific, disambiguated, and relevant for the purpose. When following already established guidelines that underpin an existing thesaurus or those specified in published thesaural standards, a grasp of the official syntax and also of the end-users' vocabularies and syntax will enable consistency as to preferred terms and patterns, and inform the means of providing access from alternative words and sequences. The creation of precoordinated strings at the compilation stage of a thesaurus, and/or at the indexing stage by precoordinating terms into strings, are clearly similar processes.

It is highly desirable that the builder of the controlled vocabulary, the indexer, and the information professional searcher should collaborate closely. Any information professional or student keen to learn thesaurus-making can request some form of rotated work plan at his/her place of employment or placement. A holistic work plan[13] ensures regular performance of multiple functions by information staff, thereby enhancing the quality and aptness of thesaurus design and application.

Where information professionals and students of information science have forgotten basic grammar and parsing, it is important that they remind themselves of the parts of speech, their functions, and their place in word order. There are numerous books on fundamental grammar currently available in bookshops or via Web booksellers. It may be objected that the specific tasks of building a thesaurus or of making index entries do not require a command of all the aspects of English grammar; however, effective subject analysis surely does involve a wide command when reading/scanning texts for indexing and for making abstracts.

Iwe extends the notions of Noam Chomsky on sentence structures per se and suggests that his "idea of generation of words and their combinations relate closely to what the cataloguer is expected to do sometimes with the subject headings list."[12] In her paper Iwe takes two subject areas of the controlled vocabulary of Library of Congress Subject Headings and illustrates and compares the syntactic structures of modification, coordination, and prepositional phrase.

Derek Austin, the creator of *PRECIS (Preferred Context Index System)*, summarized[14] a number of different relationships. His listing of logical relations was comprised of Coordination (and), Disjunction (or), and Negation (not); items that could be linked by these relations were reduced to Things, Actions, and (possibly) Properties. The categories of Grammatical relations were set out as Predication (to be), Possession (to have), Action (to do), and Location (to locate). However, Austin's experiment of teaching *PRECIS* through "reference to the familiar parts of speech and grammatical roles of English" was unsuccessful because there are both similarities and differences between *PRECIS* roles and grammatical categories.[15]

The *PRECIS* manual[16] abounds in concrete exercises on the syntax of terms, with solutions provided. The Manual also has four chapters dealing specifically with thesaural matters. The classic Penguin network[17] is shown, also its alphabetical presentation and systematic forms.[18] There is also an exercise on and solution for another concept network.[19] Working systematically through these *PRECIS* exercises should pay dividends in imparting a good grip on syntactic and semantic problems in thesaurus-making, indexing, and searching.

CLASSIFICATION AS A BASIS FOR CONSTRUCTING A THESAURUS

A systematic approach to organizing knowledge has always been implicit in the preparation of a thesaurus, even if the final result was only or mainly an alphabetical list. Increasingly, the classified approach is exhibited to the indexer/searcher in the form of one or more systematic displays.

The earlier literature featured several books and articles on how to construct a faceted classification, as well as some on building a thesaurus on a faceted foundation. Redfern features a short but rewarding basic exercise[20] in the faceted approach to organizing a domain–in this case, music. A set of titles, representing documents, is analyzed into facets, then the precoordinated syntax is determined.

Redfern can be followed by Ramsden,[21] who provides initiation into index language construction. A set of titles is subjected to facet analysis, and from the elements so identified, a classification system, an alphabetical list of subject headings, and an alphabetical thesaurus are constructed. A programmed instruction approach is adopted. Unlike a conventional textbook with numbered pages, this "scrambled" programmed text uses numbered frames. Each frame is devoted to a particular focus of instruction. Many frames pose a question and list a menu of possible answers. If the answer is correct, the student progresses to the next step in the learning, but if the response is faulty, the learner is directed to one or more frames which offer remedial material. Working through Ramsden is demanding but holds the interest of the private student, raises awareness of difficulties, and reinforces a command of techniques. A Self Test is appended together with answers.

Textbooks are well established and easily available for information and library science courses in the area of organizing knowledge, classification, and subject cataloging. They include or are devoted to general classification systems and subject headings lists. Some are in the form of programmed texts, usually devoted to a single system. Most hard copy texts today are not programmed, though some do include problems plus the answers. While the books are heavily used to show how to classify and catalog by popular systems, they inevitably throw considerable light on the structure of those systems. It must be kept in mind that the schemes dealt with are discipline-oriented, and general in scope, so embracing many domains. Even if already studied by an information professional or a student for cataloging and classification purposes, it is well worth working through them afresh but now from the standpoint of thesaurus construction and use. A few examples are Chan,[22] Downing and Downing,[23] and Intner and Weihs.[24]

UNSCRAMBLING CLASSIFICATION SYSTEMS AND THESAURI

Some of the items already suggested may be out of print and difficult to purchase, although interlibrary loan could be tried. An alternative or a supplementary, reinforcing procedure is to examine classification schemes and thesauri that are available–on sale, in collections, or downloadable. Most useful are those confined to a special subject field or to a subdiscipline, preferably an area in which the beginner has a personal or professional interest. Special subject classes may also be exploited within the detailed level fascicles of the *Universal Decimal Classification*[25] and the separate parts of the highly faceted *Bliss Bibliographic Classification*.[26]

Having chosen a narrow area of knowledge, the learner unscrambles the relevant section within a detailed general classification, special classification, or systematic part of a thesaurus, refiling the terms in alphabetical order or in random order. Then this assortment of terms is sorted into distinct main topics, facets, etc., using the various principles of helpful order. The result is then compared to the presentation in the scheme or thesaurus. In this manner much will be learnt about systematic order and collocation. The learner may also organize semantic maps and alphabetical displays and compare these to the original versions. Even better is to draw on two systems or thesauri, which may reveal that, even if the concepts and terms themselves happen to correspond to a high degree, there may not be a joint consensus or viewpoint in arrangement.

The more general topic terms will appear in general systems, but clearly those systems cannot match the specialized controlled vocabularies for specific terms. It can prove interesting and illuminating to see how Dewey Decimal Classification and Library of Congress Classification place the more general of the topics, and also how Sears and Library of Congress Subject Headings manage the vocabulary and the semantic references.

Such comparative study arouses interest in the structure of knowledge and the manipulation of vocabulary–foundation features of a thesaurus.

EXERCISES IN THESAURUS CONSTRUCTION

Basic exercises within the *PRECIS* Manual,[16,17,18,19] and Ramsden[21] have been noted already. More practice is afforded by those texts devoted to thesaurus construction, such as those of Townley and Gee[27] and Orna.[28]

The American National Standards guidelines publication appends a minithesaurus[29] of thesaurus terms; the best way to make this into a good short exercise is to form one alphabetical list from all of the terms in the flat display and the generic structure example; then derive a graphic display, a hierarchical display, an alphabetical display, and a permuted or rotated index; and finally check against the two given presentations. The 2nd edition of the British Standard Guidelines, BS5723:1987, contains excellent material[30] with which to experiment. Taking the concrete topic of cameras, it describes and illustrates terms and their relationships by showing the alphabetical display, the systematic display, the alphabetical index to the systematic display, the tree structure, the index to the tree structure, the arrow graph, and the index to the arrow graph. The earlier edition BS5723:1979, though superseded by the 2nd edition, is also well worth working with because it demonstrates thesaurus construction by using a quite different phenomenon, namely that of aircraft.[31]

By far the most comprehensive and meticulous work on making a thesaurus is Aitchison.[32] In Section J[33] the task of building a thesaurus for catering moves progressively through the various stages: listing broad categories, organizing terms within categories into facets, subfacets, and hierarchies, adding scope notes, indicating the semantic references, and deriving an alphabetical version. For self-learning, a good ploy would be to start at the end with the alphabetical thesaurus, draft try-outs of the systematic versions, compare the results with those given in the text, and ponder hard the variations.

EXAMINING SOME ACTUAL THESAURI

The exercise of unscrambling thesauri provides insights into their structures and characteristics. Real thesauri should also be explored. There are old ones and new ones, published and fugitive, hard copy and electronic. Numerous thesauri, static or dynamic, can be quickly brought up, navigated, and their characteristics examined on the Web.

All manifestations may yield valuable ideas, hints, devices, definitions. Features to watch out for include conceptual organization and syndetic referencing, various displays available, browsing and searching, linguistic solutions, evidence of liaison with users, conformity to internal and/or external Standards, and introductory guidance. Evaluating good and bad qualities becomes an active learning experience, ultimately timesaving.

Papers written *about* thesauri are well served by the professional abstracting literature. Yet important contributions to literature contained *within* actual thesauri, such as texts of Introductions, Instructions for Use, etc., are not normally summarized and therefore not found through literature search. The introductory texts of the National Monuments Record Thesauri[34] and of the Seattle City Clerk Thesaurus[35] are helpful and straightforward; the foundational material of the mda Archaeological Objects Thesaurus[4] is excellent. Introductions to thesauri sometimes show one or more excerpts from the thesaurus, and such sample sections can be dismantled and for private study and practice purposes. Tutorials aimed at improving an enquirer's searching competence are often included in thesauri, and though these do not specifically address procedures for making a thesaurus, nevertheless the beginner can infer a great deal about construction, display, terminology, etc.

Willpower Information[11] names and provides links to some lists of thesauri. The brief ASI page *Thesauri Online*[9] was noted above; a much longer guide is the *Web Thesaurus Compendium*,[36] arranged firstly as an alphabetical list and then as an annotated subject-grouped list.

USERS' PREFERENCES

There are several key aspects of thesaurus design, application, and use for which self-tuition aids and exercises are not yet easily available to a beginner, though there are many texts and professional papers published which are worth reading to inform the approach. One such subject is the identification of users' preferences. Olason[37] briefly introduces systems engineering and perspectives of users; López-Huertes[38] considers improved interaction.

A few procedures can be readily practised, with opportunities arising everyday in the work environment or even with other groups in life which the beginner is connected. Thus buzzwords that occur in people's speech–formally spoken and informally spoken; formally written and informally written as in e-mail messages and Web content; in casual and formal occasions–can be duly noted. Terms and their synonyms or near-synonyms may be elicited through interviews with individuals and groups. Simple word association tests and games afford insight into how people perceive relationships between terms. It was recommended earlier that participation in a holistic work plan[13] improved the language knowledge and skills required for collecting a useful and current vocabulary. The technique of mind mapping,[39] akin to devising tree structures and arrow graphs, has been found especially useful for group involvement in revealing locally relevant concepts, connections, and vocabulary.

FREE THESAURUS DEVELOPMENT SOFTWARE

Several vendors provide free-of-charge opportunities to gain understanding and practical mastery of their software products. The choice of which trial stand-alone package to download and engage with may be swayed by such factors as systems requirements and the beginner's future professional career plans. Later, several resources can be experimented with to discover and compare their particular advantages and disadvantages.

The MultiTes[40] system package offers free download of seven lessons to work through; there are also eleven online help chapters available. The scope includes working with terms and relationships, navigating, preparing, generating, and printing various kinds of displayed lists (alphabetical, classified, hierarchical, top term, KWOC rotated index), multilingual facilities, and import and export capabilities. Among other systems are Term Tree 2000[41] and STRIDE.[42]

Another free download is a thesaurus construction package entitled The W32,[43] devised by Tim Craven whose introductory tutorial on *Thesaurus Construction*[10] was noted above.

AN EXPLORATORY EXPERIENCE

The suggestions given above offer some degree of direction and progression but the learner may well prefer to move around in his/her own sequence.

It is the beginner's motivation to create positive opportunities for his/her self-learning that is the secret to obtaining a grasp of the intellectual processes of thesaurus-making. Some items mentioned above and others of their kind are ingeniously devised for programmed learning. Many more items, although not so programmed, come equipped with explicit problems and solutions for the learner. Where the resources do not include questions and answers, the enterprising beginner must "create" problems by rearranging excerpts and examples found in international standards, classification schedules, thesauri, and texts on the organization of knowledge. It is best to first merge both the given preferred and non-preferred vocabularies. Then the learner essays trial workouts, covering up the original versions, and examines these conjectures against the supplied reports, displays, and renderings of terms. Any differences are noted and thought about; the learner's versions may in certain respects be superior but they are more likely to expose gaps in skills and knowledge which can then be remedied. The game of deconstruction/reconstruction may be extended so as to compare similar portions of knowledge across different controlled vocabularies.

The efforts expended should result in improvement in forming a thesaurus, using one to greater effect for indexing and/or searching, and assisting and instructing end-users to better exploit the instrument. Then it will be time to advance by reading the considerable professional literature, and to embark on viewing and searching the numerous Web texts and tools now available, such as the Carnegie Mellon Software Engineering Institute's Quality Measures Taxonomy and Applications Taxonomy.[44] New challenges include how to devise multi-functional and user-sensitive vocabularies, corporate taxonomies and ontologies, and how to apply the transformative technology to them.

NOTES

Web sites were verified February 3, 2004.

1. Vladimir Slamecka, *Indexing Aids: Final Report* (Bethesda, Md.: Documentation Inc., January 1963), p.6.
2. Chris D. Paice, "A Thesaural Model of Information Retrieval," *Information Processing & Management* 27, no. 5 (1991): 433-447, p.435.
3. Richard Pollard, "A Hypertext-Based Thesaurus as a Subject Browsing Aid for Bibliographic Databases," *Information Processing & Management* 29, no. 3 (1993): 345-357, p.346.
4. <http://www.mda.org.uk/archobj/archcon.htm> [includes Introduction].
5. <http://www.picturethesaurus.gov.au/about.html>.
6. Hans Wellisch, "A Flow Chart for Indexing with a Thesaurus," *Journal of the American Society for Information Science* 23, no. 3 (May/June 1972): 185-194.
7. David Batty, "Thesaurus Construction and Maintenance: A Survival Kit," *Database* 12, no. 1 (February 1989): 13-20.
8. David Batty, "Words, Words, Words–Descriptors, Subject Headings, Index Terms," *Database* 11, no. 6 (December 1988): 109-112.
9. American Society of Indexers home page <http://www.asindexing.org/site/>. Jessica Milstead, *How Do I Build a Thesaurus?* <http://www.asindexing.org/site/thesbuild.shtml> (1996). Jessica Milstead. Thesaurus Management Software <http://www.asindexing.org/site/thessoft.shtml> (2002). American Society of Indexers, *Thesauri Online* <http://www.asindexing.org/site/thesonet.shtml> (2002).
10. <http://instruct.uwo.ca/gplis/677/thesaur/main00.htm>.
11. <http://www.willpowerinfo.co.uk>.
12. Josephine I. Iwe, "Linguistics and Information Processing: Provision of Syntactic and Semantic Consistency in the Language of Library of Congress Subject Headings (LCSH) Pertaining to Literature and Librarianship: A Comparative Analysis," *Cataloging & Classification Quarterly* 32, no. 2 (2001): 107-126, p.109.
13. Alan R. Thomas, "The Work-Wide Web: A Cataloging Career for Every Librarian?" *Cataloging & Classification Quarterly* 24, no. 1/2 (1997): 5-22.

14. Derek Austin, "Derek Austin: Developing PRECIS, Preserved Context Index System," *Cataloging & Classification Quarterly* 25, no. 2/3 (1998): 23-66, p.54.
15. as 14, p.49-50.
16. Derek Austin, *PRECIS: A Manual of Concept Analysis and Subject Indexing*, 2nd ed. (London: British Library, 1984).
17. as 16, p.242.
18. as 16, p.274-275.
19. as 16, p.248, 337.
20. Brian Redfern, *Organizing Music in Libraries* (London: Clive Bingley, 1966), p.11-19.
21. Michael J. Ramsden, *An Introduction to Index Language Construction: A Programmed Text* (London: Clive Bingley, 1974).
22. Lois Mai Chan, *Cataloging and Classification: An Introduction*, 2nd ed. (New York: McGraw-Hill, 1994).
23. Mildred Harlow Downing and David H. Downing, *Introduction to Cataloging and Classification*, 6th ed. (Jefferson, N.C.; McFarland, 1992).
24. Sheila S. Intner and Jean Weihs, *Standard Cataloging for School and Public Libraries*, 3rd ed. (Englewood, Colorado: Libraries Unlimited, 2001).
25. <http://www.udcc.org/>.
26. *Bliss Bibliographic Classification*, 2nd ed. (London: K.G. Saur, in progress).
27. Helen M. Townley and Ralph D. Gee, *Thesaurus-making: Grow Your Own Word-Stock* (London: Deutsch, 1980).
28. Elizabeth Orna, *Build Yourself a Thesaurus: A Step-by-Step Guide* (Norwich: Running Angel, 1983).
29. ANSI/NISO, *Guidelines for the Construction, Format, and Management of Monolingual Thesauri* (Bethesda, Md.: NISO 1993), p.61.
30. British Standards Institution, *British Standard Guide to Establishment and Development of Monolingual Thesauri*, 2nd ed. (London: British Standards Institute, 1987) (BS 5723), p.19-22.
31. British Standards Institution, *Guidelines for the Establishment and Development of Monolingual Thesauri* (London: BSI, 1979) (BS 5723:1979), p.12-21.
32. Jean Aitchison, Alan Gilchrist, and David Bawden, *Thesaurus Construction and Use: A Practical Manual*, 4th ed. (London: Aslib, 2000).
33. as 32, p.145-167.
34. <http://www.english-heritage.org.uk/thesaurus/newuser.htm>.
35. <http://clerk.ci.seattle.wa.us/~public/thesintr.htm>.
36. <http://www.darmstadt.gmd.de/~lutes/thesauri.html>.
37. Susan C. Olason, "Let's Get Usable! Usability Studies for Indexers," *Indexer* 22, no. 2 (October 2000): 91-95.
38. María J. López-Huertes, "Thesaurus Structure Design: A Conceptual Approach for Improved Interaction," *Journal of Documentation* 53, no. 2 (March 1997): 139-177.
39. Adrian Dale, "Building the Taxonomy or Knowledge Map," *Library + Information Update* 2, no. 4 (April 2003): 34.
40. <http://www.multites.com/>.
41. <http://www.termtree.com.au/>.
42. <http://www.questans.co.uk/>.
43. <http://publish.uwo.ca/~craven/freeware.htm>.
44. <http://www.sei.cmu.edu/str/taxonomies>.

A Practical Exercise in Building a Thesaurus

James R. Shearer

SUMMARY. A nine-stage procedure to build a thesaurus systematically is presented. Each stage offers exercises to put the theory into practice, using agriculture as the sample topic area. Model solutions are given and discussed. *[Article copies available for a fee from The Haworth Document Delivery Service: 1-800-HAWORTH. E-mail address: <docdelivery@haworthpress.com> Website: <http://www.HaworthPress.com> © 2004 by The Haworth Press, Inc. All rights reserved.]*

KEYWORDS. Alphabetical thesaurus, building a thesaurus, practical exercises, thesauro-classification, thesaurus construction

This paper introduces a systematic practical process for building a thesaurus, culminating in the end-product of either a thesauro-classification or an alphabetical presentation. The thesaurus topic is agriculture, chosen because most people have a good understanding of the subject matter. To get the most from this paper, it is recommended to

---

James R. Shearer, MA, is Senior Lecturer, Westminster Business School, University of Westminster, London, England, and an information consultant. He was formerly Head of the Department of Library and Information Studies, Thames Valley University, England.

[Haworth co-indexing entry note]: "A Practical Exercise in Building a Thesaurus." Shearer, James R. Co-published simultaneously in *Cataloging & Classification Quarterly* (The Haworth Information Press, an imprint of The Haworth Press, Inc.) Vol. 37, No. 3/4, 2004, pp. 35-56; and: *The Thesaurus: Review, Renaissance, and Revision* (ed: Sandra K. Roe, and Alan R. Thomas) The Haworth Information Press, an imprint of The Haworth Press, Inc., 2004, pp. 35-56. Single or multiple copies of this article are available for a fee from The Haworth Document Delivery Service [1-800-HAWORTH, 9:00 a.m. - 5:00 p.m. (EST). E-mail address: docdelivery@haworthpress.com].

do the exercises progressively after each distinct stage. Readers may not arrive at *exactly* the same solutions as those given in the Appendix to this paper, but careful consideration of any differences should prove informative. It is suggested, however, that the paper's solutions should be adopted at each stage so that the next stage starts from a standard position. Readers may also wish to develop their own approaches in parallel.

The stages in building a thesaurus are:

1. Collecting the raw terms from the literature and other sources
2. Linking synonyms, distinguishing homographs
3. Grouping the terms into broad categories (facets)
4. Ordering the facets and subfacets
5. Adding further terms to the thesaurus to fill in significant gaps
6. Adding notation
7. Identifying relations between terms in different facets
8. Creating the alphabetical index to the classified thesaurus
9. Developing the alphabetical presentation.

A diagram may help show this development. The numbers in parentheses link to the stages given above.

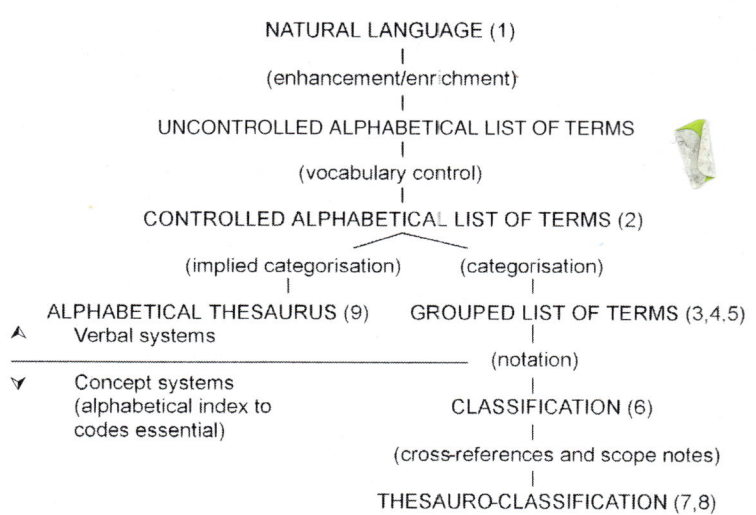

```
                    NATURAL LANGUAGE (1)
                             |
                    (enhancement/enrichment)
                             |
            UNCONTROLLED ALPHABETICAL LIST OF TERMS
                             |
                      (vocabulary control)
                             |
             CONTROLLED ALPHABETICAL LIST OF TERMS (2)
                         ___/        \___
              (implied categorisation)   (categorisation)
                        |                      |
          ALPHABETICAL THESAURUS (9)    GROUPED LIST OF TERMS (3,4,5)
       ⋏     Verbal systems                    |
       ─────────────────────────────────── (notation)
       ⋎     Concept systems                   |
             (alphabetical index to     CLASSIFICATION (6)
             codes essential)                  |
                                    (cross-references and scope notes)
                                                |
                                    THESAURO-CLASSIFICATION (7,8)
```

STAGE 1. COLLECTING THE RAW TERMS FROM THE LITERATURE AND OTHER SOURCES

Normally the initial set of terms for the thesaurus is obtained by scanning the literature in the field of interest and recording words and phrases of importance. At this stage, it is important to spread the net fairly widely to ensure that both popular and technical terms are included. It may also be appropriate to include terms used in the oral as well as the written communication in the area. Much of this will depend on the anticipated user group and their needs, and naturally, this must be a primary consideration throughout the process of thesaurus construction. It is generally considered good practice to prefer nouns and noun phrases, in the plural form, to other verbal forms.

For this exercise, using agriculture as a topic, a raw list of terms is provided in Figure 1. This contains some 170 terms (words and phrases), which we will use as the base set of terms. This is a practical number of terms to be working with initially, though naturally the final number of terms is likely to be considerably larger, on the order of 3-10,000 terms.

Exercise 1

Copy the list of terms so that it is easy to work on. A photocopy with lots of white space around is suitable, but scanning and then OCRing the text will make the mechanics of the exercise easier.

STAGE 2. LINKING SYNONYMS, DISTINGUISHING HOMOGRAPHS

Any list of terms collected as described above is likely to include synonyms (terms which have the same or nearly the same meaning, such as the *bonnet* or *hood* of a *car* or an *automobile*). One of these should be regarded as the 'preferred form,' and the other as an alternative form. Which term to prefer will depend upon the nature of the user group and its needs. Thus, *arachnids* and *spiders* are synonyms, but *arachnids* would be preferred in a list for technical users, *spiders* in one for use by the general public.

Sometimes you will find two terms in your raw list that have the same spelling but different meanings. These terms, called homographs, need to be distinguished by a qualifier (usually given in parentheses), which ultimately will probably be the next higher term in the thesaurus, but at

FIGURE 1. Raw Terms for an Agriculture Thesaurus

Afforestation
Agriculture
Agronomy
Alpine plants
Animal husbandry
Animal pests
Animals
Apiculture
Apricots
Arable farming
Asparagus
Aubergines
Bacterial diseases
Bark
Barns
Beef
Beef cattle
Beehives
Beekeepers
Beekeeping
Beetles
Beetroot
Berries
Botany
Bran
Breeding
Bulbs
Bulls
Butter
Buttermilk
Cabbages
Carrots
Cats
Cattle
Celery
Cereals
Cheese
Cheese-moulds
Cherries
Chickens
Citrus fruits
Cocoa beans
Cocoa butter
Coffee beans
Combine harvesters
Condensed milk
Corn
Cotton
Cows
Crop protection
Crops
Crops for processed foods and drinks
Crops grown for industrial processing
Cucumbers
Dairy cattle
Dairy equipment
Dairy farming
Dairy products
Diseases
Dogs
Dried fruits
Eggplants
Eggs
Farm animals
Farmers
Farmhouses
Farming
Feeding
Fertilisers
Fibre crops
Flax
Flour
Flowers
Food crops
Forage crops
Forestry
Forks
Fruits
Fungicides
Fungus diseases
Gardening
Gardening equipment
Grafting
Grain
Granaries
Grapes
Harvesting
Hay
Herbicides
Honey
Horticulture
Hoses
Insect pests
Insecticides
Juices
Lemons
Lettuces
Livestock
Locusts
Logs
Maize
Milk
Milk products
Milking machines
Mutton
Nectarines
Oils
Oranges
Ornamental plants
Pasteurised milk
Peaches
Pest control
Pesticides
Pests
Plant diseases
Plant pests
Planting
Plants
Ploughing
Ploughs
Plums
Potatoes
Poultry
Poultry farming
Propagation
Prunes
Pruning
Raisins
Reclamation and drainage
Root vegetables
Rye
Seeds
Sheep
Sheep farming
Sheep shearing
Sheepdogs
Sickles
Silos
Silviculture
Skimmed milk
Soft fruits
Soil improvement
Soil science
Solanum melongena
Solanum tuberosum
Sowing
Spades
Sprinklers
Strawberries
Tractors
Turkeys
Veal
Vegetable fruits
Vegetables
Veterinary science
Vineyards
Viniculture
Viral diseases
Watering equipment
Weeding
Weeding equipment
Weeds
Wheat
Wheatgerm
Wheelbarrows
Willows
Wines
Working animals
Yoghurt
Zoology

this point any qualifier that makes the distinction will be appropriate. Thus, *bonnet (car)* can be distinguished from *bonnet (hat)*.

Exercise 2

Read through the list carefully looking for synonyms. Choose one form as the preferred one, and link the other to it, as *cereals* used for *grain*. If your user group is mainly composed of British practical farmers, prefer *ploughs* to *plows*; but if it consists of U.S. farmers, vice versa. Check the list for homographs and qualify them appropriately.

STAGE 3. GROUPING THE TERMS INTO BROAD CATEGORIES (FACETS)

A thesaurus provides terms within an appropriate analytical structure. The next stage is therefore to start to develop that structure. The normal way to do this is to group terms that mean similar ideas, identifying the similar idea and naming it as the name of the group. Thus, *weeding* and *ploughing* are similar, and are *agricultural activities*; *ploughs*, on the other hand, are *agricultural tools*. Alternatively, it would be possible to group *ploughs* and *ploughing* together, separating them from *weeds* and *weeding tools*. These categories are termed 'facets' and 'sub-facets.' Terms within each facet and sub-facet need to be divided even more finely. For each subdivision group it is necessary to determine explicitly the characteristic that is being used to distinguish between the various terms. Where the characteristic, or principle of division, is not obvious, it is desirable to state it, for example *(by type of animal)* or *(by activity)*.

Exercise 3a

Identify the major categories (facets) of terms in the list. It may be helpful to convert these to Upper case and put the whole list into a table with two columns. Assign each facet an arbitrary number (1, 2, etc.).

Exercise 3b

Now build up sets of associated terms listed under the general category names. The easiest way to do this, using the computer, is to work through the term list adding to each term the associated number for the appropriate facet. Periodically, it will be useful to sort the list by number and term name. This helps with checking the consistency of your progress, and groups of all of the unallocated terms in one place. Keep working on this section, pulling out the easiest ones first, and so gradually reduce the list of uncategorised terms until there are only a few or even none left. If you have none left, well done. If a few terms are left over, leave them for the present. You can sort them out later as the structure development progresses.

Exercise 3c

For each list, you may well find that you can divide the terms more finely, into narrower groups. In each case you need to name the overall narrower group, and be clear what characteristic or principle of division you are using.

STAGE 4. ORDERING THE FACETS AND SUB-FACETS

More structure is added to the developing thesaurus by grouping facets and sub-facets into a useful order–useful from the point of view of your users. Various authorities have provided general orders, that of Vickery[1] being particularly useful:

- Thing (product)
- Part
- Constituent
- Property
- Measure
- Patient
- Process/Action/Operation
- Agent
- Space
- Time.

An earlier approach, that of Ranganathan,[2] is sometimes helpfully more succinct:

- Personality (the main topic area of the thesaurus–in Architecture, buildings; in Agriculture, farming)
- Matter (materials)
- Energy (activities)
- Space
- Time.

In this example, this PMEST order has generally been followed.

Terms in a hierarchy will need to be sub-grouped, and also arranged within the group. Orders that have been found useful include:

- chronological (for instance, *ploughing* comes before *harvesting* chronologically)
- evolutionary (so *plants* before *animals*)
- increasing complexity (so *hand tools* before *machinery*, perhaps)
- size
- spatial contiguity
- preferred category (*English* as the first language in a language list, perhaps)
- canonical (the standard order used in a field, such as the conventional order of the books in the Bible)
- alphabetical.

Where an order has been determined in one part of the thesaurus, it is good practice to use the same order elsewhere in the thesaurus, so if *ploughing* comes before *harvesting* in the *agronomy activity* facet, *ploughing equipment* should come before *harvesting equipment* in the *agricultural equipment* facet, and equally, *plants* should be placed before *animals* throughout. This is sometimes termed 'parallel development.'

Explanatory notes (termed 'scope notes') will be needed to clarify the use of a term where it may be ambiguous or disputable. Thus *East Africa* could be given the scope note: *Includes Ethiopia, Kenya, Somalia, Tanzania, Uganda*–this makes it clear that *Sudan* is not regarded, in this thesaurus anyway, as being in *East Africa*.

Exercise 4

Try organising your named facets into a sensible, useful order, with scope notes where necessary.

STAGE 5. ADDING FURTHER TERMS TO THE THESAURUS TO FILL IN SIGNIFICANT GAPS

At this stage in the analysis (and earlier), it becomes apparent that additional terms are needed to clarify how you have divided the terms, or because there are obvious omissions. Such terms should be added now, but it is not sensible to add many similar terms to any particular part of the thesaurus at this stage, because they will clutter up the structure and make it hard to develop the work further. Thus, if the Space facet has the continents named and grouped appropriately, and some sub-continental areas and countries added, it is not appropriate at this point to add all of the other country names that might be of importance later. Such development of the thesaurus is better left until the main structure is clearly developed and understood; it is then a simple matter to add further terms in the appropriate position. However, it may be useful to keep notes of areas that need expansion later on.

Exercise 5

Identify and add terms as necessary to clarify the structure and content of your developing thesaurus.

STAGE 6. ADDING NOTATION

The thesaurus terms are now in a highly structured order–but users will not find it easy to find specific terms. It is possible to re-order the terms in alphabetical order, indicating the structure by a standard notation. This is considered in stage 9. A classified presentation has its advantages, however, particularly in collocating related terms, and in showing the structure of the thesaurus explicitly.

To mechanise the order, ordered notation should be applied. This may take the form of numbers, letters, or a combination of the two. It is important that space be left for growth in the thesaurus, both within existing facets and sub-facets, and for new facets. The notation should therefore leave plenty of gaps. It may also be helpful to record the hierarchical level of each term at this point–normally up to about five levels prove practicable. Too few give insufficient clarity to the division, whereas too many can cause confusion.

Exercise 6

Add notation to your developing thesaurus. It may be useful to use single uppercase letters for the main classes, and four digit numbers, spread out well, for the subordinate classes. Thus, class B6000 (level 1) could be appropriate for *Agricultural equipment*, with B6400 (level 2) for *Harvesting equipment*, and B6700 (level 2) for *Dairy equipment*, B6720 (level 3) for *Milking machines*, and B7000 (level 1) for *Agricul-*

tural structures. M1200 (level 1) might be used for Food products, M3000 (level 3) for Dairy products, M3100 (level 4) for Milk products, and M4000 (level 5) for Cheese. These classification codes will replace the temporary numbers in your table, and a new column should be introduced for the levels.

Exercise 6. Solutions

Do exercise 7 before looking at the solution in the Appendix, which gives the full thesaurus for both exercises.

STAGE 7. IDENTIFYING RELATIONSHIPS BETWEEN TERMS IN DIFFERENT FACETS

The classified arrangement makes explicit the relationships between terms in the same facet. However, to help the user find other terms that relate to the same concept, it is necessary to make links to terms that are in different facets. Thus, *aircraft* in one facet should be related to *air transport* in another facet. Such relationships should be provided reciprocally, since users may need to be directed either way. The code RT is conventionally used to denote related term.

Exercise 7

Insert pairs of relationships between associated terms that are not in the same facet, giving both the term and identifying its position by including the notation. Thus *B2750 Beef cattle* will have *RT Beef (M6200)* and *M6200 Beef* will have *RT Beef cattle (B2750).* Where there are several related terms linked to a term, they are listed in classified order as this is more useful than alphabetical order.

STAGE 8. CREATING THE ALPHABETICAL INDEX TO THE CLASSIFIED THESAURUS

The classified approach gives terms in a semantic order, not accessible without an alphabetical index. The index should be a permuted one, so giving access by any element of a compound term, thus *Civil engineering* should appear as *CIVIL ENGINEERING* and as *ENGINEERING, CIVIL* in the index. *Reclamation and drainage* should appear as *RECLAMATION AND DRAINAGE*, as *AND DRAINAGE, RECLAMATION*, and as *DRAINAGE, RECLAMATION AND*

It may be appropriate to use a set of stop words, such as:

&	AT	FROM	OR
A	BY	IN	THE
AN	CAUSE	NEED	TO
AND	EXCLUDING	OF	
AS	FOR	ON	

to eliminate unhelpful permutations, or they can be excluded manually after the index is created.

Exercise 8

Create the alphabetical index for your classified thesaurus.

STAGE 9. DEVELOPING THE ALPHABETICAL PRESENTATION

The alphabetical thesaurus presentation is created by taking the hierarchical presentation and associating with each term in turn, as appropriate, other terms that link with it. The relationships are generally shown by the notation:

USE for use
UF for used for
BT for broader term
NT for narrower term
RT for related term.

Multiple terms with the same relationship are normally arranged in alphabetical order. (NB: Some thesauri put the relationships in the order UF, NT, BT, RT.)

The small sample which follows shows the approach:

Classified presentation

```
B1100      . Agronomy
              UF: Crop production
              RT: Silviculture (B8100)
B1200      . . Arable farming
B1300      . . Horticulture
              UF: Nursery practices
B1320      . . . Gardening
B1400      . . Viniculture
              UF: Vineyards
              RT: Wines (M1750)
              (by activity)
B1420      . . Ploughing
              RT: Ploughing equipment (B6300)
```

```
B1500      . . Sowing
B1510      . . Propagation
B1520      . . Planting
B1530      . . Pruning
B1540      . . Grafting
B1550      . . Weeding
              RT: Weeding equipment (B6480)
              RT: Weeds (E2200)
```

Alphabetical thesaurus entries derived from the above

Agronomy
  UF Crop production
  NT Arable farming
  NT Horticulture
  NT Viniculture
  NT Ploughing
  NT Sowing
  NT Propagation
  NT Planting
  NT Pruning
  NT Grafting
  NT Weeding
  RT Silviculture

Crop production
  USE agronomy

Production, crop
  USE agronomy

Arable farming
  BT Agronomy

Farming, arable
  USE Arable farming

Horticulture
  UF Nursery practices
  BT Agronomy

Nursery practices
  USE Horticulture

Practices, nursery
  USE Horticulture

Ploughing
  BT Agronomy
  RT Ploughing equipment

Sowing
  BT Agronomy

Propagation
  BT Agronomy

Planting
  BT Agronomy

Pruning
  BT Agronomy

Grafting
  BT Agronomy

Weeding
  BT Agronomy
  RT Weeding equipment
  RT Weeds

The alphabetical thesaurus presentation created by alphabetising the above

Agronomy
  UF Crop production
  NT Arable farming
  NT Grafting
  NT Horticulture
  NT Planting
  NT Ploughing
  NT Propagation
  NT Pruning
  NT Sowing
  NT Viniculture
  NT Weeding
  RT Silviculture

Arable farming
  BT Agronomy

Crop production
  USE Agronomy

Farming, arable
  USE Arable farming

Grafting
  BT Agronomy

Horticulture
  UF Nursery practices
  BT Agronomy

Nursery practices
  USE Horticulture

Planting
  BT Agronomy

Practices, nursery
  USE Horticulture

Production, crop
  USE Agronomy

Propagation
  BT Agronomy

Ploughing
  BT Agronomy
  RT Ploughing equipment

Pruning
  BT Agronomy

Sowing
  BT Agronomy

Weeding
  BT Agronomy
  RT Weeding equipment
  RT Weeds

Exercise 9

Provide an alphabetical presentation for the whole or part of your thesaurus. This is a purely mechanical process, so no further solution guidance is provided other than the example above.

CONCLUSION

The procedure outlines in this paper, if followed carefully and thoughtfully, can lead to the reasonably rapid development of a useful thesaurus in a limited subject area known to the developer. The most difficult stages are analysing terms and ordering them into facets and sub-facets and so on. At the same time, this is the most creative and interesting part of the work, which requires careful thought about the nature of, and relationships between, concepts on the chosen subject area.

This exercise/paper is designed to illustrate a technique for developing a thesaurus. The approach discussed is robust and reliable, but much more can be said and has been written. Aitchison, Gilchrist, and Bawden[3] give a fuller and more formal treatment. If working through this example has stimulated interest in building a really sound thesaurus, their text is recommended as a clear guide to taking the process forward. National and international standards[4,5] on thesaurus construction have also been developed, and these also contain useful advice.

NOTES

1. B. C. Vickery, *Classification and Indexing in Science* (London: Butterworths, 1958).

2. S. R. Ranganathan, *Elements of Library Classification* (Bombay: Asia Publishing, 1945).

3. Jean Aitchison and others, *Thesaurus Construction and Use: A Practical Manual*, 4th ed. (London: Aslib, 2000).

4. International Organization for Standardization, *Documentation–Guidelines for the Establishment and Development of Monolingual Thesauri*, 2nd ed. (ISO 2788) (Geneva: ISO, 1986). Also issued as British Standard BS 5723, 1987.

5. ANSI/NISO, *Guidelines for the Construction, Format, and Management of Monolingual Thesauri* (Bethesda, NISO, 1993) (ANSI/NISO Z39.19-1993).

APPENDIX. Solutions

Exercise 2 solutions
Some synonym examples

Agriculture used for Farming	[more encompassing term]
Agronomy used for Crop production	[more explicit term]
Aubergines used for Eggplants	[UK term preferred]
Aubergines used for Solanum melongena	[non-scientific term preferred]
Beekeeping used for Apiculture	[non-scientific term preferred]
Cereals used for Grain	[more explicit term]
Farm animals used for Livestock	[clearer term preferred]
Fertilisers used for Fertilizers	[UK spelling preferred]
Maize used for Corn (USA)	[unambiguous term preferred]
Ploughing used for Plowing	[UK spelling preferred]
Ploughs used for Plows	[UK spelling preferred]
Potatoes used for Solanum tuberosum	[non-scientific term preferred]
Viniculture used for Vineyards	[more encompassing term]
Wheat used for Corn (UK)	[unambiguous term preferred]

Some homograph examples

Corn in the US has a different meaning from *Corn* in the UK
If *Cheese-moulds* were not already qualified, a qualifer would be necessary to distinguish it from *Fungal moulds*

Exercise 3a solutions
Some broad classes (facets), assigned an arbitrary number

1	EQUIPMENT
2	BUILDINGS
3	PESTS AND DISEASES
4	CROPS
5	ANIMAL PRODUCTS
6	WORKING ANIMALS
8	DISCIPLINES
9	ACTIVITIES

Exercise 3b solutions
List of terms, broad classes capitalised, other terms assigned to the appropriate broad class number where it can be determined.

1	Cheese-moulds		1	Ploughs = Plows		2	Barns
1	Combine harvesters		1	Sickles		2	BUILDINGS
1	Dairy equipment		1	Spades		2	Farmhouses
1	EQUIPMENT		1	Sprinklers		2	Granaries
1	Forks		1	Tractors		2	Silos
1	Gardening equipment		1	Watering equipment		3	Animal pests
1	Hoses		1	Weeding equipment		3	Bacterial diseases
1	Milking machines		1	Wheelbarrows		3	Beetles

APPENDIX (continued)

3	Diseases	4	Flour	5	Milk
3	Fungus diseases	4	Flowers	5	Milk products
3	Insect pests	4	Forage crops	5	Mutton
3	Locusts	4	Fruits	5	Pasteurised milk
9	Pest control	4	Grapes	5	Skimmed milk
3	Pests	4	Hay	5	Veal
3	PESTS AND DISEASES	4	Juices	5	Yoghurt
		4	Lemons	6	Cats
3	Plant diseases	4	Lettuces	6	Dogs
3	Plant pests	4	Logs	6	Sheepdogs
3	Viral diseases	4	Maize = Corn (USA)	6	WORKING ANIMALS
3	Weeds	4	Nectarines	8	Agronomy = Crop production
4	Alpine plants	4	Oils		
4	Apricots	4	Oranges	8	Botany
4	Asparagus	4	Ornamental plants	8	DISCIPLINES
4	Aubergines = Eggplants = Solanum melongena	4	Peaches	8	Forestry
		4	Plants	8	Horticulture = Nursery practices
4	Bark	4	Plums	8	Silviculture
4	Beetroot = Beets	4	Potatoes = Solanum tuberosum	8	Soil science
4	Berries			8	Veterinary science
4	Bran	4	Prunes	8	Viniculture = Vineyards
4	Bulbs	4	Raisins	8	Zoology
4	Cabbages	4	Root vegetables	9	ACTIVITIES
4	Carrots	4	Rye	9	Afforestation
4	Celery	4	Soft fruits	9	Agriculture = Farming
4	Cereals = Grain	4	Strawberries	9	Animal husbandry
4	Cherries	4	Vegetable fruits	9	Arable farming
4	Citrus fruits	4	Vegetables	9	Beekeeping = Apiculture
4	Cocoa beans	4	Wheat = Corn (UK)		
4	Cocoa butter	4	Wheatgerm	9	Breeding
4	Coffee beans	4	Willows	9	Crop protection
4	Cotton	4	Wines	9	Dairy farming
4	Crops for processed foods and drinks	5	ANIMAL PRODUCTS	9	Feeding
		5	Beef	9	Gardening
4	Crops grown for industrial processing	5	Butter	9	Grafting
		5	Buttermilk	9	Harvesting
4	CROPS	5	Cheese	9	Planting
4	Cucumbers	5	Condensed milk	9	Ploughing = Plowing
4	Dried fruits	5	Dairy products	9	Poultry farming
4	Fibre crops = Fiber crops	5	Eggs	9	Propagation
		5	Honey	9	Pruning
4	Flax				

9	Reclamation and drainage
9	Sheep farming
9	Sheep shearing
9	Soil improvement
9	Sowing
9	Weeding
	Animals
	Beef cattle
	Beehives

Beekeepers
Bulls
Cattle
Chickens
Cows
Dairy cattle
Farm animals = Livestock
Farmers
Fertilisers = Fertilizers

Food crops
Fungicides
Herbicides
Insecticides
Pesticides
Poultry
Seeds
Sheep
Turkeys

Exercise 3c solutions
Some term lists
Diseases: (by agent) Bacterial diseases, Fungus diseases, Viral diseases
Fruits: Apricots, Cherries, Grapes, Lemons, Nectarines, Oranges, Peaches, Plums, etc.
Meat products: Beef, Mutton, Veal
Milk products: Butter, Buttermilk, Cheese, Condensed milk, Pasteurised milk, Skimmed milk, Yoghurt

Exercise 4 solutions
One overall broad solution is:
Agriculture –
    Agronomy, Animal husbandry, Agricultural products, Agricultural equipment, Agricultural structures
Forestry –
    Silviculture, Afforestation, Forest products
Diseases, pests, pest contol
Botany
Zoology
Veterinary science
Soil science
Food technology –
    Food products

Fruits provide an interesting problem. One solution is:
Fruits
    Citrus fruits
        Oranges
        Lemons
    Stone fruits
        Apricots
        Cherries
        Peaches
            Nectarines
        Plums
    Soft fruits
        Strawberries
    Grapes

A scope note example:
Vegetables and fruits
SN Vegetables and fruits grown primarily for man/animal consumption without intermediate processing. For treated or processed vegetables and fruits see Vegetable and fruit products.

APPENDIX (continued)

Exercise 5 solutions
Additional terms that could be added include:

Agricultural equipment	Food technology	Medicinal crops
Agricultural products	Foods of animal origin	Plant products
Agricultural structures	Forest product	Ploughing equipment
Animal diseases	General equipment	Spraying equipment
Botany	Harvesting equipment	Stone fruits
Butchered meat products	Insecta	Vegetable and fruit products
Cereal products	Leaves, stems, flowers	Vegetables and fruits
Diseases. Pests. Pest control.	Livestock equipment	
Food products	Meat products	

Exercise 6 & 7 solutions
Related terms could include:
Dairy farming, Dairy cattle, Dairy products, Dairy equipment
Beekeeping, Beekeepers, Honey, Beehives
Grapes, Viniculture, Wines
Forage crops, Feeding, Silos

Examine the resulting agricultural thesaurus carefully and compare it with your development. It may be quite different, and both solutions may well be appropriate, depending on the needs and circumstances of the users.

This thesaurus presentation and index was created using personally developed BASIC software to input, format, sort, and output the thesaurus. Several commercial software packages are available that provide similar facilities. Some of these are downloadable free for trial and learning purposes.

```
B1000   AGRICULTURE
        UF: Farming
        (by personnel)
B1020 . . Farmers
B1030 . . Beekeepers
            RT: Beekeeping (B2500)
        (by system)

B1100 . AGRONOMY
        UF: Crop production
        RT: Silviculture (B8100)
B1200 . . Arable farming
B1300 . . Horticulture
            UF: Nursery practices
B1320 . . . Gardening
B1400 . . Viniculture
            UF: Vineyards
            RT: Grapes (B3990)
            RT: Wines (M1750)
        (by activity)
B1420 . . Ploughing
            UF: Plowing
            RT: Ploughing equipment (B6300)
B1500 . . Sowing
B1510 . . Propagation
B1520 . . Planting
B1530 . . Pruning
B1540 . . Grafting
```

```
B1550 . . Weeding
            RT: Weeding equipment (B6480)
            RT: Weeds (E2200)
B1600 . . Crop protection
            RT: Pest control (E4000)
B1700 . . Harvesting
            RT: Harvesting equipment (B6650)
B1800 . . Soil improvement
            RT: Soil science (J1000)
B1820 . . . Reclamation and drainage
        (by materials)
B1880 . . Seeds
B1890 . . Bulbs
B1900 . . Fertilisers
            UF: Fertilizers

B2000 . ANIMAL HUSBANDRY
        RT: Zoology (G1000)
        RT: Veterinary science (H1000)
B2100 . . Dairy farming
            RT: Dairy cattle (B2760)
            RT: Dairy products (B5100)
            RT: Dairy equipment (B6700)
B2300 . . Poultry farming
            RT: Poultry (B2830)
B2400 . . Sheep farming
            RT: Sheep (B2800)
B2430 . . . Sheep shearing
```

```
B2500  . . Beekeeping
            UF: Apiculture
            RT: Beekeepers (B1030)
            RT: Honey (B5350)
            RT: Beehives (B6820)
         (by activity)
B2520  . . . Breeding
B2530  . . . Feeding
            RT: Forage crops (B4200)
         (by type of animal)
B2600  . . . Farm animals
            UF: Livestock
B2700  . . . . Cattle
B2720  . . . . . Cows
B2730  . . . . . Bulls
         (by product)
B2750  . . . . . Beef cattle
                RT: Beef (M6200)
B2760  . . . . . Dairy cattle
                RT: Dairy farming (B2100)
                RT: Dairy products
                    (B5100)
B2800  . . . . Sheep
                RT: Sheep farming (B2400)
                RT: Mutton (M6500)
B2830  . . . Poultry
            RT: Poultry farming (B2300)
B2850  . . . . Chickens
B2880  . . . . Turkeys
B2900  . . Working animals
B2920  . . . Dogs
B2925  . . . . Sheepdogs
B2940  . . . Cats


B3000  . AGRICULTURAL PRODUCTS
         RT: Food products (M1200)
B3100  . . Crops
         RT: Plants (F2000)
B3300  . . . Food crops
B3400  . . . . Cereals
            UF: Grain
            RT: Cereal products
                (M1320)
            RT: Granaries (B7400)
B3420  . . . . . Maize
            UF: Corn (USA)
B3440  . . . . . Rye
B3460  . . . . . Wheat
            UF: Corn (UK)
B3500  . . . . Vegetables and fruits
            SN: Vegetables and fruits
grown primarily for man/animal consumption
without intermediate processing. For treated or
processed vegetables and fruits see M1600.
B3520  . . . . . Vegetables
            (by part of plant)
B3530  . . . . . . Root vegetables
B3540  . . . . . . . Carrots
B3560  . . . . . . . Beetroot
            UF: Beets
B3580  . . . . . . . Potatoes
            UF: Solanum
                tuberosum
```

```
B3600  . . . . . . Leaves; stems; flowers
B3620  . . . . . . . Asparagus
B3630  . . . . . . . Cabbages
B3650  . . . . . . . Celery
B3680  . . . . . . . Lettuces
B3690  . . . . . . Vegetable fruits
B3700  . . . . . . . Cucumbers
B3750  . . . . . . . Aubergines
            UF: Eggplants
            UF: Solanum
                melongena
B3800  . . . . . Fruits
B3820  . . . . . . Citrus fruits
B3830  . . . . . . . Oranges
B3840  . . . . . . . Lemons
B3900  . . . . . . Stone fruits
B3910  . . . . . . . Apricots
B3920  . . . . . . . Cherries
B3940  . . . . . . . Peaches
B3945  . . . . . . . . Nectarines
B3960  . . . . . . . Plums
            RT: Prunes (M1650)
B3970  . . . . . . Soft fruits
            UF: Berries
B3980  . . . . . . . Strawberries
B3990  . . . . . . Grapes
            RT: Viniculture (B1400)
            RT: Raisins (M1680)
B4200  . . . Forage crops
            RT: Feeding (B2530)
            RT: Silos (B7300)
B4230  . . . . Hay
B4300  . . . Ornamental plants. Cut flowers
B4350  . . . . Alpine plants
B4400  . . . Crops grown for industrial
            processing
B4420  . . . . Crops for processed foods and
            drinks
B4430  . . . . . Cocoa beans
            RT: Cocoa butter (M1800)
B4440  . . . . . Coffee beans
B4500  . . . . Fibre crops
            UF: Fiber crops
B4520  . . . . . Cotton
B4530  . . . . . Flax
B4600  . . . Medicinal crops
B4620  . . . . Willows
            UF: Salicaceae
B5000  . . Animal products
            SN: Classify treated and pro-
                cessed products in M2500.
B5100  . . . Dairy products
            RT: Dairy farming (B2100)
            RT: Dairy cattle (B2760)
            RT: Dairy equipment (B6700)
B5120  . . . . Milk
            SN: Classify milk products in
                M3000
B5200  . . . Meat products
            SN: Classify butchered meat
                products in M6000
            RT: Beef cattle (B2750)
            RT: Sheep (B2800)
            RT: Poultry (B2830)
```

APPENDIX (continued)

```
B5300  . . . Eggs
              RT: Poultry (B2830)
B5350  . . . Honey
              RT: Beekeeping (B2500)

B6000  . AGRICULTURAL EQUIPMENT
B6100  . . General equipment
B6130  . . . Tractors
B6200  . . Gardening equipment
B6230  . . . Forks
B6240  . . . Spades
B6250  . . . Wheelbarrows
B6300  . . Ploughing equipment
              UF: Plowing equipment
              RT: Ploughing (B1420)
B6320  . . . Ploughs
              UF: Plows
B6480  . . Weeding equipment
              RT: Weeding (B1550)
B6500  . . Watering equipment
B6520  . . . Hoses
B6540  . . . Sprinklers
B6600  . . Spraying equipment
              RT: Crop protection (B1600)
              RT: Pesticides (E4200)
B6650  . . Harvesting equipment
              RT: Harvesting (B1700)
B6652  . . . Sickles
B6654  . . . Combine harvesters
B6700  . . Dairy equipment
              RT: Dairy farming (B2100)
              RT: Dairy products (B5100)
B6720  . . . Milking machines
              RT: Milk (B5120)
B6740  . . . Cheese-moulds
              RT: Cheese (M4000)
B6800  . . Livestock equipment
              RT: Animal husbandry (B2000)
B6820  . . . Beehives
              RT: Beekeeping (B2500)

B7000  . AGRICULTURAL STRUCTURES
B7100  . . Farmhouses
B7200  . . Barns
B7300  . . Silos
              RT: Forage crops (B4200)
B7400  . . Granaries
              RT: Cereals (B3400)

B8000  FORESTRY

B8100  . SILVICULTURE
          RT: Agronomy (B1100)
```

```
B8200  . AFFORESTATION

B8300  . FOREST PRODUCTS
B8320  . . Bark
B8340  . . Logs

E1000  DISEASES. PESTS. PEST CONTROL

E1200  . DISEASES
E1300  . . Plant diseases
              RT: Plants (F2000)
E1400  . . Animal diseases
              RT: Zoology (G1000)
              RT: Veterinary science (H1000)
          (by agent)
E1500  . . Bacterial diseases
E1520  . . Fungus diseases
              RT: Fungicides (E4300)
E1540  . . Viral diseases

E2000  . PESTS
E2100  . . Plant pests
              RT: Plants (F2000)
E2200  . . . Weeds
              RT: Weeding (B1550)
              RT: Herbicides (E4500)
              RT: Weeding equipment (B6480)
E3000  . . Animal pests
              RT: Animals (G2000)
E3100  . . . Insect pests
              RT: Insecticides (E4700)
              RT: Insecta (G4000)
E3200  . . . . Beetles
E3300  . . . . Locusts

E4000  . PEST CONTROL
          RT: Crop protection (B1600)
          (by materials)
E4200  . . Pesticides
              RT: Spraying equipment (B6600)
E4300  . . . Fungicides
              RT: Fungus diseases (E1520)
E4500  . . . Herbicides
              RT: Weeds (E2200)
E4700  . . . Insecticides
              RT: Insect pests (E3100)

F1000  BOTANY

F2000  . PLANTS
          RT: Crops (B3100)
          RT: Plant diseases (E1200)

G1000  ZOOLOGY
          RT: Animal husbandry (B2000)
          RT: Veterinary science (H1000)
```

G2000	. ANIMALS		M1630	. . . . Dried fruits
G4000	. . . . Insecta		M1650	. . . . . Prunes
	RT: Insect pests (E3100)			RT: Plums (B3960)
			M1680	. . . . . Raisins
H1000	**VETERINARY SCIENCE**			RT: Grapes (B3990)
	RT: Animal diseases (E1400)		M1700	. . . . Juices
	RT: Zoology (G1000)		M1720	. . . . Oils
			M1750	. . . . Wines
J1000	**SOIL SCIENCE**			RT: Viniculture (B1400)
	RT: Soil improvements (B1800)			RT: Grapes (B3990)
			M1800	. . . . Cocoa butter
M1000	**FOOD TECHNOLOGY**			RT: Cocoa beans (B4430)
			M2500	. . Foods of animal origin
				RT: Animal products (B5000)
M1200	. **FOOD PRODUCTS**		M3000	. . . Milk products
	SN: Treated and/or processed foods			RT: Milk (B5120)
	RT: Agricultural products (B3000)		M3200	. . . . Condensed milk
	(by origin)		M3300	. . . . Pasteurised milk
			M3400	. . . . Skimmed milk
M1300	. . Plant products		M3500	. . . . Buttermilk
M1320	. . . Cereal products		M4000	. . . . Cheese
	RT: Cereals (B3400)			RT: Cheese-moulds (B6740)
M1350	. . . . Bran		M4500	. . . . Butter
M1380	. . . . Wheatgerm		M5000	. . . . Yoghurt
M1500	. . . . Flour		M6000	. . Butchered meat products
M1600	. . . Vegetable and fruit products		M6200	. . . . Beef
	RT: Vegetables and fruits			RT: Beef cattle (B2750)
	(B3500)		M6300	. . . . . Veal
			M6500	. . . . Mutton
				RT: Sheep (B2800)

It may be helpful to highlight some points in the above display:
B2500 prefers Beekeeping to Apiculture, indicating a policy of favouring the more familiar terms, exhibited later at B3580 where Potatoes is preferred to Solanum tuberosum, and similarly elsewhere in the thesaurus.
B3620/B3680 covers a set of coordinate terms in array. There is no obviously appropriate semantic order, so alphabetical order is used to arrange the terms. A similar decision is taken in B3830/B3840.
B6000 Agricultural equipment. The order of the various types of equipment follows the order of the processes in B1100. When the thesaurus was being developed initially, this was not done correctly, and Harvesting equipment was located at B6400. It has now been moved to its more proper location, at B6650. Notice how the way the notation was initially applied made this difficult. It would have been better to reorganise the notation entirely in this area, but it has been left in this rather cramped way to show the problems encountered if the initial analysis is faulty and if the notation is not spaced adequately enough.
B7000 Agricultural structures. The implicit order is living accommodation (human), living accommodation (animals), storage accommodation. This could be stated explicity in a scope note, to provide guidance in the future as the thesaurus expands.
M1300 Plant products. Note how the order here parallels the order of B3400.

Exercise 8 solutions
Following is the rotated alphabetical index for the sample thesaurus. For clarity of display, the notation is given before the alphabetised term. Terms have been listed in upper case so that the index list is different in appearance from the classified thesaurus itself, but this is really simply a personal foible.

B3460	(UK), CORN		B3000	AGRICULTURAL PRODUCTS
B3420	(USA), CORN		B7000	AGRICULTURAL STRUCTURES
B8200	AFFORESTATION		B1000	AGRICULTURE
B6000	AGRICULTURAL EQUIPMENT		B1100	AGRONOMY

APPENDIX (continued)

B4350	ALPINE PLANTS		M3200	CONDENSED MILK
E1400	ANIMAL DISEASES		E1000	CONTROL, DISEASES. PESTS. PEST
B2000	ANIMAL HUSBANDRY			
M2500	ANIMAL ORIGIN, FOODS OF		E4000	CONTROL, PEST
E3000	ANIMAL PESTS		B3460	CORN (UK)
B5000	ANIMAL PRODUCTS		B3420	CORN (USA)
G2000	ANIMALS		B4520	COTTON
B2600	ANIMALS, FARM		B2720	COWS
B2900	ANIMALS, WORKING		B1100	CROP PRODUCTION
B2500	APICULTURE		B1600	CROP PROTECTION
B3910	APRICOTS		B3100	CROPS
B1200	ARABLE FARMING		B4420	CROPS FOR PROCESSED FOODS AND DRINKS
B3620	ASPARAGUS			
B3750	AUBERGINES		B4400	CROPS GROWN FOR INDUSTRIAL PROCESSING
E1500	BACTERIAL DISEASES			
B8320	BARK		B4500	CROPS, FIBER
B7200	BARNS		B4500	CROPS, FIBRE
B4430	BEANS, COCOA		B3300	CROPS, FOOD
B4440	BEANS, COFFEE		B4200	CROPS, FORAGE
M6200	BEEF		B4600	CROPS, MEDICINAL
B2750	BEEF CATTLE		B3700	CUCUMBERS
B6820	BEEHIVES		B4300	CUT FLOWERS, ORNAMENTAL PLANTS
B1030	BEEKEEPERS			
B2500	BEEKEEPING		B2760	DAIRY CATTLE
E3200	BEETLES		B6700	DAIRY EQUIPMENT
B3560	BEETROOT		B2100	DAIRY FARMING
B3560	BEETS		B5100	DAIRY PRODUCTS
B3970	BERRIES		E1200	DISEASES
F1000	BOTANY		E1400	DISEASES, ANIMAL
M1350	BRAN		E1500	DISEASES, BACTERIAL
B2520	BREEDING		E1520	DISEASES, FUNGUS
B1890	BULBS		E1300	DISEASES, PLANT
B2730	BULLS		E1540	DISEASES, VIRAL
M6000	BUTCHERED MEAT PRODUCTS		E1000	DISEASES. PESTS. PEST CONTROL
M4500	BUTTER			
M1800	BUTTER, COCOA		B2920	DOGS
M3500	BUTTERMILK		B1820	DRAINAGE, RECLAMATION AND
B3630	CABBAGES		M1630	DRIED FRUITS
B3540	CARROTS		B4420	DRINKS, CROPS FOR PROCESSED FOODS AND
B2940	CATS			
B2700	CATTLE		B3750	EGGPLANTS
B2750	CATTLE, BEEF		B5300	EGGS
B2760	CATTLE, DAIRY		B6000	EQUIPMENT, AGRICULTURAL
B3650	CELERY		B6700	EQUIPMENT, DAIRY
M1320	CEREAL PRODUCTS		B6200	EQUIPMENT, GARDENING
B3400	CEREALS		B6100	EQUIPMENT, GENERAL
M4000	CHEESE		B6650	EQUIPMENT, HARVESTING
B6740	CHEESE-MOULDS		B6800	EQUIPMENT, LIVESTOCK
B3920	CHERRIES		B6300	EQUIPMENT, PLOUGHING
B2850	CHICKENS		B6300	EQUIPMENT, PLOWING
B3820	CITRUS FRUITS		B6600	EQUIPMENT, SPRAYING
B4430	COCOA BEANS		B6500	EQUIPMENT, WATERING
M1800	COCOA BUTTER		B6480	EQUIPMENT, WEEDING
B4440	COFFEE BEANS		B2600	FARM ANIMALS
B6654	COMBINE HARVESTERS		B1020	FARMERS

B7100	FARMHOUSES	E3100	INSECT PESTS
B1000	FARMING	G4000	INSECTA
B1200	FARMING, ARABLE	E4700	INSECTICIDES
B2100	FARMING, DAIRY	M1700	JUICES
B2300	FARMING, POULTRY	B2500	KEEPING, BEE
B2400	FARMING, SHEEP	B3600	LEAVES; STEMS; FLOWERS
B2530	FEEDING	B3840	LEMONS
B1900	FERTILISERS	B3680	LETTUCES
B1900	FERTILIZERS	B2600	LIVESTOCK
B4500	FIBER CROPS	B6800	LIVESTOCK EQUIPMENT
B4500	FIBRE CROPS	E3300	LOCUSTS
B4530	FLAX	B8340	LOGS
M1500	FLOUR	B6720	MACHINES, MILKING
B3600	FLOWERS, LEAVES; STEMS;	B3420	MAIZE
B4300	FLOWERS, ORNAMENTAL PLANTS. CUT	B5200	MEAT PRODUCTS
		M6000	MEAT PRODUCTS, BUTCHERED
B3300	FOOD CROPS	B4600	MEDICINAL CROPS
M1200	FOOD PRODUCTS	B3750	MELONGENA, SOLANUM
M1000	FOOD TECHNOLOGY	B5120	MILK
B4420	FOODS AND DRINKS, CROPS FOR PROCESSED	M3000	MILK PRODUCTS
		M3200	MILK, CONDENSED
M2500	FOODS OF ANIMAL ORIGIN	M3300	MILK, PASTEURISED
B4200	FORAGE CROPS	M3400	MILK, SKIMMED
B8300	FOREST PRODUCTS	B6720	MILKING MACHINES
B8000	FORESTRY	B6740	MOULDS, CHEESE
B6230	FORKS	M6500	MUTTON
M1600	FRUIT PRODUCTS, VEGETABLE AND	B3945	NECTARINES
		B1300	NURSERY PRACTICES
B3800	FRUITS	M1720	OILS
B3820	FRUITS, CITRUS	B3830	ORANGES
M1630	FRUITS, DRIED	M2500	ORIGIN, FOODS OF ANIMAL
B3970	FRUITS, SOFT	B4300	ORNAMENTAL PLANTS. CUT FLOWERS
B3900	FRUITS, STONE		
B3690	FRUITS, VEGETABLE	M3300	PASTEURISED MILK
B3500	FRUITS, VEGETABLES AND	B3940	PEACHES
E4300	FUNGICIDES	E4000	PEST CONTROL
E1520	FUNGUS DISEASES	E1000	PEST CONTROL, DISEASES. PESTS.
B1320	GARDENING		
B6200	GARDENING EQUIPMENT	E4200	PESTICIDES
B6100	GENERAL EQUIPMENT	E2000	PESTS
B1540	GRAFTING	E3000	PESTS, ANIMAL
B3400	GRAIN	E3100	PESTS, INSECT
B7400	GRANARIES	E2100	PESTS, PLANT
B3990	GRAPES	E1000	PESTS. PEST CONTROL, DISEASES.
B4400	GROWN FOR INDUSTRIAL PROCESSING, CROPS		
		E1300	PLANT DISEASES
B6654	HARVESTERS, COMBINE	E2100	PLANT PESTS
B1700	HARVESTING	M1300	PLANT PRODUCTS
B6650	HARVESTING EQUIPMENT	B1520	PLANTING
B4230	HAY	F2000	PLANTS
E4500	HERBICIDES	B4350	PLANTS, ALPINE
B5350	HONEY	B4300	PLANTS. CUT FLOWERS, ORNAMENTAL
B1300	HORTICULTURE		
B6520	HOSES	B1420	PLOUGHING
B2000	HUSBANDRY, ANIMAL	B6300	PLOUGHING EQUIPMENT
B1800	IMPROVEMENT, SOIL	B6320	PLOUGHS
B4400	INDUSTRIAL PROCESSING, CROPS GROWN FOR	B1420	PLOWING
		B6300	PLOWING EQUIPMENT

APPENDIX (continued)

B6320	PLOWS	B8100	SILVICULTURE
B3960	PLUMS	M3400	SKIMMED MILK
B3580	POTATOES	B3970	SOFT FRUITS
B2830	POULTRY	B1800	SOIL IMPROVEMENT
B2300	POULTRY FARMING	J1000	SOIL SCIENCE
B1300	PRACTICES, NURSERY	B3750	SOLANUM MELONGENA
B4420	PROCESSED FOODS AND DRINKS, CROPS FOR	B3580	SOLANUM TUBEROSUM
		B1500	SOWING
B4400	PROCESSING, CROPS GROWN FOR INDUSTRIAL	B6240	SPADES
		B6600	SPRAYING EQUIPMENT
B1100	PRODUCTION, CROP	B6540	SPRINKLERS
B3000	PRODUCTS, AGRICULTURAL	B3600	STEMS; FLOWERS, LEAVES;
B5000	PRODUCTS, ANIMAL	B3900	STONE FRUITS
M6000	PRODUCTS, BUTCHERED MEAT	B3980	STRAWBERRIES
M1320	PRODUCTS, CEREAL	B7000	STRUCTURES, AGRICULTURAL
B5100	PRODUCTS, DAIRY	M1000	TECHNOLOGY, FOOD
M1200	PRODUCTS, FOOD	B6130	TRACTORS
B8300	PRODUCTS, FOREST	B3580	TUBEROSUM, SOLANUM
B5200	PRODUCTS, MEAT	B2880	TURKEYS
M3000	PRODUCTS, MILK	M6300	VEAL
M1300	PRODUCTS, PLANT	M1600	VEGETABLE AND FRUIT PRODUCTS
M1600	PRODUCTS, VEGETABLE AND FRUIT		
		B3690	VEGETABLE FRUITS
B1510	PROPAGATION	B3520	VEGETABLES
B1600	PROTECTION, CROP	B3500	VEGETABLES AND FRUITS
M1650	PRUNES	B3530	VEGETABLES, ROOT
B1530	PRUNING	H1000	VETERINARY SCIENCE
M1680	RAISINS	B1400	VINEYARDS
B1820	RECLAMATION AND DRAINAGE	B1400	VINICULTURE
B3530	ROOT VEGETABLES	E1540	VIRAL DISEASES
B3440	RYE	B6500	WATERING EQUIPMENT
B4620	SALICACEAE	B1550	WEEDING
J1000	SCIENCE, SOIL	B6480	WEEDING EQUIPMENT
H1000	SCIENCE, VETERINARY	E2200	WEEDS
B1880	SEEDS	B3460	WHEAT
B2430	SHEARING, SHEEP	M1380	WHEATGERM
B2800	SHEEP	B6250	WHEELBARROWS
B2400	SHEEP FARMING	B4620	WILLOWS
B2430	SHEEP SHEARING	M1750	WINES
B2925	SHEEPDOGS	B2900	WORKING ANIMALS
B6652	SICKLES	M5000	YOGHURT
B7300	SILOS	G1000	ZOOLOGY

Thesaurus Construction: Key Issues and Selected Readings

Marianne Lykke Nielsen

SUMMARY. The purpose of this selected bibliography is to introduce issues and problems in relation to thesaurus construction and to present a set of readings that may be used in practical thesaurus design. The concept of thesaurus is discussed, including the purpose of the thesaurus and how the concept has evolved over the years according to new IR technologies. Different approaches to thesaurus construction are introduced, and readings dealing with specific problems and developments in the collection, formation, and organisation of thesaurus concepts and terms are presented. Primarily manual construction methods are discussed, but the bibliography also refers to research about techniques for automatic thesaurus construction. *[Article copies available for a fee from The Haworth Document Delivery Service: 1-800-HAWORTH. E-mail address: <docdelivery@haworthpress.com> Website: <http://www.HaworthPress.com> © 2004 by The Haworth Press, Inc. All rights reserved.]*

KEYWORDS. Thesaurus construction, thesauri, bibliography, methodologies

---

Marianne Lykke Nielsen, MLISc, PhD, holds an academic position at the Department of Information Studies, Royal School of Library and Information Science, Sohngardsholmsvej 2, DK 9000 Aalborg, Denmark (E-mail: mln@db.dk). She teaches courses in indexing, classification, thesaurus construction, and database design, and her research focuses on methodologies for the development of systems for knowledge organization.

[Haworth co-indexing entry note]: "Thesaurus Construction: Key Issues and Selected Readings." Nielsen, Marianne Lykke. Co-published simultaneously in *Cataloging & Classification Quarterly* (The Haworth Information Press, an imprint of The Haworth Press, Inc.) Vol. 37, No. 3/4, 2004, pp. 57-74; and: *The Thesaurus: Review, Renaissance, and Revision* (ed: Sandra K. Roe, and Alan R. Thomas) The Haworth Information Press, an imprint of The Haworth Press, Inc., 2004, pp. 57-74. Single or multiple copies of this article are available for a fee from The Haworth Document Delivery Service [1-800-HAWORTH, 9:00 a.m. - 5:00 p.m. (EST). E-mail address: docdelivery@haworthpress.com].

http://www.haworthpress.com/web/CCQ
© 2004 by The Haworth Press, Inc. All rights reserved.
Digital Object Identifier: 10.1300/J104v37n03_05

INTRODUCTION

The aim of this selected bibliography is to present a set of readings that may be used as the basis for practical thesaurus design projects. The intention is not to provide a complete list, but to introduce issues and problems to consider when constructing a thesaurus and to present methods how to handle the problems.

The thesaurus is a well-known and well-established tool in information retrieval that is used to guide indexing and retrieval based on controlled as well as natural language indexing. Within the last years the thesaurus has experienced a renaissance. Many organisations focus on knowledge management. In the context of different types of knowledge management systems–intranets, content management systems, document management systems–the thesaurus is used both as a traditional tool supporting indexing and retrieval, and a tool to manage and communicate the specific language that is used within the organisation. In this last situation the thesaurus is used as a meaning mapper and as a tool for teaching and communication. In knowledge management systems, the thesaurus is furthermore used for computer-based techniques like automatic classification of documents, automatic indexing, and for automatic query expansion. The hierarchical structure of the thesaurus may also be used as the basis for a navigational taxonomy.

The increased interest and the new environment in which the thesaurus is used are reflected in the literature. New roles for the thesaurus are discussed in several papers, and also the impact on thesaurus construction is discussed in recent publications.

This bibliography is structured in themes related to thesaurus construction. In the first section, readings about the concept of thesaurus are presented, then follows a list of general readings about thesaurus construction. Different approaches to thesaurus construction are introduced in the next section, followed by sections about the sub-processes: collection, formation, and organisation. Then follows a section about automatic thesaurus construction, and the last section sums up the discussion.

THE CONCEPT OF THESAURUS

The thesaurus has been used in Information Retrieval (IR) for the last 50 years. Over the years the definition and use of thesauri have changed, from a tool primarily to aid searching in the early days to a tool for indexing. During the 1980s the thesaurus tended to relinquish its role as an authority for indexing, again becoming a tool to aid searching. The following papers discuss the concept and role of the thesaurus, and taken together, they outline the history of the thesaurus and define it:

Aitchison, Jean, Alan Gilchrist, and David Bawden. *Thesaurus Construction and Use: A Practical Manual*, 4th ed. London: Aslib, 2000.
Bernier, Charles L. and Karl F. Heumann, "Correlative Indexes III. Semantic Relations Among Semantemes–The Technical Thesaurus." *American Documentation* 8, no. 3 (1957): 211-220.
Cochrane, Pauline A. "Indexing and Searching Thesauri, the Janus or Proteus of Information Retrieval." In *Classification Research for Knowledge Representation and Organization. Proceedings of the 5th International Study Conference on Classification Research, Toronto, Canada, 24-28 June, 1991*, edited by N. J. Williamson and M. Hudon, 161-177. Amsterdam: Elsevier Science Publishers BV and FID, 1992.
Foskett, Douglas J. "Thesaurus." In *Encyclopedia of Library and Information Science*, 30, edited by Allen Kent, Harold Lancour and Jay E. Daily, 416-463. New York: Marcel Dekker, 1980.
Gilchrist, Alan. *The Thesaurus in Retrieval*. London: Aslib, 1971.
Holm, B. E. and L. E. Rasmussen, "Development of a Technical Thesaurus." *American Documentation* 12 (July 1961): 184-190.
Joyce, T. and R. M. Needham, "The Thesaurus Approach to Information Retrieval." *American Documentation* 9 (1958): 192-197.
Lancaster, F. Wilfrid. *Vocabulary Control for Information Retrieval*. Arlington, Virginia: Information Resources Press, 1986.
Milstead, J. L. "Invisible Thesauri: The Year 2000." *Online and CDROM Review* 19, no. 2 (1995): 93-94.
Mooers, Calvin N. "The Next Twenty Years in Information Retrieval." *American Documentation* 11, no. 3 (1960): 229-236.
Reisner, Phyllis. *Evaluation of a "Growing" Thesaurus*. Yorktown Heights: IBM Watson Research Center, 1966.
Roberts, N. "The Pre-History of the Information Retrieval Thesaurus." *Journal of Documentation* 40, no. 4 (1984): 271-285.
Soergel, D. *Indexing Languages and Thesauri: Construction and Maintenance*. Wiley Information Science Series. Los Angeles, CA: Melville, 1974.
Sparck Jones, K. "Some Thesauric History." *Aslib Proceedings* 24, no. 7 (1972): 400-411.
Vickery, B. C. "Thesaurus–A New Word in Documentation." *Journal of Documentation* 16, no. 4 (1960): 181-189.
Wall, E. "Information Systems." *Chemical Engineering Progress* 55, no. 1 (1959): 55-59.

The searching thesaurus was introduced in the 1980s, and the role of this specific type of thesaurus is to assist in searching by suggesting additional search terms, especially synonyms and narrower terms. The searching thesaurus, also called end-user thesaurus, is regarded as a search-only vocabulary rather than an indexing vocabulary. The searching thesaurus is supposed to be a specialized tool for the process of defining and formulating the request and query. In contrast to the classical thesaurus, the searching thesaurus does not seek to control and standardise the term choices, but, instead, provide alternatives to the terms that the searcher has in mind and help the searcher to recall relevant related concepts and terms. The searching thesaurus is independent of any specific information system and guides the user to an alternative set of retrieval synonyms. However, the thesaurus may divide and define the set of terms indicating how the concept of interest is named in selected information systems.

Bates, Marcia J. "Subject Access in Online Catalogs: A Design Model." *Journal of the American Society for Information Science* 37, no. 6 (1986): 357-376.

Cochrane, Pauline A. "Indexing and Searching Thesauri, the Janus or Proteus of Information Retrieval." In *Classification Research for Knowledge Representation and Organization. Proceedings of the 5th International Study Conference on Classification Research, Toronto, Canada, 24-28 June, 1991*, edited by N. J. Williamson and M. Hudon, 161-177. Amsterdam: Elsevier Science Publishers BV and FID, 1992.

Gillman, Peter. "Thesauri to Aid Retrieval from Very Large Text Bases: Subject Term Retrieval from Large Text Resources, and the Problems of Ambiguity." In *Knowledge Organization for Information Retrieval. Proceedings of the 6th International Study Conference on Classification Research, University College London, 16-18 June 1997*, 113-119. FID 716. The Hague, Netherlands: International Federation for Information and Documentation, 1997.

Johnson, Eric H. and Pauline A. Cochrane. "A Hypertextual Interface for a Searcher's Thesaurus." In *Proceedings of Digital Libraries '95: The Second Annual Conference on the Theory and Practice of Digital Libraries: June 11-13, 1995, Austin, Texas, USA*, 77-86. College Station, Texas: Hypermedia Research Laboratory, 1995.

Knapp, Sara D. "Creating BRS/Term, a Vocabulary Database for Searchers." *Database* 7, no. 4 (1984): 70-75.

Knapp, Sara D. *The Contemporary Thesaurus of Social Science Terms and Synonyms: A Guide for Natural Language Computer Searching*. Phoenix, AZ: Oryx Press, 1993.

Knapp, Sara D., Laura B. Cohen, and D. R. Juedes. "A Natural Language Thesaurus for the Humanities: The Need for a Database Search Aid." *Library Quarterly* 68, no. 4 (1998): 406-430.
Lykke Nielsen, M. "What Kind of Structure and Relations Do Searchers Need?" In *Structures and Relations in Knowledge Organization. Proceedings of the Fifth International ISKO Conference, 25-29 August 1998, Lille, France*, edited by W. Mustafa el Hadi, J. Maniez and S. A. Pollitt, 152-159. Würzburg: Argon Verlag, 1998.
Piternick, Anne Brearley. "Searching Vocabularies: A Developing Category of Online Search Tools." *Online Review* 8, no. 5 (1984): 441-449.
Schatz, Bruce R., Eric H. Johnson, Pauline A. Cochrane, and Hsinchun Chen. "Interactive Term Suggestion for Users of Digital Libraries: Using Subject Thesauri and Co-occurrence Lists for Information Retrieval." In *Proceedings of the 1st ACM International Conference on Digital Libraries: March 20-23, 1996, Bethesda, Maryland*, edited by Edward A. Fox and Gary Marchionini, 126-133. New York: Association for Computing Machinery, 1996.

A recent development of the thesaurus is the corporate taxonomy that incorporates elements of both classification systems and thesauri. The corporate taxonomy originates in operational, professional information environments. It is not a prototypical thesaurus but a system to arrange and label metadata, provide access to the primary data or information by a hierarchical structure, and allow the data to be systematically managed and manipulated. The role is, furthermore, to gather all jargon or special language practiced in an organization to one location and to give clear and simple definitions that communicate the basic and essential meaning. The goal is to facilitate both understanding at a conceptual level and communication on a linguistic level, as well as to create a vocabulary that can be learned and that can provide a tool for corporate communication. The objective of the corporate taxonomy is twofold: (1) securing and supporting information retrieval, and (2) aiding in the understanding and use of a subject area or vocabulary.

Conway, Susan and Char Sligar. "Unlocking Knowledge Assets." Chap. 6 in *Building Taxonomies*. Redmond, Wash.: Microsoft Press, 2002.
Gilchrist, Alan. "The Corporate Taxonomy: The Latest Tool in the Battle Against Information Overload." *Records Management Bulletin* 100 (Dec. 2000): 11-15.
Gilchrist, Alan. "Thesauri, Taxonomies and Ontologies–An Etymological Note." *Journal of Documentation* 59, no. 1 (2003): 7-18.

Gilchrist, Alan and Peter Kibby. *Taxonomies for Business: Access and Connectivity in a Wired World.* London: TFPL, 2000.

Hagedorn, K. *Extracting Value from Automated Classification Tools: The Role of Manual Involvement and Controlled Vocabularies.* Available online at URL: http://argus-acia.com/white_papers/classification.html.

International Organization for Standardization. *Information and Documentation: Record Management.* ISO 15489. Geneva: ISO, 2001.

Lykke Nielsen, M. and A. Gjerluf Eslau. "Corporate Thesauri–How to Ensure Integration of Knowledge and Reflection of Diversity." In *Challenges in Knowledge Representation and Organization for the 21st Century: Integration of Knowledge Across Boundaries. Proceedings of the Seventh International ISKO Conference, 10-13 July 2002, Granada, Spain,* edited by María J. López-Huertas, 324-331. Würzburg: Ergon-Verlag, 2002.

Mahon, Bally, Rubin Hourican, and Alan Gilchrist. *Research into Information Architecture: The Roles of Software, Taxonomies and People: A Report.* London: TFPL, 2001.

Soergel, D. "SemWeb: Proposal for an Open, Multifunctional, Multilingual System for Integrated Access to Knowledge About Concepts and Terminology." In *Proceedings of the Fourth International ISKO Conference, 15-18 July, 1996, Washington, DC, USA,* edited by R. Green, 165-173. Frankfurt/Main: Indeks Verlag, 1996.

GENERAL WRITINGS ABOUT THESAURUS CONSTRUCTION

The process of thesaurus construction is traditionally divided into three technical sub-processes:

- Collection of concepts and terms
- Formation and definition of concepts and terms
- Organisation of concept and terms.

These technical processes are well-described in textbooks, guidelines, and standards. International standards exist for both monolingual and multilingual thesauri:

Association Française de Normalisation. *Principes directeurs pour l'établissement de thésaurus multilingues.* NFZ 47-101. Paris: AFNOR, 1990.

Association Française de Normalisation. *Règles d'établissement des thésaurus monolingues.* NFZ 47-100. Paris: AFNOR, 1981.
British Standards Institution. *British Standard Guide to Establishment and Development of Monolingual Thesauri,* 2nd ed. BS5723. London: British Standards Institute, 1987.
British Standards Institution. *British Standard Guide to Establishment and Development of Multilingual Thesauri.* BS6723. London: British Standards Institute, 1985.
Deutsches Institut für Normung (DIN). *Erstellung und Weiterentwicklung von Thesauri; Einsprachige Thesauri.* DIN 1463-1, Ausgabe: 1987-11. Berlin: DIN, 1987.
Deutsches Institut für Normung (DIN). *Erstellung und Weiterentwicklung von Thesauri; Mehrsprachige Thesauri.* DIN 1463-2, Ausgabe 1993-10. Berlin: DIN, 1993.
International Organization for Standardization. *Documentation–Guidelines for the Establishment and Development of Monolingual Thesauri,* 2nd ed. ISO 2788. Geneva: ISO, 1986.
International Organization for Standardization. *Documentation–Guidelines for the Establishment and Development of Multilingual Thesauri.* ISO 5964. Geneva: ISO, 1985.
National Information Standards Organisation. *Guidelines for the Construction, Format, and Management of Monolingual Thesauri.* ANSI/NISO Z39.19-1993. Bethesda: NISO Press, 1994.

Issues and problems related to thesaurus construction have also been thoroughly discussed in practical guidelines and books, which all are considered classical works on thesaurus construction:

Aitchison, Jean, Alan Gilchrist and David Bawden. *Thesaurus Construction and Use: A Practical Manual,* 4th ed. London: Aslib, 2000.
Lancaster, F. Wilfrid. *Vocabulary Control for Information Retrieval.* Arlington, Virginia: Information Resources Press, 1986.
Soergel, Dagobert. *Indexing Languages and Thesauri: Construction and Maintenance.* Wiley Information Science Series. Los Angeles: Melville, 1974.
Svenonious, Elaine. "Design of Controlled Vocabularies." In *Encyclopedia of Library and Information Science,* 45, edited by Allen Kent, Harold Lancour and Jay E. Daily, 82-109. New York: Marcel Dekker, 1990.

Principles and guidelines have evolved over a long period and are widely accepted. In practice, there may be some doubt as to how much direct impact the guidelines have had on actual thesaurus construction, as there exists a wide variation in the nature and quality of thesauri. In 1990, in his paper on the "The Standards Jungle," Alan Gilchrist (1991) stated that virtually the only recommendation in ISO 2788 which has become "standard" is the use of the symbols BT, NT, RT, etc. The impact of standards is discussed in the following writings:

Dextre Clarke, S. G. "Thesaural Relationships." In *Relationships in the Organization of Knowledge*, edited by Carol A. Bean and Rebecca Green, 37-52. Dordrecht: Kluwer Academic Publishers, 2001.

Gilchrist, A. "The Standards Jungle." In *Standards for the International Exchange of Bibliographic Information: Papers presented at a course held at the School of Library, Archive and Information Studies, University College London, 3-18 August 1990*, edited by Ia C. McLlaine. London: Library Association, 1991.

Krooks, D. A. and F. W. Lancaster. "The Evolution of Guidelines for Thesaurus Construction." *Libri* 43, no. 4 (1993): 326-342.

Williamson, Nancy J. "Standards and Rules for Subject Access." *Cataloging & Classification Quarterly* 21, no. 3/4 (1996): 155-176.

APPROACHES TO THESAURUS CONSTRUCTION

The processes mentioned earlier–collection, formation and organisation–are technical processes for which a set of general principles has been developed, and the thesaurus compiler must apply the guidelines according to situational and environmental needs. Decisions regarding, for instance, associative relationships must be taken according to the way concepts are used and related within the information environment. The guidelines and standards may suggest alternative types of relationship, but it is domain-related factors that make it possible to choose among the alternatives. Therefore, the thesaurus compiler should have thorough knowledge of the information environment.

In the early literature about thesaurus construction, no methodology was mentioned to help gain the needed knowledge about the information environment. During the eighties a user-centred approach to thesaurus construction emerged, which introduced strategies of basing the development of indexing systems, including thesauri, on field studies of the users' information use and information needs. The thesaurus construction process was considered as a system design process, and focus was on information systems and thesauri supporting people in their daily activities.

Allen, Bryce. *Information Tasks: Toward a User-centered Approach to Information Systems.* San Diego: Academic Press, 1996.

Pejtersen, A. M. "Design of a Classification Scheme for Fiction Based on an Analysis of Actual User-Librarian Communication, and Use of the Scheme for Control of Librarians' Search Strategies." In *Theory and Application of Information Research: Proceedings of the Second International Research Forum on Information Science, 3-6 August 1977, Royal School of Librarianship, Copenhagen,* edited by Ole Harbo and Leif Kajberg, 146-159. London: Mansell, 1980.

Pejtersen, Annelise Mark and Raya Fidel. "A Framework for Work Centered Evaluation and Design: A Case Study of IR on the Web." Report for MIRA. Grenoble, France, 1998.

Soergel, Dagobert. *Organizing Information: Principles of Data Base and Retrieval Systems.* San Diego: Academic Press, 1985.

Wilson, T. D. "On User Studies and Information Needs." *Journal of Documentation* 37 (1981): 3-15.

Later, the user-centred approach within information science evolved and turned into a holistic view of all of the interactive communication processes, stressing the importance of the situational context that surrounds the user. This development of the user-centred approach is called the "person-in-situation" approach or the holistic cognitive approach.

Allen, B. "Information Needs: A Person-in-Situation Approach." In *Information Seeking in Context: Proceedings of an International Conference on Research in Information Needs, Seeking and Use in Different Contexts,* 14-16 August, 1996, Tampere, Finland, edited by Pertti Vakkari, Reijo Savolainen and Brenda Dervin, 111-122. London: Taylor Graham, 1997.

Ingwersen, Peter. "Users in Context." In *Lectures on Information Retrieval: Third European Summer-School,* ESSIR 2000, Varenna, Italy, September 11-15, 2000, edited by Maristella Agosti, Fabio Crestani, and Gabriella Pasi, 157-178. Berlin: Springer, 2001.

Kuhlthau, Carol C. and Pertti Vakkari. "Editorial: Information Seeking in Context (ISIC)." *Information Processing & Management* 35, no. 6 (1999): 723-725.

Lykke Nielsen, Marianne. "A Framework for Work Task Based Thesaurus Design." *Journal of Documentation* 57, no. 6 (2001): 774-797.

Vakkari, P. "Information Seeking in Context: A Challenging Metatheory." In *Information Seeking in Context: Proceedings of an International Conference on Research in Information Needs, Seeking and Use in Different Contexts,* 14-16 August, 1996, Tampere, Finland, edited by Pertti Vakkari, Reijo Savolainen and Brenda Dervin, 451-464. London: Taylor Graham, 1997.

Wilson, T. D. "Models in Information Behaviour Research." *Journal of Documentation* 55, no. 3 (1999): 249-270.

The user-centred and the cognitive approaches have been criticised for being defective in being based solely on studies of individual users detached from their context. It is argued that the individual user's knowledge structures and behaviour are shaped through participation in socially grounded domains. Knowledge is constructed through and embedded within acting, and system analysis should study the information environment itself and not the individuals acting in it. The critics stress the importance of seeing the individual user as member of a particular knowledge domain. Individuals do not operate in isolation but work, instead, within the dynamical contexts provided by complex socio-cultural and historical systems. Any attempt to construct an adequate explanation and understanding of human cognitive activities should focus on the nature of the knowledge domain.

Thus, there exist different approaches on how to gain the needed knowledge about the information environment. The boundary between the different approaches is less marked today. It seems to be generally accepted that the study of information behaviour must take into account the users, their particular role or function and, especially, the information environment that influences information seeking and use. Anyway, the discussion and consciousness about how to approach the construction process is useful and provides a fruitful theoretical basis for the process of constructing systems for knowledge organization.

Hjørland, Birger. "Domain Analysis in Information Science: Eleven Approaches–Traditional as Well as Innovative." *Journal of Documentation* 58, no. 4 (2002): 422-462.

Hjørland, Biger. "Epistemology and the Socio-Cognitive Perspective in Information Science." *Journal of the American Society for Information Science and Technology* 53, no. 4 (2002): 257-270.

Hjørland, B. and H. Albrechtsen. "Toward a New Horizon in Information Science: Domain-Analysis." *Journal of the American Society for Information Science* 46, no. 6 (1995): 400-425.

Jacob, Elin K. and Debora Shaw. "Sociocognitive Perspectives on Representation." *Annual Review of Information Science and Technology* 33 (1998): 131-185.

Talja, S., R. Heinisuo, S. Luukkainen, and K. Järvelin. "Discourse Analysis in the Development of a Regional Information Service." In *Library and Information Studies: Research and Professional Practice: Proceedings of the 2nd British-Nordic Conference on Library and Information Studies, Queen Margaret College, Edinburgh, 1997*, edited by Micheline Beaulieu, Elisabeth Davenport and Niels Ole Pors, 109-128. London: Taylor Graham, 1997.

COLLECTION OF TERMS AND CONCEPTS

After defining the purpose and scope of the thesaurus through a domain study of the information environment, the next logical step in thesaurus construction is collection of terms and concepts. A thesaurus may be compiled using a deductive method, attempting to collect a broad set of terms that cover the subject field as widely as possible before starting the examination of the selected terms. Alternately, the thesaurus compiler may use the inductive method, admitting terms and concepts to the thesaurus as soon as they are encountered in the literature and used in indexing. Using the inductive method, the terms collected primarily derive from the indexed documents and are collected during the indexing process. Using the deductive method, the compiler may use a wide range of written and unwritten sources for collection. Unwritten sources are, for instance, the knowledge and experience of users and subject experts, obtained by interviews, focus groups, word association tests, or workshops. Written sources may be divided into: terms in standardized, prearranged form; non-standardized terminology found in the literature; or in users' recorded questions and profiles. Terms may be extracted by manual, intellectual selection or by automatic, computer-based extraction. Collection methods are covered thoroughly by the general textbooks and guidelines. The following readings are presented, because they present new approaches to term collection:

Haas, S. W. and C. A. Hert. "Terminology Development and Organization in Multi-Community Environments: The Case of Statistical Information." In *Classification for User Support and Learning: Proceedings of the 11th ASIS & T SIG/CR Classification Research Workshop: November 12, 2000*, edited by Dagobert Soergel, Padmini Srinivasan, and Barbara Kwasnik, 51-72. Silver Spring, Maryland: American Society for Information Science, 2000.

Lykke Nielsen, Marianne. "The Word Association Test in the Methodology of Thesaurus Construction." In *Advances in Classification Research: Proceedings of the 8th ASIS SIG/CR Classification Research Workshop, Washington, D.C., November 1-6, 1997*, edited by Efthimis N. Efthimiadis, 43-58. Medford, N.J.: Information Today, 1998.

Lykke Nielsen, Marianne and A. Gjerluf Eslau. "Corporate Thesauri–How to Ensure Integration of Knowledge and Reflection of Diversity." In *Challenges in Knowledge Representation and Organization for the 21st Century: Integration of Knowledge Across Boundaries: Proceedings of the Seventh International ISKO Conference, 10-13 July 2002, Granada, Spain*, edited by María J. López-Huertas, 324-331. Würzburg: Ergon-Verlag, 2002.

Lykke Nielsen, Marianne. "The Word Association Method: A Gateway to Work-Task Based Retrieval." Ph.D. diss., Åbo Akademi University Press, 2002.

Talja, S., R. Heinisuo, S. Luukkainen, and K. Järvelin. "Discourse Analysis in the Development of a Regional Information Service." In *Library and Information Studies: Research and Professional Practice: Proceedings of the 2nd British-Nordic Conference on Library and Information Studies, Queen Margaret College, Edinburgh, 1997*, edited by Micheline Beaulieu, Elisabeth Davenport and Niels Ole Pors, 109-128. London: Taylor Graham, 1997.

FORMATION AND DEFINITION OF CONCEPTS

Terms and concepts are controlled in various ways in thesauri. The form of the terms is controlled, whether this involves grammatical form, spelling, singular and plural form, abbreviations, or compound form of the term. Meaning of concepts is controlled and a choice is made between synonyms available to express the same concept. Understanding and restrictions of use are indicated by the addition of scope notes and, in the case of homographs, definitions and qualifying phrases. In a thesaurus used for controlled indexing, the preferred, controlled representation (the descriptor) is chosen.

Standards and guidelines describe techniques based on general principles that apply to all subject fields. But it is also recognised that these general principles and guidelines must be applied according to the situation, the purpose of the thesaurus, and the characteristics of the information environment. Current awareness of the fuzziness of language has provoked an increased focus on integrating more profound definitions in order to clarify meaning and differentiate perspective in language use. The following readings discuss the dynamics and fuzziness of language and provide guidelines on how to better understand the vocabulary.

Hudon, Michele. "Preparing Terminological Definitions for Indexing and Retrieval Thesauri: A Model." In *Knowledge Organization and Change: Proceedings of the Fourth International ISKO Conference, 15-18 July 1996, Washington, DC, USA*, edited by Rebecca Green, 363-369. Frankfurt/Main: Indeks Verlag, 1996.

Hudon, Michele. "Multilingual Thesaurus Construction–Integrating the Views of Different Cultures in One Gateway to Knowledge and Concepts." *Information Services and Use* 17, no. 2/3 (1997): 112-123.

Hudon, Michele. "A Preliminary Investigation of the Usefulness of Semantic Relations and of Standardized Definitions for the Purpose of Specifying Meaning in a Thesaurus." In *Structures and Relations in Knowledge Organization: Proceedings of the Fifth International ISKO Conference, 25-29 August 1998, Lille, France*, edited by Widad Mustafa el Hadi, Jacques Maniez and Steven A. Pollitt, 139-145. Würzburg: Ergon Verlag, 1998.

Jacob, E. K. and H. Albrechtsen. "Constructing Reality: The Role of Dialogue in the Development of Classificatory Structures." In *Knowledge Organization for Information Retrieval: Proceedings of the Sixth International Study Conference on Classification Research held at University College London, 16-18 June 1997*, 42-50. FID 716. The Hague, Netherlands: International Federation for Information and Documentation, 1997.

Svenonius, E. "Definitional Approaches in the Design of Classification and Thesauri and Their Implications for Retrieval and for Automatic Classification." In *Knowledge Organization for Information Retrieval: Proceedings of the Sixth International Study Conference on Classification Research held at University College London, 16-18 June 1997*, 12-16. FID 716. The Hague, Netherlands: International Federation for Information and Documentation, 1997.

ORGANISATION OF CONCEPTS

The ability to distinguish and display relationships between concepts and terms is an intrinsic feature of the thesaurus, and the classification provides important conceptual knowledge and understanding to the thesaurus user. The structuring and classification of terms signal the meaning and usage of the vocabulary; browsing the structure gives the user a feeling for the knowledge domain. Three basic inter-term relationships are used: the equivalence relationship, the hierarchical relationship, and the associative relationship.

Recently, there has been increased research of hierarchical and associative relationships. The interest is related to the growing awareness of the dynamic and context-dependent character of language and the derived need for conceptual information to explain the use and meaning of terms and concepts. Relationships play an important role in disambiguation; perspective hierarchical and associative relations, especially, show the different meanings that terms can assume in a particular knowledge domain. The current interest is furthermore related to the fact that well-structured queries perform better than poorly structured queries. The thesaurus is seen as a means to support the inexperienced searcher in characterising their information need, and to be used automatically through retrieval algorithms that formulate or modify search queries. The following papers treat the issue of relationships from different aspects:

Bean, Carol. "Analysis of Non-Hierarchical Associative Relationships Among Medical Subject Headings (MeSH): Anatomical and Related Terminology." In *Knowledge Organization and Change: Proceedings of the Fourth International ISKO Conference, 15-18 July 1996, Washington, DC, USA*, edited by Rebecca Green, 80-86. *Advances in Knowledge Organization*, vol. 5. Frankfurt/Main: Indeks Verlag, 1996.

Bean, Carol A. and Rebecca Green, eds. *Relationships in the Organization of Knowledge*. Dordrecht: Kluwer Academic Publishers, 2001.

Dextre Clarke, Stella G. "Thesaural Relationships." In *Relationships in the Organization of Knowledge*, edited by Carol A. Bean and Rebecca Green, 37-52. Dordrecht: Kluwer Academic Publishers, 2001.

Green, Rebecca. "Development of a Relational Thesaurus." In *Knowledge Organization and Change: Proceedings of the Fourth International ISKO Conference, 15-18 July 1996, Washington, DC, USA,* edited by Rebecca Green, 72-79. *Advances in Knowledge Organization*, vol. 5. Frankfurt/Main: Indeks Verlag, 1996.

López-Huertas, María J. "Thesaurus Structure Design: A Conceptual Approach for Improved Interaction." *Journal of Documentation* 53, no. 2 (1997): 139-177.

Lykke Nielsen, Marianne. "A Framework for Work Task Based Thesaurus Design." *Journal of Documentation* 57 no. 6 (2001): 774-797.

Milstead, Jessica L. "Standards for Relationships Between Subject Indexing Terms." In *Relationships in the Organization of Knowledge*, edited by Carol A. Bean and Rebecca Green, 53-66. Dordrecht: Kluwer Academic Publishers, 2001.

Schmitz-Esser, Winfried. "Thesaurus and Beyond: An Advanced Formula for Linguistic Engineering and Information Retrieval." *Knowledge Organization* 26, no. 1 (1999): 10-22.

Talja, S., R. Heinisuo, S. Luukkainen, and K. Järvelin. "Discourse Analysis in the Development of a Regional Information Service." In *Library and Information Studies: Research and Professional Practice: Proceedings of the 2nd British-Nordic Conference on Library and Information Studies, Queen Margaret College, Edinburgh, 1997*, edited by Micheline Beaulieu, Elisabeth Davenport and Niels Ole Pors, 109-128. London: Taylor Graham, 1997.

Tudlope, Douglas, Harith Alani, and Christopher Jones. "Augmenting Thesaurus Relationships: Possibilities for Retrieval." *Journal of Digital Information* 1, no. 8 (2001). Available online at URL: http://jodi.ecs.soton.ac.uk/Articles/v01/i08/Tudhope/.

Tudhope, Douglas, Ceri Binding, Dorothee Blocks and Daniel Cunliffe. "Representation and Retrieval in Facetted Systems." In *Challenges in Knowledge Representation and Organization for the 21st Century: Integration of Knowledge Across Boundaries. Proceedings of the Seventh International ISKO Conference, 10-13 July 2002, Granada, Spain*, edited by María J. López-Huertas, 191-197. Würzburg: Ergon-Verlag, 2002. Also available online at URL: http://www.glam.ac.uk/soc/research/hypermedia/publications/presentationdocs/ISKOn.doc.

Vakkari, Pertti. "Subject Knowledge, Source of Terms, and Term Selection in Query Expansion: An Analytical Study." In *Advances in information retrieval: 24th BCS-IRSG European Colloquium on IR Research, Glasgow, UK, March 25-27, 2002: Proceedings*, edited by Fabio Crestani, Mark Girolami, and Cornelis Joost van Rijsbergern, 110-123. Berlin: Springer-Verlag, 2002.

AUTOMATIC THESAURUS CONSTRUCTION

Over the years a considerable amount of research has been performed on automatic approaches to the operations of information systems, including automatic construction of thesauri. Techniques for automatic thesaurus generation are based on automatic extraction of terms and on statistical clustering of terms or phrases. The construction operations, collection and structuring of terms, are assisted by statistical techniques or computational linguistics.

Basically, two approaches exist to automatic construction of thesauri: construction of global thesauri or local thesauri. In a global approach thesaurus classes, once constructed, are used to index both documents and queries, like a traditional thesaurus. In contrast, the local thesaurus uses information obtained from the documents retrieved in response to a particular query to modify that query, which is then resubmitted to the retrieval system for processing. Thus a global thesaurus is constructed prior to the indexing process and is used to index both documents and queries, whereas a local thesaurus is constructed dynamically during the query processing and is used as a searching thesaurus to modify only that query.

The use of automatic techniques is still not widely applied in the operational, practical situation, but as the computer-based construction techniques have become a natural part of software products for information management, the balance of the intellectual effort is shifting from human to computing processes. However, there is a widespread agreement on the importance of human intervention (Gilchrist & Kibby, 2000).

Chen, Hsinchun and Kevin J. Lynch. "Automatic Construction of Networks of Concepts Characterizing Document Databases." *IEEE Transactions on Systems, Man, and Cybernetics* 22, no. 5 (1992): 885-902.

Chen, Hsinchun and T. Ng. "An Algorithmic Approach to Concept Exploration in a Large Knowledge Network (Automatic Thesaurus Consultation): Symbolic Branch-and-Bound Search vs. Connectionist Hopfield Net Activation." *Journal of the American Society for Information Science* 46, no. 5 (1995): 348-369.

Chen, Hsinchun, Tak Yim, David Fye, and Bruce Schatz. "Automatic Thesaurus Generation for an Electronic Community System." *Journal of the American Society for Information Science* 46, no. 3 (1995): 175-193.

Crouch, Carolyn J. "An Approach to Automatic Construction of Global Thesauri." *Information Processing & Management* 26, no. 5 (1990): 629-640.

Gilchrist, Alan. "The Corporate Taxonomy: The Latest Tool in the Battle Against Information Overload." *Records Management Bulletin* 100 (Dec. 2000): 11-15.

Lancaster, F. Wilfred. *Indexing and Abstracting in Theory and Practice.* London: Library Association, 1998.

Lesk, M. E. "Word-Word Association in Document Retrieval Systems." *American Documentation* 20, no. 1 (1969): 27-38.

Mahon, Barry, Robin Hourican and Alan Gilchrist. *Research Into Information Architecture: The Roles of Software, Taxonomies and People: A Report.* London: TFPL, 2001.

Peat, H. J. and P. Willett. "The Limitations of Term Co-occurrence Data for Query Expansion in Document Retrieval Systems." *Journal of the American Society for Information Science* 42, no. 5 (1991): 378-383.

Rees-Potter, Lorna K. "Dynamic Thesaural Systems: A Bibliometric Study of Terminological and Conceptual Change in Sociology and Economics with Application to the Design of Dynamic Thesaural Systems." *Information Processing & Management* 25, no. 6 (1989): 677-691.

Salton, Gerald and Michael McGill. *Introduction to Modern Information Retrieval.* New York, NY: McGraw Hill, 1983.

Schatz, Bruce R., Eric H. Johnson, Pauline A. Cochrane, and Hsinchun Chen. "Interactive Term Suggestion for Users of Digital Libraries: Using Subject Thesauri and Co-occurrence Lists for Information Retrieval." In *Proceedings of the 1st ACM International Conference on Digital Libraries: March 20-23, 1996, Bethesda, Maryland*, edited by Edward A. Fox and Gary Marchionini, 126-133. New York: Association for Computing Machinery, 1996.

Schneider, Jesper W. and P. Borlund. "Preliminary Study of the Potentiality of Bibliometric Methods for the Construction of Thesauri." In *Emerging Frameworks and Methods: CoLIS 4: Proceedings of the Fourth International Conference on Conceptions of Library and Information Science, Seattle, WA, USA, July 21-25, 2002*, edited by Harry Bruce, R. Fidel, P. Ingwersen and P. Vakkari, 151-165. Colorado: Libraries Unlimited, 2002.

Schütze, Hinrich and Jan O. Pedersen. "A Cooccurrence-Based Thesaurus and Two Applications to Information Retrieval." *Information Processing & Management* 33, no. 3 (1997): 307-318.

Sparck Jones, Karen. *Automatic Keyword Classification for Information Retrieval.* London: Butterworths, 1971.

Sparck Jones, Karen. "Automatic Indexing." *Journal of Documentation* 30, no. 4 (1974): 393-432.

Sparck Jones, Karen. "Thesaurus." In *Encyclopedia of Artificial Intelligence*, 2, edited by S. C. Shapiro, 1605-1613. New York, NY: John Wiley, 1992.

Stiles, H. Edmund. "The Association Factor in Information Retrieval." *Journal of the ACM* 8, no. 2 (1961): 271-279.

Van Rijsbergen, C. J., D. J. Harper, and M. F. Porter. "The Selection of Good Search Terms." *Information Processing & Management* 17, no. 2 (1981): 77-91.

CONCLUDING REMARKS

The thesaurus is a well-defined concept, widely used within information science to aid indexers and searchers in finding their way around the vocabulary of a certain knowledge domain. The thesaurus is a tool to map and handle the fuzziness of language and provide security in information retrieval and knowledge sharing. The latest adaptation and development of the thesaurus is the corporate taxonomy that captures corporate and disciplinary jargons in order to facilitate communication and information exchange within an organisation. The taxonomy is used to structure intranets and portals, to control metadata, and to relate to external data structures and vocabularies.

Thesaurus construction involves three primary technical processes: collection of terms and concepts, formation of concepts and control of terms, and organisation of concepts and terms. Particular problems are related to each process. Over the years, principles concerning form, definition, and organisation have been developed and evolved, and recommendations and experiences have been embodied in a variety of standards and guidelines. The guidelines and standards suggest alternative solutions to problems faced by the thesaurus compiler, but it is these domain-related factors which make it possible to choose among those alternatives. The thesaurus should be developed according to the nature and needs of the information environment in which it is going to be used. This implies a thorough knowledge of the information environment and the discourses and languages in play. This knowledge may be gathered by different methodologies. Recently, there has been some discussion about what approach to take in order to get the needed insight. However, it is generally accepted to take a holistic approach and study the information environment and its users as an interacting whole.

Thesaurus Consultancy

Leonard Will

SUMMARY. The role and functions of a consultant in thesaurus development are reviewed, with guidance given on when and how a consultant can be selected. The need for a contract is discussed, and the steps of a thesaurus project are outlined. The cost of thesaurus development is seen to be subject to many variables, which makes it difficult to estimate accurately, but some guidelines are given. Testing and feedback are important, and the use of a thesaurus requires an ongoing commitment from the client organisation to maintain and develop it to keep pace with change. Ways in which thesaurus development software can be used are discussed, and attention is drawn to the need for interaction between thesaurus developers and user interface designers to allow the benefits of a thesaurus-based information retrieval system to be fully realised. *[Article copies available for a fee from The Haworth Document Delivery Service: 1-800-HAWORTH. E-mail address: <docdelivery@haworthpress.com> Website: <http://www.HaworthPress.com> © 2004 by The Haworth Press, Inc. All rights reserved.]*

KEYWORDS. Thesauri–consultants, thesaurus construction, thesaurus software, thesauri–functions

---

Leonard Will, Willpower Information, Enfield, UK (http://www.willpowerinfo.co.uk), is a consultant in information management, specializing in thesauri, classification schemes, and other means of subject retrieval in museums, libraries, and archives. He was previously Head of Library and Information Services at the Science Museum, London.

The author is grateful to Stella Dextre Clarke for her interesting comments on this topic.

[Haworth co-indexing entry note]: "Thesaurus Consultancy." Will, Leonard. Co-published simultaneously in *Cataloging & Classification Quarterly* (The Haworth Information Press, an imprint of The Haworth Press, Inc.) Vol. 37, No. 3/4, 2004, pp. 75-85; and: *The Thesaurus: Review, Renaissance, and Revision* (ed: Sandra K. Roe, and Alan R. Thomas) The Haworth Information Press, an imprint of The Haworth Press, Inc., 2004, pp. 75-85. Single or multiple copies of this article are available for a fee from The Haworth Document Delivery Service [1-800-HAWORTH, 9:00 a.m. - 5:00 p.m. (EST). E-mail address: docdelivery@haworthpress.com].

INTRODUCTION

"A thesaurus is a growing organism," to adapt one of Ranganathan's "Laws of Library Science." Organisations have to learn that they cannot just ask a consultant to produce a thesaurus which they can then use in its original form for the foreseeable future. A thesaurus is a dynamic part of an organisation's information and knowledge management system, and it needs to be nurtured so that it can grow and change with the organisation itself. Only a committed internal owner can give it the continuing tender loving care it needs.

However, an external consultant can help an organisation to decide whether a thesaurus is appropriate and, if so, to set them on the right track to developing and using it effectively. We shall discuss some aspects of consultancy from the standpoints of both consultant and client.

THE ROLE OF A CONSULTANT

The term "consultant" is sometimes used where "contractor" would be more appropriate. Although there is often no clear boundary, and a single person can perform both roles, it is useful to think of a consultant as someone who helps you to decide what should be done, whereas a contractor is someone who helps you to do it or does it for you.

It is probably too narrow to think of someone as a "thesaurus consultant" because the decision to use a thesaurus would not normally be made until after quite a lot of investigation and analysis of the organisation's needs. This investigation can benefit from the input of a consultant able to advise on the whole area of "information management." There are many different names for schemes of indexing and subject organisation, such as classifications, thesauri, taxonomies, ontologies, subject metadata, topic maps and semantic nets; these overlap in meaning and are not clearly defined–terminology control in this area is seriously deficient! There are also important decisions to be made to achieve the right balance between relying on computer processing and categorisation of text on the one hand and subject analysis and indexing by humans on the other. A consultant with a broad understanding of the underlying principles will help to cut through the hype and choose an appropriate and realistic solution.

WHAT BENEFITS CAN A CONSULTANT BRING?

A consultancy project will only be fully successful if it is seen as a cooperative commitment between the organisation and the consultant. The end result must be that, when the consultant leaves, the organisation is equipped with the staff, the knowledge, and the tools to manage its information system effectively into the future. A consultant should not be seen as someone who can tell an organisation what they should do, but someone who can help them to clarify their needs and objectives and plan and implement a way forward. A consultant's role is to help the organisation to make informed decisions, not to make those decisions for it. It would be very worrying for a consultant if his/her advice were to be followed in blind faith–any recommendations need to be backed up by argument, and a consultancy report may well contain various options, with the arguments for and against each.

A consultant is nevertheless often expected to make a judgement between options, and this should be given due weight, as it embodies the greater breadth and depth of knowledge and experience which led to the consultant being engaged in the first place. In particular, a consultant can look at an organisation's needs with a fresh and objective approach, unhampered by assumptions about "the way things have always been done." A consultant can also assess proposals in the knowledge of what has been tried elsewhere and how successful it was.

Different people within an organisation may have different views on what should be done; there may be conflicts or stresses between the priorities of different departments or functions. By avoiding taking sides, by listening to everyone with an open mind, and by analysing the problems objectively, a consultant can bring these matters into the open and help to reach agreement. Not least, an enthusiastic consultant can provide inspiration and encouragement to help an organisation not only to see that its problems are not insuperable but also to widen its horizons to greater challenges and opportunities.

As I have said, there is no clear dividing line between the role of a consultant and a contractor, and in many cases it may be desirable for a consultant to do some of the work rather than just advising. This would be the case where special skills are needed to accomplish a task more effectively or efficiently than internal staff could do it. Setting up the framework of a thesaurus or classification scheme, for example, and populating it with an initial set of concepts, would ensure that the structure was correct and consistent, and would act as a good set of examples of the principles on which staff could build as later change and development became necessary. Even when the internal staff have the skills and experience to do the work, they may not have the time to undertake a major project, and then it is useful to be able to buy in extra resources to develop and implement a new system within a realistic time frame.

DECISION TO SEEK HELP

A project usually starts when an organisation decides that it needs help. This may be at a fairly early stage, when it decides to have a general look at its information policy, being aware of the developments elsewhere in information and knowledge management but not being sure where to start. On the other hand, it may occur after some basic decisions have been made–a computer system selected and installed and some material catalogued–when the organisation realises that they are not quite sure what they should do to implement the thesaurus module of the package they have bought. Sometimes there are many different and incompatible systems that have been developed in the past by various parts of the organisation, and someone thinks that it would be a good idea if these could be integrated.

FINDING A CONSULTANT

Consultants are often chosen on the basis of personal recommendation from people who have used the consultants in the past or know of them through professional contacts, publications, or reputation. From the consultant's point of view, this indicates the importance of becoming known, contributing usefully to professional discussions at conferences and on electronic newsgroups and mailing lists, and of publishing regularly. Thesaurus consultants may come from many different backgrounds, including librarianship, information science, indexing, and computing. They may have worked for libraries, museums, archives, or business organisations. Generally it is more important to find someone who has a good all-round background and understanding of the principles of information management and who is prepared to listen and grasp your needs quickly, than to insist on someone who already has a knowledge of your special subject field. A client normally has plenty of people with subject knowledge, but it is the complementary skills that are needed.

Depending on personal recommendations makes it more difficult for a new consultant to enter the profession. Most people probably gain experience through employment, where they can develop a professional reputation, before setting up on their own. One possibility is to join an established firm of consultants, whose reputation will underpin the work of the individual. Some professional bodies maintain directories of consultants, and membership of such a body may provide some assurance about professional competence and compliance with a code of ethics.

For substantial projects, particularly those paid for from public funds, a formal process of advertised competitive tendering may be used. Although this requires additional work by the client and the consultant, it has some benefits; it gives an opportunity for new entrants to the profession to compete with more established players and does not limit the field to those consultants whom the client already knows. The necessity to prepare a statement of requirements makes the client think carefully about what is really needed, but this can have disadvantages if it embodies the requirement for a particular type of solution, as the client may not be best able to judge what this should be. It might then be better to split the project into two parts: first an analysis and feasibility study phase to investigate the problem and determine a way forward, and second an implementation phase to put the agreed solution into place.

SCOPE OF THE PROJECT

Initial discussions with a consultant can be very useful before deciding the precise scope of a project, because a thesaurus cannot be developed in isolation. It should take account of the actual material which the thesaurus will be used to index, the people who will use it for indexing and retrieval, and the systems within which it will be implemented. A consultant should help an organisation to take a broader view, considering not just the immediate problem but also how things might develop in the future, including the integration of the information system with other systems within the organisation and with external resources. It might be appropriate for an information audit to be carried out to review existing information resources, needs, and use. It might be desirable to have the consultant provide some discussion and training sessions for staff who will use and develop the thesaurus, so as to ensure that they understand how it is constructed and how to use it effectively. This high level system design and project planning may well take more time than the development of the thesaurus itself. Graef[1] quotes a typical time frame of four to fourteen months at a cost of US$150,000 or more for this stage.

CONTRACTS

Once the scope of the project has been decided, it is highly desirable that this should be embodied in a written contract. This is not just a formality but the way to ensure an effective and satisfactory relationship between consultant and client, making sure that they both know what they have undertaken to do. A good contract will also answer many "what if" questions in advance, so that if anything unexpected happens, there will be no need to try to negotiate an agreement after difficulties have arisen. Some points that the contract should cover are:

- The work the consultant will do, the time when it will be done, and the amount to be charged
- Liability for tax and payment of expenses
- Obligations of the consultant in carrying out the work
- Obligations of the client, including making information and documents available and responding to the consultant's enquiries
- Confidentiality of information, including whether the consultant may publicise the project and discuss it with colleagues and other organisations. Allowing such discussion will generally help the consultant to use a wider range of information sources and thus give better advice.
- Copyright and ownership of products, including the moral rights of the consultant to be identified as the author of the thesaurus and of any accompanying report, and restricting the publication of modified versions without the consultant's approval
- Conditions on which the contract can be terminated by either party
- Calculation of the fee payable if the project is terminated before completion
- Force majeure: excusing either party from obligations under the contract due to circumstances beyond their control
- Arrangements for variations to the contract after commencement, including possible adjustment of the fee to be paid
- Arbitration or other arrangements for resolving disputes.

THESAURUS COMPILATION

The actual work of thesaurus compilation can be broken down into the following stages.

Definition of Style and Scope

Initial discussions will have to determine what kind of thesaurus is required, and the ways in which it is to be presented. What will be the depth and breadth of its coverage? Will the users be subject specialists, the general public, or both? Roughly how many terms are expected to be needed? Will the main use be for retrieval of specific subjects, or for browsing around an area? Will terms need to be arranged within subject fields as well as in hierarchies under primary facets? Will this amount to a classification scheme, requiring a notation? Will there need to be provision for the creation of pre-coordinated subject headings, either as strings of terms or as synthesised class numbers? What standards will be followed? Can any departure from these standards be justified? Does the software on which it will be used impose any constraints, such as not supporting polyhierarchy or not handling facet and subfacet indicators?

Starting Points

Has anyone else produced a thesaurus that can be adopted, or are there pre-existing lists of terms that can be used as a basis for a new one? These may be in the form of a previous subject organisation scheme, a list of document titles or object names, or a glossary or dictionary. In practice, account often has to be taken of all of these. If concepts are not clearly defined, then much discussion may be required to draw up scope notes that are acceptable to all parties and to obtain agreement on the most appropriate term to use for each concept. Tact is necessary in explaining the artificial nature of an indexing language; it may be necessary to persuade members of staff that designating their favourite term as "non-preferred" does not imply that it is "wrong" or that it cannot be used to retrieve information when searching.

Building the Thesaurus

Once terms have been identified, the work of creating relationships can begin. Concepts have to be analysed into facets and built into hierarchies; overlaps of meaning have to be resolved and associative relationships identified. The time required for this varies greatly from one project to another, but personal experience indicates that a list of straightforward, understandable terms can be built into a hierarchy at an average rate of about 25 terms per hour. On the other hand, when investigation of scope and definitions is necessary, the number of terms that can be processed per day can reduce to 10 to 20 or fewer. This figure, and estimates of the time required for the other elements of thesaurus construction, are contained in an Excel spreadsheet prepared by the Data Standards Unit of English Heritage and available from them.[2] Graef indicates that a typical time frame for developing a thesaurus structure is one week to three months, at a cost of US$5,000+.

Reviewing and Amending Draft

Once a draft thesaurus has been prepared, an introduction has to be written that explains the principles on which it has been constructed, the decisions that have been taken about options, and how it should be used and maintained. Then the draft has to be reviewed by potential users and subject experts, and their feedback used to prepare a revised version. Only then will the thesaurus be ready to put into use.

Maintenance and Development

A consultant may be retained to advise from time to time on the ongoing maintenance of a thesaurus, but the actual work of doing this should normally be the responsibility of a permanent member of the client's staff. There needs to be someone within the organisation who can give immediate informed help to users. When the thesaurus is used, candidate terms will be submitted by users, and these need to be considered and dealt with promptly and accurately if confidence in the system is to be maintained. It is desirable that the thesaurus should be evaluated more fully to ensure that it meets users' needs, that they understand it, and are able to use it effectively. Evaluation of thesauri is discussed in an article by Leslie Ann Owens and Pauline Atherton Cochrane elsewhere in this volume.

COSTS

Consultants may contract to work on a project for a fixed fee, or may be paid an agreed rate per day for the work that they do. Typical rates would be in the region of US$500 to $1000 per day, though these can vary greatly. These may seem high compared with the daily rate for a permanent employee, but a consultant cannot expect continuous employment and must spend quite an amount of non-paid time on keeping up to date with developments, professional contacts, and business administration, as well as having to cover overhead costs.

With a fixed fee the consultant has to estimate the time the project will take, and takes the risk that it will turn out more complicated than expected. The work and the deliverables have to be clearly defined, and the consultant has to have substantial control of the project so that delays or changes by the clients do not affect the time required. The clients know what they will get, when they will get it and what it will cost, with a minimum of uncertainty.

If the work cannot be clearly defined at the outset, or if the project is being managed by the client, with the consultant called in from time to time to give advice or to do parts of the work, then payment for the time taken will be more appropriate. There is less risk for the consultant in this case, though the need to record the time used for each part of the work is an increased burden. "Thinking time" and background reading are hard to account for on this basis. If the project is not under the consultant's control, it will be more difficult to predict when he/she will be needed, so there are constraints on his/her ability to schedule other work. The client may have to accept that the consultant may not be available when needed, or else may have to pay a retainer fee to guarantee a certain amount of time per week or per month.

THESAURUS SOFTWARE

There are many software packages that can be used for thesaurus development,[3] and consultants may wish to use one that they are familiar with and have installed on their own computers. On the other hand, if a thesaurus module of an integrated information storage and retrieval system is to be used, it may be preferable for the consultant to do the thesaurus development work using the client's system. This may mean working on the client's premises; remote electronic access would often be more convenient, but IT departments are often reluctant to arrange this because of security concerns. Some thesaurus software development systems allow for distributed access and cooperative thesaurus development by many people simultaneously. In this case thesauri may be hosted on the Web site of a software provider, who takes responsibility for the security aspects. Such systems are generally designed and priced with large corporate organisations in mind.

However the thesaurus is developed, it may need to be transferred from one software system to another. There is, as yet, no standard exchange format for thesaurus data, though some are being developed and tested using XML.[4,5] However, most thesaurus software packages can import and export thesaurus data in a tagged text format, essentially the same as the normal alphabetical presentation of the thesaurus designed for human use. In any thesaurus development project, it is important to clarify in what format the thesaurus is to be delivered and whether the consultant will be responsible for loading it into the client's computer system.

If the thesaurus is to be made accessible through a Web browser interface, there may be a need for the thesaurus consultant to collaborate with Web page designers, so as to ensure that an appropriate level of thesaurus functionality is made available to the users. Many users do not understand the structure of a thesaurus or how to use one effectively, and often do not take time to read explanatory "help" pages. By working together with the software developers, a thesaurus consultant can help to embody some tutorial help in the interface itself. A good system can emulate the "reference interview" that would be conducted by a live librarian, asking questions such as "You have asked for X; we have this in the following contexts–which do you want?" "Would you also be interested in Y?" "That is a very broad topic. Can you be more specific–would one or more of the following narrower terms reflect your need more accurately?" "Do you mean '(A or B) and C' or do you mean 'A or (B and C)'?"

Similarly, if the interface is not fixed in an existing system, it might be possible to work with the client to allow queries to be progressively refined by combining terms from different facets of a thesaurus or classification, as is done in systems such as *Flamenco* [6] and *Waypoint*.[7]

CONCLUSION

Thesauri and faceted classifications are powerful resources which are being rediscovered as adjuncts to the techniques of text searching and automatic categorisation. Information providers and users do not yet understand and use them as widely and effectively as they might. Thesaurus consultants can help to spread the word and make these tools available to the many organisations and their users who can benefit from them.

NOTES

1. Jean Graef, "Taxonomy Consultants: What They Do, Where to Find Them." *Montague Institute Review*, 2001. <http://www.montague.com/E1/society/review/consultants.html>. Restricted by password to members of the Society of Knowledge Base Publishers.

2. Edmund Lee. *RE: Cost/benefit of Controlled Vocabularies.* Contribution to discussion on the NKOS mailing list, 2001. <http://orc.dev.oclc.org:5103/nkos/msg00201.html>.

3. Leonard Will. *Software for Building and Editing Thesauri.* Web page. 2002. <http://www.willpowerinfo.co.uk/thessoft.htm>.

4. Mike Taylor. *Zthes: A Z39.50 Profile for Thesaurus Navigation.* Version 0.4. Washington, DC: Library of Congress. Z39.50 International Standard Maintenance Agency, 1999. <http://lcweb.loc.gov/z3950/agency/profiles/zthes-04.html>.

5. Joseph Busch. *Vocabulary ML: Metacode Strawman DTD.* MS Word document 2000. <http://nkos.slis.kent.edu/VOCML-1.DOC>.

6. BAILANDO projects. *FLAMENCO.* Berkeley: University of California, 2002. <http://bailando.sims.berkeley.edu/flamenco.html>.

7. C. A. McMahon and others, "'No Zero Match' Browsing for Hierarchically Categorised Information Entities," *Artificial Intelligence for Engineering Design, Analysis and Manufacturing* 16, no. 3 (2002): 243-256. This system is now commercially available as Adiuri Systems' Waypoint™ <http://www.adiuri.com/waypoint.htm> and an application of it may be seen at Arkive <http://www.arkive.org>.

Thesaurus Evaluation

Leslie Ann Owens
Pauline Atherton Cochrane

SUMMARY. The process of thesaurus evaluation can enhance the value of a thesaurus in terms of usability, scope, precision and recall. Structural, formative, observational, and comparative evaluation techniques are explained along with specific examples of their use. These methods of evaluation can be applied in the assessment of an existing thesaurus or the construction of a new thesaurus. The history of thesauri since 1960, the development of national and international standards, and sources of evaluative literature are also discussed. *[Article copies available for a fee from The Haworth Document Delivery Service: 1-800-HAWORTH. E-mail address: <docdelivery@haworthpress.com> Website: <http://www.HaworthPress.com> © 2004 by The Haworth Press, Inc. All rights reserved.]*

KEYWORDS. Thesauri, thesaurus construction and use, evaluation, international standards, usability

---

Leslie Ann Owens, MLIS, works as a consultant in the areas of knowledge management, thesaurus construction, and indexing. Pauline Atherton Cochrane is Professor Emerita from both University of Illinois at Urbana-Champaign and Syracuse University. She has consulted with many organizations about their thesauri and conducted research in information retrieval for over forty years.

[Haworth co-indexing entry note]: "Thesaurus Evaluation." Owens, Leslie Ann, and Pauline Atherton Cochrane. Co-published simultaneously in *Cataloging & Classification Quarterly* (The Haworth Information Press, an imprint of The Haworth Press, Inc.) Vol. 37, No. 3/4, 2004, pp. 87-102; and: *The Thesaurus: Review, Renaissance, and Revision* (ed: Sandra K. Roe, and Alan R. Thomas) The Haworth Information Press, an imprint of The Haworth Press, Inc., 2004, pp. 87-102. Single or multiple copies of this article are available for a fee from The Haworth Document Delivery Service [1-800-HAWORTH, 9:00 a.m. - 5:00 p.m. (EST). E-mail address: docdelivery@haworthpress.com].

http://www.haworthpress.com/web/CCQ
© 2004 by The Haworth Press, Inc. All rights reserved.
Digital Object Identifier: 10.1300/J104v37n03_07

INTRODUCTION

The library world has had classification schemes and subject heading lists for centuries, but the device for controlling index vocabularies called the thesaurus has only been in existence since the late 1950s. As the paper by Vickery[1] shows, the thesaurus adds rigorous discipline to the formation of the structure of index vocabularies. Very soon after the ASTIA[2] and ERIC[3] thesaurus projects in the 1960s, a standard was developed in the United States and in the United Kingdom and then at the international level. Anyone developing a thesaurus for their special collection could refer to these standards and compare and evaluate the features in their thesaurus with those mentioned in the appropriate standard. For example, were all index terms in the list related by BT-NT and RT relationships to other terms? Did all terms have synonyms expressed by the UF-Use relationship? Did the form of the term, e.g., singular vs. plural, spelling variations, conform to the standard? This form of evaluation could be undertaken by the "thesaurus maker" or lexicographer. It insured consistency within the word list, but would not cover the other forms of evaluation that linked the thesaurus to the objectives of the retrieval system. This paper will mention other forms of thesaurus evaluation vis-à-vis retrieval and user studies which comment on access, assistance, browsability, failure analysis, and successful retrieval scores. This latter type of evaluation gets closest to "value" for the user, while the earlier mentioned studies cover "value" for the system operators, checking on efficiency, effectiveness, recall, and precision.

Comparing thesauri within the same domain such as education, medicine, or physics represents another form of evaluation that will be mentioned in this paper. Such studies were performed frequently in the 1960s and 1970s when subject-oriented online retrieval systems were being developed and some vocabulary control mechanism had to be chosen. The National Science Foundation and other government agencies funded several such studies such as AUDACIOUS, SUPARS, ERIC, MEDICINE, PSYCHOLOGY, and ENVIRONMENT.

Eventually some of these efforts led to attempts to map across the various index languages and to move more automatically between free text searching/processing and controlled vocabulary mechanisms. This area of work has the general rubric of "vocabulary switching," about which more will be said in this paper.

Given the present state of retrieval, not all software designs or search features on the Internet take advantage of thesauri generated by humans. When designers of software are ignorant of the availability of such thesauri, they tend to use only keyword co-occurrence lists generated from full-text processing and call this an "automatic thesaurus." Unfortunately such systems do not contain any of the structure of relationships mentioned in the thesaurus standards, such as synonym control, spelling, hierarchical relationships, scope notes, and class category placements for each thesaurus term. More and more we hear of efforts to devise "ontologies" and "topic maps" to organize and improve access to the electronic collections in a given domain. In our opinion these efforts are related to the earlier work of thesaurus construction, and often provide broader scope to express the associations between concepts, names, dates, and places extracted from text. They will enhance earlier forms of thesauri if they provide for structure, relationships and various displays for access and retrieval. Formative evaluations of these innovations need to be carried out. If ontologies and topic maps change as much as thesauri have changed in the past forty years, we can be more confident that users will be well-served.

Although we will not consider the cost of thesaurus construction as a part of thesaurus evaluation, it is still timely to consider what Eugene Wall, the early pioneer in this field, had to say about costs in 1975:

> At best, a thesaurus is not inexpensive. Overall, for example, the Thesaurus of Engineering and Scientific Terms (TEST) probably cost almost $1 million dollars in 1967 dollars . . . equivalent to about $40 per term. This high cost resulted from a very large coordinating effort on the part of Department of Defense, and from the use of thesaurus assembly computer programs which did not enable efficient editing . . . In our opinion, however, the expenditure today [1975] of more than $20 per term (excluding publication costs) must mean that the creators of the thesaurus are doing something wrong . . . If a previous thesaurus is merely to be built upon, and if all computer programs, and input procedures are optimal, costs may be $10 per term or even less . . . When viewed in the light of the ubiquitous utility of the thesaurus in both system operations and user applications, and considering that the same approximate cost has been saved in indexing effort (at the same quality level), [this amount] seems not an unacceptable expenditure.[4]

HISTORY OF THESAURUS DEVELOPMENTS AND EARLY EVALUATION EFFORTS

According to Norman Roberts, the modern history of the information retrieval thesaurus may be dated from 1947, while the Engineering Information Center of E. I. DuPont de Nemours is credited with developing the first full-scale operational thesaurus in 1959.[5] The DuPont thesaurus was not widely circulated; therefore, the *Thesaurus of ASTIA Descriptors* (1960) and the *Chemical Engineering Thesaurus* of the American Institute of Chemical Engineers (1961) are recognized as the first published information retrieval thesauri. Roberts notes that "the information retrieval thesaurus emerged in its operational form, following a lengthy and confused intellectual history, as a secondary, supplementary, indexing aid. In similar fashion to the literary thesaurus, it was intended to enlarge the vocabulary of indexers and to indicate the place of concepts in larger schemes of relationships."[6]

In what can be considered an early example of knowledge management, "experience gained in thesaurus construction was recorded and codified, eventually leading to the appearance of guidelines and standards for the process."[7] Indeed, Krooks and Lancaster suggest that from 1959-1974 thesauri were constructed by a small group of lexicographers who shared skills and influenced each other.[8] For more on the history of thesaurus construction, standards and their influences, see F. W. Lancaster's *Vocabulary Control for Information Retrieval* and Krooks and Lancaster (1993).

As thesauri grew, "major aspects of the problems of entry vocabulary, hierarchical organization, the associative relationship, scope notes, and reciprocal relations between terms were identified."[9] F. W. Lancaster has observed that standards for proper thesaurus construction grew out of work done in bibliographic classification as well as alphabetic subject indexing.

The ANSI/NISO *Guidelines for the Construction, Format, and Management of Monolingual Thesauri* are embraced in part because they include an official and workable definition of a thesaurus: "A thesaurus is a controlled vocabulary arranged in a known order and structured so that equivalence, homographic, hierarchical and associative relationships among terms are displayed clearly and identified by standardized relationship indicators that are employed reciprocally."[10] The guidelines specify the four principal purposes served by a thesaurus, namely:

1. Translation: To provide a means for translating the natural language of authors, indexers, and users into a controlled vocabulary used for indexing and retrieval.
2. Consistency: To promote consistency in the assignment of index terms.

3. Indication of relationships: To indicate semantic relationships among terms.
4. Retrieval: To serve as a searching aid in retrieval of documents.[11]

Thesaurus evaluation is the process of determining if a given thesaurus meets these objectives. Depending on the primary purpose of the thesaurus, different criteria may be weighted to guide the revision and evaluation process.

By following the ANSI/NISO guidelines during the construction process, a lexicographer will create a thesaurus that meets the standard for monolingual thesauri. The guidelines offer rules for formulating the descriptors and establishing relationships among terms; they give some information on effectively presenting the information in print and electronically. Thesaurus maintenance procedures and recommended features of thesaurus management systems are also covered.[12]

Despite a revision in 1998, the guidelines do not sufficiently address issues related to publishing thesauri electronically. Limitations of the existing standards are considered in NISO's 1999 *Report on the Workshop on Electronic Thesauri*.[13] Since compliance is voluntary, the ANSI/NISO standards do not establish true "standards" for interoperability. Nevertheless, they serve as an authoritative resource for the broad community of those interested in improving information retrieval (IR), including software developers and artificial intelligence specialists, and represent the shared wisdom of the past fifty years.

In addition to codifying specifications, the ANSI/NISO standards promote access to existing thesauri. To that end, they include the mailing address of a thesaurus clearinghouse where lexicographers are to deposit compliant thesauri to be stored and presumably shared. Outside of academia, however, customized thesauri are often considered intellectual property and are "owned" by the consulting firms and businesses that develop them. Additionally, since printed thesauri are rare in today's information retrieval environment, this repository would be more useful as a searchable online database. A collection of thesaurus-related resources is available at the Web site for Willpower Information.[14]

Yet, that suggestion is unlikely to take hold in the contemporary thesaurus construction environment, owing to the fact that thesauri come in so many shapes and forms. David Batty outlines three levels of thesauri–(1) *Universal* (LCSH, LCC, Dewey); (2) *Broad* (MeSH, AAT); (3) *Specific* (Transportation Research Thesaurus (TRT), ERIC)[15]–to which we would add custom-made thesauri developed for corporate intranets and e-commerce Web sites. Of course, a thesaurus which covers the vocabulary of a specific industry—such as finance—or within a corporation, differs significantly in terms of scope and purpose from something like LCSH, and may, or may not, be compliant with the standards. In fact some thesaurus construction and evaluation tutorials do not mention compliance with the standards as an objective in developing a usable controlled vocabulary. Fortunately, thesauri created with thesaurus construction software such as MultiTes (http://www.multites.com) are programmed to comply with the general expectations set out by the ANSI/NISO standard. This compliance results in time-saving features such as the automatic creation of reciprocal headings.

While much research addresses the quality of "universal" and "broad" thesauri, less attention is paid to domain-specific thesauri. We suggest that if a subject-specific thesaurus conforms to the ANSI/NISO standard, its compliance should be made clear through some sort of recognition. Such a rating system or "seal of approval" might help librarians in assessing the utility of a subject-specific thesaurus, and its acceptability for electronic vocabulary switching endeavors.

In addition to supporting thesaurus construction, the standards can be used to evaluate the structure and rigor of an existing thesaurus. "It is possible to confirm that the thesaurus adheres to international standards in terms of singular/plural conventions, acceptable word forms, direct entry and other matters of consistency. Aesthetic aspects of layout and typography can also be considered."[16] Ideally this *structural* evaluation would be combined with a subjective evaluation by subject experts to confirm the effectiveness of the controlled vocabulary in satisfying the user's information need.

From the 1960s on, there have been evaluation tests and reports about thesauri as indexing languages. The Cranfield studies, undertaken in England by Cyril Cleverdon, with Jean Aitchison as lexicographer/indexer/searcher, pioneered comparative evaluation and relevance measures such as precision and recall. Not only did the test results impact retrieval system design as the computer-based systems were being built, but they also impacted thesaurus standards. The extent that hierarchy, synonymy control, indexer consistency, and user search strategy affected retrieval scores was now known. Failure analysis was a new tool for vocabulary improvement. The *Annual Review of Information Science and Technology* (ARIST)[17] has compiled reviewers' comments on such evaluation tests since Volume 1 in the late 1960s. Don King[18] and Raya Fidel[19] have done retrospective reviews in a recent publication.

The perceived value of controlled vocabularies such as thesauri has fluctuated with innovations in online retrieval. Milstead notes, "The first thesauri were produced before electronic searching became widely available, but their full development coincided with the growth of online bibliographic databases."[20] As the full text of information–as opposed to just the bibliographic record–became accessible and search engines became more sophisticated, some online database providers "were dissuaded from using a thesaurus for what seemed to be valid economic considerations: fear of the apparent expense of designing and using a thesaurus, and doubt that the size of the database would justify that expense."[21] Cost is still an issue of concern today, often without objective evidence that a well-designed thesaurus might not be as costly as poor retrieval by other techniques of subject access.

The need for and potential of controlled indexing languages is now back in vogue. It is recognized that certain retrieval problems such as homonymy and synonymy are caused by the use of natural language and can be obviated by a controlled vocabulary.[22] For more on the "dramatic change in the text retrieval scene," see Aitchison's fourth edition of *Thesaurus Construction and Use*.[23]

METHODS OF THESAURUS EVALUATION

When a thesaurus is being analyzed by an expert, criticized by users, checked against other indexing and access vocabularies, or its features compared with national or international standards, then that thesaurus is being evaluated. If access and retrieval tests are being conducted on a system or Web site that includes a thesaurus, then the thesaurus is being evaluated. Each of these processes will involve different methodologies. We will illustrate some of them here. Often the "sample test" is just that and may not be comprehensive; the conclusions drawn from such a study may not be conclusive, but all observations have some value and may help in revising the thesaurus, updating its vocabulary or increasing the number of lead-in terms and associative relationships.

Because the Library of Congress List of Subject Headings (LCSH) has the longest history, now in existence for over a century, it probably has the largest body of evaluative literature pointing to its flaws and concluding that its value would be improved if this or that were to be done. *The LCSH Century: One Hundred Years with the Library of Congress Subject Headings System*[24] includes a paper written by the second author of this paper.[25] In the bibliography for that paper several evaluative studies are mentioned and two comprehensive bibliographies of "Critical Views of LCSH" are cited, which will help the reader find evaluative literature published before 1992.[26,27] Most of this literature is of the type we would call "expert evaluation," but the comparison of LSCH and PRECIS, and the user studies of LCSH done at the advent of online catalogs broaden the scope of the criticism of LCSH and suggest many improvements which would aid the user.

A search of the ERIC database using the terms "ERIC Thesaurus" and "Evaluation" would uncover another body of evaluative literature as this thesaurus was under constant scrutiny by users, indexers, and retrieval experts for almost fifty years. Add to this the Barbara Booth 1979 article on the ERIC Vocabulary Improvement Project[28] and you can see how evaluative comments can reap their own reward. Finally, ARIST (cited earlier) has had many chapters reviewing thesaurus evaluation, indexing languages and retrieval tests.

Oftentimes, as a thesaurus is being developed from scratch, some *formative* evaluation will be performed before the thesaurus is released for use in indexing and searching. For example, lexicographers can review the search logs of an existing IR system in which an organization has invested time and money. The terms from the search logs can be used to augment lead-in vocabulary and gain insight on users' terminology and search sophistication. Conducting hands-on exercises such as card sorting with potential users can reveal user perspectives of hierarchical groupings. A focus group of potential users may be asked to comment on the language of the thesaurus. Discussion questions might include:

- Should acronyms and abbreviations or full terms be used?
- Are the terms in the list precise enough?
- Does the thesaurus reflect the context of the domain for which it is to be used?
- Are synonyms properly controlled?
- Are the top level terms mutually exclusive?
- Are the terms properly categorized?

If necessary, feedback on the usability and desired design features of the thesaurus can be gathered using preliminary sketches of the interface.[29] All of the comments made during such a focus group are evaluative and should prove useful for revising the thesaurus before it is released. A technique such as a focus group is usually performed by someone other than the thesaurus builder, but a recording is made for that person. In this way the participants are not as reluctant to be critical. During OPAC studies in the 1980s, this technique was used at several locations, including the Library of Congress, to gather data from users doing subject searching where LCSH was the controlled vocabulary.[30]

Another type of formative evaluation done while a thesaurus is being developed consists of retrieval tests on a test collection of documents indexed using the thesaurus. Searchers phrase their queries and then an asker and an expert examine every item in the collection to determine relevance. This file of relevance assessments is used to assess quality of indexing, the thesaurus, and retrieval results. The system–which can be truly automated or simulated by an individual–tries to retrieve all of the relevant documents, but it may fail if there is no match between the search vocabulary and the thesaurus, or if the indexer did not use the thesaurus properly. With such findings, the thesaurus builder will know how to improve the thesaurus and thereby improve indexing and retrieval. Figures 1 and 2 lay out the research design and demonstrate how thesaurus improvements can come from both the indexer's and the searcher's use of the thesaurus.

If time permits, such an evaluation can also concentrate on procedures for indexing of documents for the test collection to ensure that all concepts needed to be indexed are represented. The evaluation will help achieve the four principle purposes served by a thesaurus: translation, consistency in indexing, indication of relationships, and retrieval.[31] Figures 1 and 2 lay out the research design and demonstrate how thesaurus improvements can come from both the indexer's and the searcher's use of the thesaurus.

Once a thesaurus is well-established, evaluations by users can be aided by transaction logs or controlled tests of use that are not artificial. If a view or display of the thesaurus is available, then an *observational* report can become an assessment of the thesaurus as well as the software. Such a study was done by the second author. The data collection instrument is displayed in Figure 3, but the source must be hidden as this was a "not for publication" report.

Comparative evaluation methods are used both to determine the best audience for a thesaurus and to generate specific suggestions for improvement. Jane Greenberg compared the *Art & Architecture Thesaurus* (AAT) and the *LC Thesaurus for Graphic Materials* (LCTGM) in 1993. In her analysis, she wrote:

> The overall result is that the AAT has a faceted structure and is currently geared towards a more specialized audience of art and architecture researchers. LCTGM is very similar to LCSH and aims to service the widespread archival community . . . Perhaps at some point there could be reconciliation between the AAT and LCTGM. Already there have been several attempts to match GMGPC terminology with that of the AAT . . . A project cataloging a series of visual images with both the AAT and LCTGM may

reveal useful information. However, further investigations cannot be fully realized unless catalogers understand the structure and application of thesauri in comparison with subject heading lists in today's online environment.[32]

Data from comparative evaluation of thesauri can have a great impact on retrieval. If retrieval is ever to be improved for cross-file searching, the search mechanism will need to operate on a thesaurus file with vocabu-

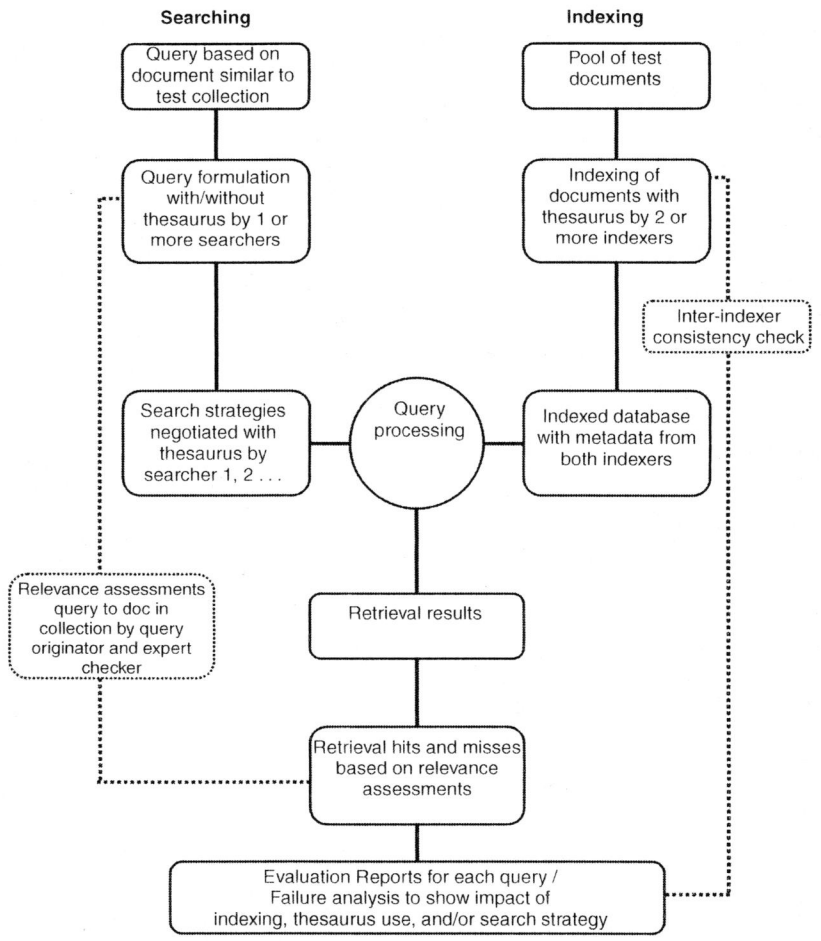

FIGURE 1. Thesaurus Evaluation Project: Outline of Tasks

FIGURE 2. Thesaurus Evaluation Project: Searching

Query:

What are the essential areas in which school boards and teacher organizations have had differences of opinion in which resolution was at least attempted in a negotiating relationship?

Relevant Documents:

Query Originator: 3 4 5 7 8 12 19 21 51
Expert Checker: 3 4 5 51

Common Relevance Assessment: 3 4 5 51 (base for recall and precision in this analysis)

Search Strategies and Retrieval Results:

Participant 1:

School Board (and) Teacher (and) Collective Bargaining
          (or)   (or)
        Education   Negotiation

Retrieval Output: Document 22 (non-relevant)

Participant 2:

School Board (and) Labor Dispute Settlement

Retrieval Output: No Documents

Failure Analysis:

The term "School Board" in the thesaurus was used in the indexing record of only document 22. Both indexers agreed that it was a major term in that case.

None of the titles of the documents judged relevant reflect a discussion of "School Board." This does not necessarily mean, however, that this is not a concept in the articles.

Two possible ways to renegotiate the query provide better results. In an operational environment unsatisfactory retrieval would warrant this iterative process.

---

lary switching possibilities. What first began as a comparative study or mapping of several thesauri in the same field could now become a retrieval tool when used to access related databases. Ruan in Fire Service,[33] Chaplan in Industrial and Labor Relations,[34] and many others have done the groundwork. Mapping has three purposes: (1) to initiate a new thesaurus with a base of general subject terms; (2) to enhance a subject area with extra terminology from a related discipline; (3) to aid in thesaurus maintenance and growth.

See Figure 4 for an example of mapped data in Ruan's thesaurus, called FireTalk. It is easy to see from this illustration that users of all four databases (FSI, LCSH, NETC, and New York) would be better served if this mapping data were used during cross-file searching and their search term "Firemen" were automatically converted to either "Firefighters"

FIGURE 3. Navigating the Thesaurus: Evaluation Form Developed by Pauline Atherton Cochrane

Name: _____

Please describe the main topic of your search:

1) Were you able to find a key term for your main topic in either the alphabetic thesaurus or the Top Term Cluster Displays?

   Thesaurus: Yes _____   No _____
   Top Term: Yes _____   No _____

2) If Yes, comment on the usefulness of the depth and structure of the hierarchy:

   In thesaurus: _____

   In Top Term display: _____

3) Did you examine the Related Terms list? If yes, comment on its usefulness:

   _____

4) If you did NOT find a key term for your topic from either display, did you proceed to do a next search?
   Yes _____   No _____

   Comment on the result:

5) Please list the concepts in your search which you could not translate into thesaurus terms:

6) Comments on the thesaurus browser software:

FIGURE 4. Sample Record with Mapping Data from the FireTalk Thesaurus

FIREFIGHTERS (NETC, New York, FSI)	
TT	01 Management
BT	Fire department personnel (NETC, FSI)
NT	Forest firefighters (FSI) Marine firefighters (FSI) Rural firefighters (FSI) Volunteer firefighters (NETC, New York, FSI) Women firefighters (NETC, New York, FSI)
RT	Fire officers (NETC, New York, FSI)
UF	Firefighter Fire fighters (LCSH) Fire fighter Firemen

Source: Lian Ruan, "Providing Better Subject Access to Nonprint Fire Emergency Materials for Illinois Firefighters," *Cataloging & Classification Quarterly*, 31:3/4 (2001): 213-235.

(NETC, New York, FSI) or "Fire Fighters" (LCSH). If the browser software also displayed the broader (BT), narrower (NT) and related (RT) terms, then more precise or more general information could be found in each database. Mapping and vocabulary switching is not as easy as this illustration might have you believe, but it does show how valuable comparison studies, evaluative reports and standards can be and how they can lead to better retrieval.

The successful FireTalk mapping resulted from manual effort and analysis. On a larger scale, mapping depends not only on similar terminology and structured relationships, but also on how those relationships are built or coded. For this reason, the World Wide Web Consortium (W3C) is directing many initiatives on the Semantic Web, including a specification for an XML/RDF thesaurus schema.[35] Indeed, interoperability is considered the principle "success factor" for the future of thesauri and is a fertile research area.

CONCLUSION

In this paper we have explored comparative, observational, formative, and structural methods for evaluating thesauri. We hope this will help the reader determine the quality and utility of a thesaurus, regardless of whether it is online or printed, machine or human-generated, stand-alone or integrated, monolingual or multilingual, standards-compliant or not.

RECOMMENDED ADDITIONAL READING

Aitchison, Jean, Alan Gilchrist and David Bawden. *Thesaurus Construction and Use: A Practical Manual,* 4th. ed. Chicago: Fitzroy Dearborn Publishers, 2000.

Chaplan, Margaret A. "Mapping Laborline Thesaurus Terms to Library of Congress Subject Headings: Implications for Vocabulary Switching." *Library Quarterly* 65, no. 1 (1995): 39-61.

Cochrane, Pauline A. *Improving LCSH for Use in Online Catalogs.* Littleton, Colorado: Libraries Unlimited, 1986.

Dubois, C.P.R. "The Use of Thesauri in Online Retrieval." *Journal of Information Science* 8, no. 2 (1984): 63-66.

Miller, Uri. "Thesaurus Construction: Problems and Their Roots." *Information Processing & Management* 33, no. 4 (1997): 481-493.

Rada, Roy. "Connecting and Evaluating Thesauri: Issues and Cases." *International Classification* 14, no. 2 (1987): 63-69.

Rada, Roy and Brian K. Martin, "Augmenting Thesauri for Information Systems." *ACM Transactions on Office Information Systems* 5, no. 4 (1987): 378-392.

Ruan, Lian. "Providing Better Subject Access to Nonprint Fire Emergency Materials for Illinois Firefighters." *Cataloging & Classification Quarterly* 31, no. 3/4 (2001): 213-235.

Stone, Alva T., ed. *The LCSH Century: One Hundred Years with the Library of Congress Subject Headings System.* New York: The Haworth Information Press, Inc., 2000.

NOTES

1. B.C. Vickery, "Thesaurus–A New Word in Documentation," *Journal of Documentation* 16, no. 4 (1960): 181-189.

2. Defense Documentation Center (U.S.), Document Processing Division, *Thesaurus of ASTIA Descriptors* (Arlington, Virginia: Armed Services Technical Information Agency, 1960).

3. Educational Resources Information Center (U.S.), *Thesaurus of ERIC Descriptors* (Washington, D.C.: U.S. Dept. of Health, Education and Welfare, Office of Education, 1968-).

4. Eugene Wall, "Symbiotic Development of Thesauri and Information Systems: A Case History," *Journal of the American Society for Information Science* 26, no. 2 (March-April 1975): 71-79.

5. Norman Roberts, "The Pre-history of the Information Retrieval Thesaurus," *Journal of Documentation* 40, no. 4 (1984): 271-285, p. 282.

6. Ibid.

7. F. Wilfrid Lancaster, *Vocabulary Control for Information Retrieval*, 2nd ed. (Arlington, Va.: Information Resources Press, 1986), 29.

8. David A. Krooks and F. Wilfrid Lancaster, "The Evolution of Guidelines for Thesaurus Construction," *Libri* 43, no. 4 (1993): 326-342.

9. Ibid., 337.

10. National Information Standards Organization, *Guidelines for the Construction, Format, and Management of Monolingual Thesauri* (Bethesda, Maryland: NISO Press, 1994), 1.

11. Ibid.

12. Ibid.

13. Jessica Milstead. *Report on the Workshop on Electronic Thesauri, November 4-5, 1999* <http://www.niso.org/news/events_workshops/thes99rprt.html> (26 Oct 01). Seen 27 March 2003. *[Editor's note: In 2003 a NISO initiative to revise Z39.19 grew out of the recommendations developed at this workshop. See "Developing the Next Generation of Standards for Controlled Vocabularies and Thesauri" for more information. Available online at URL: http://www.niso.org/committees/MT-info.html. Seen 7 Feb. 2004.]*

14. *Publications on Thesaurus Construction and Use: Lists of Thesauri* <http://www.willpower.demon.co.uk/thesbibl.htm> (07 Aug 02). Seen 7 Feb. 2004. According to Leonard Will, "The University of Toronto Library maintains an international clearinghouse for thesauri in the English language, including multilingual thesauri containing English language sections. These are included in the library cata-

logue, and records may be retrieved by doing a subject search for 'subject headings.' Searching for 'classification' also retrieves many relevant items."

15. David Batty, "WWW–Wealth, Weariness or Waste," *D-Lib* (November 1998): 4. <http://www.dlib.org/dlib/november98/11batty.html>. Seen 7 Feb. 2004.

16. F. Wilfrid Lancaster, *Vocabulary Control for Information Retrieval*, 2nd ed. (Arlington, Virginia: Information Resources Press, 1986), 156.

17. *Annual Review of Information Science and Technology*. (Medford, New Jersey: Learned Information, 1966-).

18. Don King, "Blazing New Trails: In Celebration of an Audacious Career," in *Saving the User's Time Through Subject Access Innovation*, William J. Wheeler, ed. (Champaign: University of Illinois, 2000), 59-78.

19. Raya Fidel, "The User Centered Approach: How We Got Here," in *Saving the User's Time Through Subject Access Innovation*, William J. Wheeler, ed. (Champaign: University of Illinois, 2000), 79-100.

20. Jessica L. Milstead, "Use of Thesauri in the Full-Text Environment," p. 1. Based on a paper presented at the 34th Clinic on Library Applications of Data Processing (Cochrane & Johnson, 1998) <http://www.bayside-indexing.com/Milstead/useoff.htm> (Sep 98). Seen 7 Feb. 2004.

21. David Batty, "WWW–Wealth, Weariness or Waste," *D-Lib* (November 1998): 4. <http://www.dlib.org/dlib/november98/11batty.html>. Seen 7 Feb. 2004.

22. Elaine Svenonius, "Unanswered Questions in the Design of Controlled Vocabularies," *Journal of the American Society for Information Science* 37, no. 5 (1986): 331-340 p. 331.

23. Jean Aitchison, Alan Gilchrist and David Bawden, *Thesaurus Construction and Use: A Practical Manual*, 4th ed. (Chicago: Fitzroy Dearborn Publishers, 2000).

24. Alva T. Stone, ed., *The LCSH Century: One Hundred Years with the Library of Congress Subject Headings System* (New York: The Haworth Information Press, Inc., 2000).

25. Pauline Atherton Cochrane, "Improving LCSH for Use in Online Catalogs Revisited–What Progress Has Been Made? What Issues Still Remain?" *Cataloging & Classification Quarterly* 29, no. 1/2 (2000): 73-89.

26. Monika Kirtland and Pauline A. Cochrane, "An ERIC Information Analysis Product in Two Parts: I. Critical Views of LCSH, a Bibliographic and Bibliometric Essay," *Cataloging & Classification Quarterly* 1, no. 2/3 (1982): 71-94.

27. Steven Blake Shubert, "Critical Views of LCSH–Ten Years Later: A Bibliographic Essay," *Cataloging & Classification Quarterly* 15, no. 2 (1992): 37-97.

28. Barbara Booth, "A 'New' ERIC Thesaurus, Fine-Tuned for Searching," *Online* (July 1979): 20-29.

29. The Internet offers exciting mechanisms to present traditional thesaurus concepts with graphics and hypertext. See, for example, the 3-D interface of the Plumb Design Visual thesaurus at http://www.visualthesaurus.com/.

30. Karen M. Drabenstott and Marjorie S. Weller, "Failure Analysis of Subject Searches in a Test of a New Design for Subject Access to Online Catalogs," *Journal of the American Society for Information Science* 47, no. 7 (1996): 519-537.

31. National Information Standards Organization, *Guidelines for the Construction, Format, and Management of Monolingual Thesauri* (Bethesda, Maryland: NISO Press, 1993) p. 1.

32. Jane Greenberg, "Intellectual Control of Visual Archives," *Cataloging & Classification Quarterly* 16, no. 1 (1993): 85-117 p. 97.

33. Lian Ruan, "Providing Better Subject Access to Nonprint Fire Emergency Materials for Illinois Firefighters," *Cataloging & Classification Quarterly* 31, no. 3/4 (2001): 213-235.

34. Margaret A. Chaplan, "Mapping Laborline Thesaurus Terms to Library of Congress Subject Headings: Implications for Vocabulary Switching," *Library Quarterly* 65, no. 1 (Jan 1995): 39-61.

35. *RDF Thesaurus Draft Specification* <http://ilrt.org/discovery/2001/01/rdf-thes/> (24 Jan 00). Seen 7 Feb. 2004.

User Comprehension and Searching with Information Retrieval Thesauri

Jane Greenberg

SUMMARY. While information retrieval thesauri may improve search results, there is little research documenting whether general information system users employ these vocabulary tools. This article explores user comprehension and searching with thesauri. Data were gathered as part of a larger empirical query-expansion study involving the *ProQuest® Controlled Vocabulary*. The results suggest that users' knowledge of thesauri is extremely limited. After receiving a basic thesaurus introduction, however, users indicate a desire to employ these tools. The most significant result was that users expressed a preference for thesauri employment through interactive processing or a combination of automatic and interactive processing, compared to exclusively automatic processing. This article defines information retrieval thesauri, summarizes research results, considers circumstances underlying users' knowledge and searching with thesauri, and highlights future research needs. *[Article copies available for a fee from The Haworth Document Delivery Service: 1-800-HAWORTH. E-mail address: <docdelivery@haworthpress.com> Website: <http://www.HaworthPress.com> © 2004 by The Haworth Press, Inc. All rights reserved.]*

KEYWORDS. Thesaurus, thesauri, information retrieval, automatic processing, interactive processing

---

Jane Greenberg is Assistant Professor, School of Information and Library Science, University of North Carolina at Chapel Hill (SILS/UNC-CH). Her research and teaching activities focus on metadata and classification problems.

[Haworth co-indexing entry note]: "User Comprehension and Searching with Information Retrieval Thesauri." Greenberg, Jane. Co-published simultaneously in *Cataloging & Classification Quarterly* (The Haworth Information Press, an imprint of The Haworth Press, Inc.) Vol. 37, No. 3/4, 2004, pp. 103-120; and: *The Thesaurus: Review, Renaissance, and Revision* (ed: Sandra K. Roe, and Alan R. Thomas) The Haworth Information Press, an imprint of The Haworth Press, Inc., 2004, pp. 103-120. Single or multiple copies of this article are available for a fee from The Haworth Document Delivery Service [1-800-HAWORTH, 9:00 a.m. - 5:00 p.m. (EST). E-mail address: docdelivery@haworthpress.com].

http://www.haworthpress.com/web/CCQ
© 2004 by The Haworth Press, Inc. All rights reserved.
Digital Object Identifier: 10.1300/J104v37n03_08

INFORMATION RETRIEVAL THESAURI

Information retrieval thesauri, also identified as structured thesauri (Greenberg, 1998, 2001a), present rich semantic networks of vocabulary terms. These tools (hereafter referred to as *thesauri*) are constructed to support document indexing and retrieval. Among several significant features defining information retrieval thesauri and distinguishing them from other vocabulary tools are the following:

- They are created according to an established set of standards. The ANSI/NISO Z39.19-1993, *Guidelines for the Construction, Format, and Management of Monolingual Thesauri* (1994), is one of the most frequently used standards.
- They generally encode equivalent, hierarchical and associative relationships among vocabulary terms (Aitchison et al., 1997, p. 47-66; ANSI//NISO Z39.19 1994, p. 15-21; Lancaster, 1986, p. 35-49).
- They are produced by human processes. Initial construction may stem from automatic processing of electronic discipline-specific text(s), although human intervention is required to encode distinct types of lexical-semantic relationships (e.g., equivalent, hierarchical, and associative relationships).
- They are generally domain-specific tools. For example, the *Thesaurus of ERIC Descriptors* (2001) includes language in the education domain; and the *ASIS Thesaurus of Information Science and Librarianship* (Milstead, 1998) includes language in the library and information science domain.
- Their construction is guided by the principle of *literary warrant* in that thesaurus terminology corresponds to the language used in the published literature of a selected discipline (or disciplines) (Aitchison et al., 1997, p. 47-66, p. 123; ANSI/NISO Z39.19, 1994; and Lancaster, 1986, p. 24-26). Their construction is also guided by *end-user warrant* in that authorized headings are the terms most commonly used by the community(s) for which the thesaurus is designed (Lancaster, p. 26-27).
- They are distinct from both algorithmic or similarity thesauri, which are generated via statistical techniques based on term frequencies, co-occurrence equations, and weighting techniques (e.g., Chen et al., 1995). They are also distinct from general-purpose thesauri, such as *Roget's Thesaurus of English Words and Phrases* (1990), which distinguish grammatical treatments of

words (e.g., nouns, adjectives, adverbs, and verbs) and different senses of these grammatical treatments.
- Finally, they are distinct from subject heading lists because they have been primarily designed to support "post-coordinate searching," whereas subject heading lists contain subject heading strings (e.g., Chinese Americans–Education), inverted subject headings (e.g., Art, Roman), and many more multi-term headings (e.g., Women in Business) because they were initially designed to support "pre-coordinate searching" (Dykstra, 1988).[1]

The features outlined here identify thesauri as unique tools that facilitate the organization and access of information. Studying the current and potential application of thesauri is important–particularly as people increasingly search information systems from the comfort of their own home, wireless network connections, such as the campus coffee shop, or other places without assistance from an information professional. This paper explores questions concerning current thesauri/user relationships in an effort to improve the use of these tools.

THESAURI RESEARCH AND USERS

Studying the interaction between "users and thesauri" is a growing trend. Two key factors motivating this growth include: (1) intensified research efforts in human computer interaction and information seeking behavior, and (2) increased public access to thesauri-supported information systems via the World Wide Web.

The User

A common focus of human computer interaction and information seeking behavior research is the *general information system user* (hereafter referred to as the *user*). This type of user is generally without any professional training in online searching. It's possible that the user may have learned about information retrieval thesauri or controlled vocabularies by participating in a library's bibliographic instruction session. Even so, such users lack the information professional's experience and knowledge garnered from searching thesaurus-supported information systems daily to help clients solve problems. Library and information science researchers want to circumvent general users' searching limitations, increase thesaurus use, and ultimately improve users' retrieval results.

Research Trend-Setters

Setting the "thesauri/user" research trend is a growing body research on thesaurus interface design, end-user warrant, and processing options.

Most *thesaurus interface design* research is construction-oriented, testing new technologies and techniques. The overriding goal is to design user-friendly interfaces that invite and encourage thesaurus use. Hypertext supports easy navigation of terminological semantic relationships encoded in thesauri (e.g., broader term [BT], narrower terms [NT], related terms [RT]) and appears to be one of the most favored technologies (e.g., Shapiro & Yan, 1996). Researchers experimenting with innovative technologies are also developing prototype thesauri with interfaces representing semantic term-relationships via graphical visualization techniques (Rorvig et al., 1999; Ramsey et al., 1999), in three-dimensional space (Hemmje et al., 1994; LyberWorld, 1999), and through animated spatial maps (*Plumb Design Visual Thesaurus*, 1999). *"End-user" warrant* studies assess the degree of matching between users' search terms and thesauri or controlled vocabulary terms (e.g., Carlyle, 1989; Greenberg, 2001a; Humphreys, McCray, and Cheh, 1997). A high degree of matching indicates that a thesaurus is effective, whereas a poor degree of matching leads to questions about thesaurus currency and functionality (Aitchison et al., 1997, p. 1-22; Lancaster, 1986).

Bates' (1986, 1990) influential work on the *end-user thesaurus* advances our thinking in the area of end-user warrant. Through writings, Bates proposes the design of an end-user thesaurus containing "rich" entry vocabulary, allowing users to easily connect to thesaurus terminology. Bates explains this idea with the phrase of "hitting the side of the barn" (1986, p. 365), whereby a user's search need only to map to the thesaurus, but need not exactly match an authorized term. Additionally, end-user thesaurus entry vocabulary may grow over time. In Bates' discussions, the end-user thesaurus supports a much greater degree of mapping compared to an indexing thesaurus (a thesaurus with authorized terms used by an indexer). The end-user thesaurus allows users to benefit from professional indexing without having to learn about the rules and restriction inherent in the indexing thesaurus.

The final thesauri/user trend to note in this literature review is the exploration of *user preferences for automatic* or *interactive thesaurus processing*. Automatic processing requires users to input their initial search term(s). User search terms are then seamlessly mapped to "authorized" thesaurus terminology for search execution. This method appeals to users practicing the *principle of least effort* (Mann, 1993)–that is, the user not wanting to put time in to the search process and not necessarily worried about retrieving the best documents. Automatic processing can be frustrating for users wanting to understand how their search is manipulated, particularly users wanting to have some control over the search process. Interactive thesaurus processing requires users to select thesaurus terms when initiating a search, or more commonly select additional thesaurus terms through means of query expansion (an iterative process) after evaluating retrieval results of an initial search. A good example of interactive searching with controlled vocabulary is provided with the Okapi experimental system underlying the online catalog at City University, London (Beaulieu et al., 1996; Beaulieu, 1997). Interactive processing appeals to users who want to have some control over their search, although research has shown that users give up during interactive term selection due to the labor intensity surrounding their involvement (Drabenstott & Weller, 1996).

It's likely that the most effective thesaurus processing will come from research exploring both automatic and interactive processing methods. One example in this area is the DARPA Unfamiliar Metadata Project (http://metadata.sims.berkeley.edu/GrantSupported/unfamiliar.html) in the School of Information Management & Systems (SIMS) at the University of California at Berkeley. A part of this project explores "automatic" mapping algorithms for the initial search and cross-language information retrieval. "Interactive" and "automatic" processing methods are then combined for the relevance feedback term selection activities (Buckland et al, 1999). This research also includes statistical means for matching terminology. Research like this seeks to exploit the strengths and minimize the weaknesses of both automatic and interactive processes.

Research Summary

Research highlighted here discusses thesauri and users and addresses thesauri processing for information retrieval. Research needs to also address fundamental questions about user comprehension and employment of thesauri. For example: Do users actually know what an information retrieval thesaurus is and how it operates? Given basic knowledge about thesauri, will users search with a thesaurus? Do users prefer that thesauri be employed via automatic and/or interactive processes during a search activity? Examining these questions will complement existing thesauri/user research, advance our knowledge on this topic, and help improve thesauri implementation in information retrieval systems.

RESEARCH QUESTIONS

The research presented in this article explores user comprehension and searching with thesauri. The research is part of a recent study that focused on automatic and interactive query expansion via lexical semantic relationships encoded in the *ProQuest Controlled Vocabulary and Classification Codes* (1997) (hereafter referred to as the *ProQuest Thesaurus*). This article reports on the portion of the study that explored users' thesauri knowledge, desire to employ a thesaurus when searching, and the preferred processing methods for working with thesauri. Research questions explored were:

1. What knowledge base do general information system users (users) have of information retrieval thesauri (thesauri)?
2. Given basic thesauri knowledge, and assuming thesaurus availability, will users employ a thesaurus when searching?
3. Given basic thesauri knowledge, and assuming thesaurus availability, what thesaurus processing methods do users prefer, if any?

RESEARCH METHODS

The survey method was the primary means for examining the above research questions. Two surveys were implemented: A "Participant Profile Survey," and a "Thesaurus Use Survey," which was a subset of a larger study's Post-evaluation Questionnaire. The surveys used are presented in Appendix A-1 and A-3 in Greenberg (2001a). The examination was also supported by a brief thesaurus introduction. The study took place in an operational setting defined by the real users, real queries, the ABI/Inform database and its underlying thesaurus, the *ProQuest Thesaurus*.

PROCEDURES

Graduate students at Katz Graduate School of Business, University of Pittsburgh, who intended to search ABI/Inform, were recruited for the study. Potential participants had to submit a query where at least one search term mapped to the *ProQuest Thesaurus* via a series of mapping rules. Searches were limited to topical terms and could not include *named entities* (e.g., names of corporate, personal, geographical, or architectural entities). Qualification and mapping rules for participants are found in Appendix B-1 and B-2 of Greenberg (2001a). The Participant Profile Survey was implemented as part of the recruitment process to gather data on participants' backgrounds, online searching experiences, and thesauri knowledge.

Participants' queries were mapped to the *ProQuest Thesaurus* (at least the one term that matched) and then searched using semantically related thesauri terminology and an extended Boolean algorithm. Participants were then asked to evaluate the relevancy of the retrieval results.

After the relevance evaluations for the retrieval results, participants were given a "brief thesaurus introduction." The introduction included presenting participants with a vocabulary list from the *ProQuest Thesaurus* in the immediate vicinity of their mapped search terms. That is, the *ProQuest Thesaurus* "BT" (broader term), "NT" (narrower term), "RT" (related term), "Use," and "UF" (use for) terms directly connected to their mapped search term(s). These *ProQuest Thesaurus* terms were classified and alphabetically arranged by each participant's original search terms. Common thesaural identifiers of BT, NT, RT, Use, and UF were eliminated from this introduction in order to emphasize the thesaurus as a searching vocabulary. Section A-1 of the Appendix illustrates the presentation of *ProQuest Thesaurus* terms in a classified alphabetized fashion without thesaural identifiers. Thesaurual identifiers are removed because it was speculated that their inclusion and distinguishing authorized headings would distract users from learning about thesauri as basic searching vocabulary tools. For comparison purposes, Section A-2 of the Appendix shows the actual thesaural identifiers (the reference structure) for the terms listed in Section A-1. Participants did *not* see this second display. As an extension of the presentation of thesaurus terms, participants were asked to select any terms that they thought would retrieve additional useful documents. This request was part of a larger interactive query expansion study (Greenberg, 2001b). The thesaurus introduction was followed by the Thesaurus Use Survey, which gathered data about users' desire to employ thesauri and preferred processing methods for working with these tools.

DATA ANALYSIS

Data gathered provided information on participants' backgrounds and online searching experience, thesaurus experience, and preferred processing methods for working with thesauri.

Participants' Backgrounds and Online Searching Experience

Forty-two M.B.A. students participated in the study. The majority of participants (83.4%, 35) were in the first of six required modules (similar to semesters). English was the native language for slightly over half of the participants (52.4%, 22 participants). Comfort level with the English language for non-native English-speakers was recorded on a semantic differential scale ranging from "1" (not very comfortable) to and "5" (very comfortable). Nineteen (95.0%) of the 20 non-native English-speaking participants gave a score 4.0 or higher, 15 of which gave a score of 5.0–the highest value. One participant gave a score of 3.5, which was still above average. It was concluded that the participants' comfort level would not interfere with interpreting of the study's results.

Participants identified themselves as fairly regular searchers of online information retrieval systems (hereafter referred to as *information systems*), as indicated in Table 1.

Searching comfort level for each participant was recorded on a 5-point semantic differential scale ranging from "1" (not very comfortable) to "5" (very comfortable). The mean comfort level score was 4.1, with a mode of 5.0 (45.2%, 19 participants selected 5.0) demonstrating a high degree of comfort in searching information systems.

About one-fifth (8 participants, 19.0%) had searched ABI/Inform prior to participation in the larger query expansion study. Four of these participants indicated they search ABI/Inform one to three times a month. The other four participants selected the "other" option for frequency. Two of these participants indicated that their ABI/Inform searching varied, depending on current assignments and information needs; one participant

TABLE 1. Use of Information Systems*

Search frequency per month	No. of participants
8 or more times	26 (61.9%)
4 to 7 times	9 (21.4%)
1 to 3 times	4 (9.5%)
Varied per month	2 (4.8%)
Never	1 (2.4%)

Information systems were defined as PITTCAT (the University of Pittsburgh's online library catalog), newspaper indexes, digital library resources, but excluded larger Internet databases underlying commercial search engines, such as Yahoo!, Google, Lycos, etc.

noted that ABI/Inform was used at a previous job; and one participant indicated that ABI/Inform is used at a current job, although not on any regular basis and not recently. A 5-point semantic differential scale ranging from "1" (not very comfortable) to "5" (very comfortable) was used to record participants' ABI/Inform comfort level. Only eight responses could be examined for this question. Responses ranged from 1 to 4, with a mean of 2.8. Comfort level corresponded with participants' use frequency in that the participants who searched ABI/Inform more had provided higher comfort-level scores for this system.

Experience with Thesauri

Data gathered on participants' experiences with thesauri provided insight into their knowledge of these tools. Only six participants (14.3%) indicated that they had previously used a thesaurus to aid online searching. Searching thesauri identified by participants are recorded in Table 2. Column three in Table 2 provides a verification note for each identified thesaurus.

Two participants indicated that they had used *Roget's Thesaurus of English Words and Phrases* (hereafter referred to as *Roget's Thesaurus*) for online searching. Although *Roget's Thesaurus* is available online through the University of Pittsburgh Digital Library, it is not available

TABLE 2. Thesaurus Use and Availability Verification

No. of Participants	Thesauri "Named" by participants	Verification Note
2	Roget's Thesaurus [of English Words and Phrases]	Thesaurus is available online via the University Library's digital resources webpage, although it is not attached to any online information system.
1	Wilson Marketing Database Thesaurus	Thesaurus could not be verified. Participant might be referring to the controlled vocabulary underlying the H. W. Wilson's™ Business Periodicals database.
1	Web Thesaurus for Business Books	Thesaurus could not be verified.
2	Could not recall thesaurus used	N/A

as a searching device for any of the online information systems to which the University subscribes. It is conceivable that these two participants have looked up a term in *Roget's Thesaurus* before searching an online information system, but it is more likely that these participants recorded the title "*Roget's Thesaurus*" because it was a thesaurus with which they were familiar. The other two thesaurus titles provided by participants could not be verified, and two participants could not recall the thesaurus previously used.

Only two participants (4.8%) indicated that they were aware that ABI/Inform had a thesaurus. These two participants were among the six participants who indicated they had previously used a thesaurus for online searching. A discrepancy was found as one of these two participants indicated the larger query expansion experiment was their first time using ABI/Inform. In a follow-up question, the participant indicated that this answer was based on an assumption that "many [information] systems have a thesaurus." It is possible that the presentation of this question after the basic thesaurus introduction and term selection activity influenced the participant's response.

Preferred Processing Methods for Working with Thesauri

The third research question posited in this research explored the preferred processing methods for working with thesauri. The Thesaurus Use Survey asked participants if they would consider using a thesaurus next time they searched ABI/Inform. This inquiry took place after participants completed the relevancy evaluations from larger query expansion study and partook in the thesaurus introduction. Figure 1 presents participants' desire to employ a thesaurus when searching ABI/Inform next time.

A little over half of the participants (54.8%, 23 participants) selected the "yes" option, 42.9% (18 participants) selected "maybe," and one participant (2.4%) selected "no."

Following the thesaurus employment question, participants were asked to select the preferred processing methods for selecting additional search terms from a thesaurus to aid searching. The researcher was on hand to explain the different methods, and participants were encouraged to ask for clarification if they did not understand the different options. A little over ten percent of the participants (5 participants, 11.9%) asked for clarification. Results for preferred processing methods are presented in Table 3.

FIGURE 1. Future Thesaurus Employment During ABI/Inform Searching

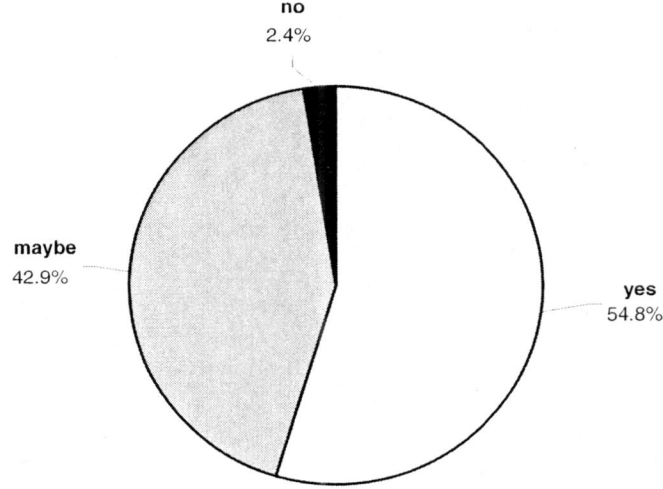

Results indicate that the majority of participants favor automatic processing as long as they have the option to manually interact and select terms. Preference for some control is further evidenced by the fact that 15 participants (33.3%) favored exclusively interactive term selection over the four participants (9.5%) that favored exclusively automatic processing. Only two participants (4.8%) didn't indicate a preference.

DISCUSSION

This study gathered data on participants' backgrounds and online searching experience, thesauri experience, and preferred processing methods for working with thesauri. The data gathered permitted exploration of the research questions posited above and provide insight into the topic of thesauri and users.

Users' Thesauri Knowledge

Results found that participants' thesauri knowledge was extremely limited. This was evidenced by the fact that only 14.3% of the participants (6 participants) said they had used a thesaurus for searching before

TABLE 3. Preferred Thesaurus Processing

Options	No. of participants
Automatically.	4 (9.5%)
By giving you a list to choose from.	15 (33.3%)
Automatically and also by giving you a list to choose from.	22 (52.4%)
I don't care.	2 (4.8%)

participating in the study. Only three different thesauri were identified by four participants, and none of the thesauri could be verified as devices associated with any specific information system (see Table 2).

To some extent these results are surprising, given participants' education level and frequency of and comfort with online searching. All participants were pursuing graduate education at the M.B.A. level–a program that requires an earned undergraduate degree. It's likely that these participants had more library experience and interaction with library information systems compared to general "users" at less-advanced educational levels. In turn, it is likely that various information systems used throughout their educational tenure had thesauri, although clearly system interaction doesn't confirm thesaurus use. Nevertheless, the *thesaurus use expectation* for this study was further influenced by the fact that over half of the participants (61.9%, 26 participants) search information systems eight or more times a month. This figure excludes searching databases underlying commercial search engines (e.g., the Yahoo! database). Additionally, close to half of the participants (45.2%, 19 participants) selected the very highest comfort-level score of "5" for online searching, with an average of "4.1" on a 5-point scale. In other words, it was not unreasonable to anticipate greater interaction with thesauri, given the fairly frequent use and high comfort-level found with users' online searching. Contrary to these results, it's possible that access to information systems with thesauri was limited during participants' college education. Data on participants' age, place of undergraduate education, and year of completion were not gathered in this study.

Plans for Thesaurus Employment When Searching ABI/Inform

This study found that a little over half of the participants (54.8%, 23 participants) plan on thesauri searching next time they work with ABI/Inform and that 18 participants (42.9%) might consider thesaurus searching in ABI/Inform given their response of "maybe" (see Figure 1). It's likely that the basic thesaurus introduction, whereby users were presented with *ProQuest Thesaurus* terms related to their search term, contributed to the positive responses. To reiterate, the thesaurus introduction emphasized the thesaurus as a searching vocabulary, and eliminated thesaurus identifiers and the identification of authorized headings. The results suggest that a good way to encourage thesaurus use is to present searchers with thesauri terms related to their search after they have evaluated an initial set of retrieved documents. Spink (1997) found that search term modification as part of the relevance feedback process improved search results, although participants' search terms were not mapped to a thesaurus in this earlier research. The results of the study reported on here have implication for educating users about thesauri and relate to the following discussion on thesaurus processing methods.

Preferred Processing Methods for Working with Thesauri

Exploring the preferred processing methods for working with thesauri is the final research topic reported on in this paper. Slightly over half of participants (22 participants, 52.4%) were in favor of combining automatic and interactive processing methods. Participants in this group may have been generally pleased with the initial retrieval results from the automatic processing, although they may have wanted to retrieve a greater number of documents–and may have thought that they could have by interactive term selection.

There are very few operational systems supporting both automatic and interactive thesaurus processing. The Okapi system underlying City University's online catalog, which was mentioned above, supports both methods in a unique way. Controlled vocabulary terms are extracted from bibliographic records that the user judges relevant, and these terms are then presented to the user for interactive term selection (Beaulieu et al., 1996; Beaulieu, 1997). Although this system deals with subject headings, it provides a potential model for an information system that could facilitate both automatic and interactive thesaurus processing.

A strong preference for both automatic and interactive processing was followed by a third of the participants (15 participants, 33.3%) favoring *only* interactive processing. This group of participants may have been less pleased with the initial retrieval results from the automatic processing. It's likely that this group of 15 participants perceived a greater potential to retrieve additional relevant documents via interactive processing.

It's possible that some participants in this group and the group preferring both processing methods may have been aware of the advantages associated with human/manual indexing compared to the weaknesses of automatic indexing. Data supporting this possibility were not gathered.

Reasons given for participants' preferences are difficult to verify. This is in part because the results reported on here stem from a larger query expansion study. Participants' relevance evaluations were based on records retrieved via both their initial search terms and *ProQuest Thesaurus* terms semantically related to their initial search terms. Participants were therefore exposed to thesaurus terms at this early phase of the experiment without being informed.

Despite the limitations noted here, the complete set of results show that 37 participants (85.7%) favor some form of interactive thesaurus use, compared to only four participants (9.5%) exclusively in favor of automatic processing. The population of 37 participants is based on the 22 participants endorsing automatic and interactive processing together and the 15 participants endorsing, exclusively, interactive processing of thesauri. Those preferring only automatic processing may have perceived this as the easiest means of getting information and were likely pleased with their initial retrieval results. Additionally, the two participants (4.8%) with no preference may have predicted that both methods produced equally satisfactory results, although it's conceivable that they didn't understand or take time to think about the difference between both processes. Regardless of the exact reasons behind preferences found, the high percentage of participants supporting some level of interactive processing is a *significant* finding that researchers need to take into account in designing thesauri applications.

CONCLUSIONS AND FUTURE RESEARCH DIRECTIONS

The study explored user comprehension of information retrieval thesauri, thesaurus searching, and preferred processing methods for working with thesauri. Participants were educationally advanced students pursing M.B.A. degrees, with business queries that were mapped to the *ProQuest Thesaurus*. The results suggest that:

- Users' thesauri comprehension is extremely limited.
- Given a basic thesaurus introduction, users indicate a desire to employ these tools.
- Given a basic thesaurus introduction, users favor either interactive or a combination of automatic and interactive thesaurus processing compared to completely automatic processing.

The results of this study are useful in that they provide insight into user comprehension of thesauri, their desire to use these tools, and processing preferences. The results are, however, limited by the participant population, the nature of queries, ABI/Inform's contents, and the *ProQuest Thesaurus*. Other limitations are attributed to the fact that the study was a peripheral part of a larger query expansion study. Even so, the study provides a framework for future thesauri/user examinations. Future investigations addressing the topics underlying this study might be improved by gathering data about participants' previous information system use during college or other advanced education, and by specifically asking for feedback about the thesaurus processes preferences.

This study raises questions about the emphasis thesaurus developers and researchers place on producing systems seamlessly linking user search terms to thesaurus terms during information retrieval activities. Indeed, these efforts are important because they aim to eliminate user burdens associated with learning about thesauri intricacies. The emphasis in this area has, however, limited the attention given to different types of users, particularly users who may prefer some degree of thesaurus interaction. In efforts to fully take advantage of thesauri, research needs to also consider how to stimulate user exploration of thesauri and meet the needs of users like the participants in this study.

Future thesauri research needs to also consider current system design limitations and user behavior. Current thesaurus-supported systems often fail to adequately highlight a thesaurus search option. Information systems may include the word "Thesaurus" on a navigation bar or as a hypertext button, but the explanation of how this feature can assist with the selection of search terms may be hidden. Additionally, systems that include a thesaurus often provide confusing interfaces. They use thesaural identifiers like "BT" and "NT" or phrases like "broader term," which may not be clear to a user (non-professional searcher), and they have limited tutorials or explanations of the thesaurus feature.

In the area of user behavior, attention needs to be given to increasing participation in bibliographic instruction sessions and also to creating and improving thesauri tutorials that invite user exploration. Additional research may help determine what factors influence a user's decision to retain knowledge about information retrieval thesauri. For example, how might ease of thesaurus access, a good or intuitive thesaurus tutorial (online or personal), improved results during first-time use, or repetitive use impact a user's acquisition and ability to retain thesauri knowledge? Answers to these questions may improve thesauri employment by users.

Thesauri are intellectual creations. They are valuable for indexing and retrieving information. Increasingly, information systems with thesauri are being linked to web portals. Digital libraries and other web initiatives are adopting thesauri for organizing information. People are searching these and other information systems that include thesauri twenty-four/seven (around the clock), without assistance from an information professional. Thesauri developers and researchers need to better understand the current thesauri/user relationship, and highlight the splendid nature of these tools in order to improve user thesauri employment.

NOTE

1. This distinction is becoming less of an issue, as *subject heading lists* go through a process of *thesaurification*. For example, string headings are disconnected, inverted headings are reversed, multi-term headings are deconstructed, and thesaural abbreviations are added (e.g., BT, NT, etc.) to identify semantic relationships. At the same time, online systems increasingly support post-coordinate searching of individual terms still found in subject headings strings, inverted subject headings, and multi-term concepts.

REFERENCES

Aitchison, Jean, Alan Gilchrist, and David Bawden. *Thesaurus Construction and Use: A Practical Manual*, 3rd ed. London: Aslib, 1997.

ANSI/NISO. *Guidelines for the Construction, Format, and Management of Monolingual Thesauri*. Bethesda, MD: NISO Press, 1994. ANSI/NISO Z39.19-1993.

Bates, M. J. "Design for a Subject Search Interface and Online Thesaurus for a Very Large Records Management Database." In *Proceedings of the 53rd ASIS Annual Meeting, Toronto, Ontario, November 4-8, 1990*, edited by Diane Henderson, 20-28. Medford, N.J.: Published for the American Society for Information Science by Information Today, 1990.

Bates, M. J. "Subject Access in Online Catalogs: A Design Model." *Journal of the American Society for Information Science* 37, no. 6 (1986): 357-376.

Beaulieu, M. "Experiments of Interfaces to Support Query Expansion." *Journal of Documentation* 53, no. 1 (1997): 8-19.

Beaulieu, M., S. Robertson, and E. Rasmussen. "Evaluating Interactive Systems in TREC." *Journal of the American Society for Information Science* 47, no. 1 (1996): 85-94.

Buckland, Michael, Aitao Chen, Hui-Min Chen, Youngin Kim, Byron Larn, Ray Larson, Barbara Norgard, and Jacek Purat. "Mapping Entry Vocabulary to Unfamiliar Metadata Vocabularies." *D-Lib Magazine* 5, no. 1 (1999). Available online at URL: http://www.dlib.org/dlib/january99/buckland/01buckland.html.

Carlyle, A. "Matching *LCSH* and User Vocabulary in the Library Catalog." *Cataloging & Classification Quarterly* 10, no. 1/2 (1989): 37-63.

Chen, Hsinchun, Tak Yim, David Fye and Bruce Schatz. "Automatic Thesaurus Generation for an Electronic Community System." *Journal of the American Society for Information Science* 46, no. 3 (1995): 175-193.

Drabenstott, Karen Markey and Marjorie S. Weller. "Failure Analysis of Subject Searches in a Test of a New Design for Subject Access to Online Catalogs." *Journal of the American Society for Information Science* 47, no. 7 (1996): 519-537.
Dykstra, M. "LC Subject Headings Disguised as a Thesaurus." *Library Journal* 113, no. 4 (1988): 42-46.
Greenberg, Jane. "An Examination of the Impact of Lexical-Semantic Relationships on Retrieval Effectiveness During the Query Expansion (QE) Process." Completed in partial fulfillment of University of Pittsburgh, School of Information Sciences, 1998.
Greenberg, Jane. "Automatic Query Expansion via Lexical-Semantic Relationships." *Journal of the American Society for Information Science and Technology* 52, no. 5 (2001a): 402-415.
Greenberg, Jane. "Optimal Query Expansion (QE) Processing Methods with Semantically Encoded Structured Thesauri Terminology." *Journal of the American Society for Information Science and Technology* 52, no. 6 (2001b): 487-498.
Hemmje, Matthias, Clemens Kunkel, and Alexander Willet. "LyberWorld–A Visualization User Interface Supporting Fulltext Retrieval." In *Proceedings of 17th Annual International ACM SIGIR Conference on Research and Development in Information Retrieval, 1994 July 3-4, Dublin, Ireland*, 249-259. Berlin: Springer-Verlag, 1994.
Humphreys, B. L., A. T. McCray and M. L. Cheh. "Evaluating the Coverage of Controlled Health Data Terminologies: Report on the Results of the NLM/AHCPR Large Scale Vocabulary Test." *Journal of the American Medical Informatics Association* 4, no. 6 (1997): 484-500.
Lancaster, F. W. *Vocabulary Control for Information Retrieval*, 2nd ed. Arlington, VA: Information Resources Press, 1986.
LyberWorld homepage. (2002): http://www.darmstadt.gmd.de/~hemmje/Activities/Lyberworld/.
Mann, Thomas. *Library Research Models: A Guide to Classification, Cataloging, and Computers.* New York: Oxford University Press, 1993.
Milstead, Jessica L., ed. *ASIS Thesaurus of Information Science and Librarianship*, 2nd ed. Medford, NJ: Published for the American Society for Information Science by Information Today, 1998.
Plumb Design Visual Thesaurus. (1998). http://www.visualthesaurus.com/index.jsp.
ProQuest® Controlled Vocabulary and Classification Codes. Ann Arbor, MI: UMI, 1997.
Ramsey, Marshall C., Hsinchun Chen, Bin Zhu, and Bruce R. Schatz. "A Collection of Visual Thesauri for Browsing Large Collections of Geographic Images." *Journal of the American Society for Information Science* 50, no. 9 (1999): 826-834.
Roget's Thesaurus of English Words and Phrases. New York: Portland House, 1990. [Originally authored by Dr. Peter Mark Roget in 1852.]
Rorvig, M. E., C. H. Turner and J. Moncada. "The NASA Image Collection Visual Thesaurus." *Journal of the American Society for Information Science* 50, no. 9 (1999): 794-798.
Shapiro, Celia D. and Puck-Fai Yan. "Generous Tools: Thesauri in Digital Libraries." *National Online Meeting Proceedings–1996, Proceedings of the 17th National Online Meeting, New York, May 14-16, 1996*, 323-332. Medford, NJ: Information Today, 1996.
Spink, Amanda. "Information Science: A Third Feedback Framework." *Journal of the American Society for Information Science* 48, no. 8 (1997): 728-740.
Thesaurus of ERIC Descriptors, 14th ed. James E. Houston, editor/lexicographer. Phoenix, AZ: Oryx Press, 2001.

APPENDIX. Term Selection Test (Part of the Thesaurus Introduction)

A-1

Classified-alphabetized lists presented to a participant.*
The query submitted by the participant was: "Entertainment Industry AND Market Potential."

Dear Participant:
Please circle the search terms that appear to be, or that you think would have been useful to your search.

Entertainment Industry
Amusement industry
Amusement parks
Broadcasting industry
Casinos
Celebrities
Entertainers
Entertainment technology &
 design
Home entertainment industry
Motion picture industry
Music industry
Radio broadcasting
Recording industry

Reservation systems
Sports & recreation clubs
Television broadcasting
Tickets
Video industry

Market Potential
Commercial markets
Commercialization
Demand analysis
Market research
Market saturation
Market strategy

*The presentation of these terms introduced participants to thesauri as a source for additional searching terminology. The request for the selection of additional search terms was part of a larger interactive query expansion study (Greenberg, 2001b).

A-2

***ProQuest® Controlled Vocabulary* (1997) reference structure for the terms listed in A-1.**

Entertainment Industry
UF: Amusement industry
NT: Amusement parks
 Broadcasting industry
 Casinos
 Home entertainment
  industry
 Motion picture industry
 Music industry
 Radio broadcasting
 Recording industry
 Reservation systems
 Video industry

RT: Celebrities
 Entertainers
 Entertainment technology
  & design
 Sports & recreation clubs
 Television broadcasting
 Tickets

Market Potential
RT: Commercial markets
 Commercialization
 Demand analysis
 Market research
 Market saturation
 Market strategy

Distributed Thesaurus Web Services

Eric H. Johnson

SUMMARY. HTML-based information services provide access to online information sources but do not make them useful for much more than viewing in a Web browser. There is also no cohesive cataloging or subject access scheme for the Internet. XML and Web services provide the framework for enhancing the information content of all types of data delivered over the Internet and for enhancing the functionality of specialized yet interoperable networked information retrieval applications. The Thesauro-Web, a proposed network of thesaurus access and navigation services, could provide enhanced subject access for the World Wide Web and enhance the functionality of information retrieval applications. The idea behind the Thesauro-Web is described here in detail, with examples of applicable XML protocols and descriptions of possible uses. *[Article copies available for a fee from The Haworth Document Delivery Service: 1-800-HAWORTH. E-mail address: <docdelivery@haworthpress.com> Website: <http://www.HaworthPress.com> © 2004 by The Haworth Press, Inc. All rights reserved.]*

KEYWORDS. Internet, World Wide Web, Web portals, Web services, XML, HTML, subject access, thesauri, digital libraries, ADL Thesaurus Protocol, KWIC, UDDI, information retrieval applications

---

Eric H. Johnson, MS (Library and Information Science), MA (Sociology), MS (Computer science), is a knowledge architect, AOL Tucson.

[Haworth co-indexing entry note]: "Distributed Thesaurus Web Services." Johnson, Eric H. Co-published simultaneously in *Cataloging & Classification Quarterly* (The Haworth Information Press, an imprint of The Haworth Press, Inc.) Vol. 37, No. 3/4, 2004, pp. 121-153; and: *The Thesaurus: Review, Renaissance, and Revision* (ed: Sandra K. Roe, and Alan R. Thomas) The Haworth Information Press, an imprint of The Haworth Press, Inc., 2004, pp. 121-153. Single or multiple copies of this article are available for a fee from The Haworth Document Delivery Service [1-800-HAWORTH, 9:00 a.m. - 5:00 p.m. (EST). E-mail address: docdelivery@haworthpress.com].

http://www.haworthpress.com/web/CCQ
© 2004 by The Haworth Press, Inc. All rights reserved.
Digital Object Identifier: 10.1300/J104v37n03_09

INTRODUCTION

The World Wide Web and the use of HTML-based information displays has greatly increased access to online information sources, but at the same time limits the ways in which they can be used. By the same token, Web-based indexing and search engines give us access to the full text of billions of online documents, but make it difficult to access them in any kind of organized, systematic way. For years before the advent of the Internet, lexicographers built well-structured subject thesauri to organize large collections of documents. These have since been converted into electronic form and even put online, but in ways that are largely uncoordinated and not useful for searching. Until they can be brought together in a coordinated, semantically interoperable way, and offer to searchers dynamic and easy-to-use applications for subject access, they will continue to lie dormant while chaos reigns on the Internet.

This paper describes some of the ways in which XML-based Web services[1] could be used to coordinate subject thesauri and other online vocabulary sources to create a "Thesauro-Web" that could be used by both searchers and indexers to improve subject access on the Internet.

THE PROBLEM

Despite the enormous computing power applied to indexing and searching the Internet, and all of the clever algorithms (e.g., Larry Page's PageRank algorithm used by Google[2]) applied to ranking result sets, it is still just too difficult to find anything on the Web unless it has a specific and unique name. The organization of the Web could therefore benefit greatly from the use of controlled vocabularies, and for reasons that I don't need to explain here.

In terms of information organization and management, the Web's greatest strength also turns out to be its greatest weakness. The idea of the Web–a globally interlinked collection of documents–precludes an overarching organizational principle by which a searcher might begin to navigate the collection. The Domain Name Service (DNS) does provide a kind of organization, but only by server locations and not by some sort of topical scheme, and thus is of little use to the searcher who wants to navigate the Web topically. It is of no help to an information seeker to know that a particular website is, for example, under the ".org" as opposed to the ".com" top-level domain when relevant documents could be under either or both, or neither.

Web portals, such as Yahoo.com, offer communities of users specially organized navigational hierarchies of links to Web pages of interest. However, in these cases portal developers, rather than searchers, determine which documents are "relevant" and therefore included. Also, Web portals with significant levels of commercial and/or political sponsorship can bias the categories and sets of included documents, with many authors finding their documents excluded altogether from popular Web portals. Searchers have many Web portals from which to choose, but often have difficulty locating the most relevant to their information need, and they often must rely on networks of friends and colleagues to locate relevant and useful portals and Web pages instead of being able to find them directly.

One major source of the problem is that the Web presents topical and/or logical organization using the same tools as it does to present the actual target information (HTML documents). This means that catalogs and indexes are lost in the mix of all Web pages until searchers go in and find them. To draw an analogy to a traditional library of printed books, suppose that when you walked in to the library you saw only book stacks instead of the catalog and the book stacks as separate entities. Randomly dispersed throughout the book stacks would be various special volumes, not readily distinguishable from the rest of the collection, serving as catalogs to some fraction of the whole. You might know, through experience, about particular catalog volumes of interest to you, but you would have to rely on other people to know where certain other catalogs and indexes were that you might need at certain times, never knowing for certain that there were not others that would be more helpful. And no one person could claim to know the location of all the catalog volumes or even if all of the books in the library were cataloged (unfortunately, the scheme proposed here still won't solve this latter problem). The order of books on the shelves would be of no help, as there would be no sense of topical collocation either. Once you found one or a few catalogs that satisfied your need for information, you would tend to go back to those same catalogs even though they would not necessarily include the most relevant or up-to-date material. Here the Rosenberg principle applies–searchers select information sources based on their familiarity and ease of use rather than the quality of the information that they contain. So when we search the Web, we focus on what we can access through a few favorite portals or search engines when we are probably missing much relevant information. That characterizes the current state of the Internet as a searchable collection. Unless there is some fundamental change in how we can link this information in a catalog or topical form, and allow for a networked, decentralized way of doing so, the problem will only continue to get much worse. Fortunately, the Internet, with its decentralized, non-authoritative architecture, provides the means to do it, even though specialized software will be required.

In the physical library, the advent of a catalog as a specialized tool physically distinguishable from the collection gave searchers a separate and distinct (though not mandatory) means of locating items in the collection, and catalogers a way of ensuring that the catalog included each item. The catalog had a different look and feel from the collection (drawers of cards rather than shelves of books), had much finer granularity, offered different affordances, and had a different organizational structure, most notably that each item in the collection had multiple access points in the catalog corresponding to the multiple ways that searchers might want to find it. These were necessary because of the differences in use, organization, and granularity between the collection and the catalog. The same applies to the World Wide Web, its catalogs and indexes, and the subject navigation tools that it needs. As with a physical library collection, the Web needs a separate and distinct, though not mandatory, means of subject access as well as author and title access that operates outside of the means for document delivery (the Web browser).

Another more serious problem with presenting thesauri in HTML is the lack of coordination and coherency between different thesauri, even thesauri covering the same domain. HTML offers no way to identify the information in a page, and therefore cannot provide a basis for relating the content of two different thesauri, even though they may cover the same subject domain. From a user interaction perspective, the current practice of displaying thesaurus hierarchies on Web pages, and then having to fetch updated displays from the server each time you select a different term or change the display in any way, leaves much to be desired, in terms of excessive client/server interaction, unnecessary bandwidth use, and sheer user annoyance. HTML also provides no consistent way to display vocabularies, relate terms residing in different thesauri, link terms between thesauri, provide metathesauri, or discover new thesauri. Thesauri therefore require their own markup language and user interface to coherently express relations between concepts, efficiently transport semantic structures, and provide the user with an enjoyable and productive information retrieval experience.

Despite the variety of disciplines covered by thesauri and the variety of semantic structures that they employ, this is not an insurmountable problem, and in fact much of the current Web infrastructure provides the means for solving it. What makes the World Wide Web work as well as it does is not agreement about the content that each community produces, nor the form in which it is presented, but rather that they use common standards by which documents can refer to other documents (HTML-based hypertext links) and by which documents are transported (HTTP). A system of networked thesauri would similarly use a common protocol and basis for providing markup but in a way suitable for thesaurus use and interaction. However, thesauri, in contrast to the linear documents delivered over HTTP, have complex internal structures and must provide highly granular, non-sequential access to multiple features and database records, using typically dozens of such records to compose a single display. This further underscores the need for specialized design of both thesaurus server and thesaurus client browser software.

The solution is not to propose (nor impose) one enormous "thesaurus of everything" but rather to allow each community of practice to build its own thesaurus, or perhaps a number of microthesauri, and then provide the means for linking them together into a kind of "Thesauro-Web." The technology of the Internet does not require regimented, inflexible organization. It should have a logical organization separate from and independent of its physical organization, and the searcher should be able to change its logical organization according to his or her preferences. The World Wide Web today represents an enormous collection of commonly accessible documents, even though each online author or community of authors maintains only their own. As with the current Web of HTML documents accessed via HTTP, a lexicographer could create a thesaurus (or convert an existing one) with a common markup scheme, use specialized server software to make it available online, and provide links to other thesauri that use the same protocol and markup language. In addition to UDDI-driven access (described later), directory services and conventional HTML Web pages could provide entry points into the Thesauro-Web. Distributed applications similar to the Web crawlers that index Web pages could provide common keyword indexes to all thesauri.

The use of a Thesauro-Web would not require eliminating the existing use of HTML links, but rather would provide additional access points to Web documents and documents in digital collections that wish to employ the Thesauro-Web as a subject thesaurus. As with any thesaurus, the searcher would only use it when necessary and could ignore it until needed.

Effective and coherent thesaurus interaction and access to thesaurus and vocabulary services require more information-rich markup than HTML, and also more lightweight and flexible protocols than HTTP. Until lightweight protocols come into widespread use, we could still use HTTP without significantly degrading performance.

USER INTERACTION AND SPECIALIZED APPLICATIONS vs. THE WEB

"Web-based" applications currently use Web browsers as thin clients–requiring no installation or administration of the client from the Web server–and many IT experts (particularly server administrators) argue that Web-based technologies provide the most flexible and economical implementation of a particular application. However, when it comes to usability, the Web compares poorly to specialized applications that require any but the most trivial kinds of user interaction. The Web prompted unprecedented Internet growth because it made user interaction so simple. But this had the unfortunate side-effect of causing Web designers to attempt to reduce the use of all kinds of applications to that of pointing and clicking on links, which for almost everything besides hypertext navigation makes for a tedious and frustrating user experience.

Comparison of existing Web-based vs. specialized applications bears this out. If, for example, you have ever used Web-based email, such as Hotmail or Yahoo!, and then used an email application such as Eudora or Microsoft Outlook, you probably liked using the email application much better. This is because email applications have user interfaces specially designed for the kinds of tasks that users do when using email: reading email messages, replying to them, copying and pasting text between messages, filing messages in special folders, searching for text in messages, using and maintaining address books, and so on. Specialized applications also provide far better performance because they only communicate with a remote server when actually sending and receiving new content, without HTML formatting, instead of every time the display changes. This means that specialized applications not only move smaller messages between client and server, but fewer of them. Anything requiring manipulation of already fetched data takes place on the local machine and can therefore respond to each user action without network lag and without having to wait for the server to generate and send a new HTML page. Even more significantly, the user interface can incorporate graphical user interface (GUI) elements and types of GUI interaction, such as drag and drop, which Web browsers cannot provide.

Web searching can also benefit from the use of specialized applications, but this fact is less widely recognized because Web search engines always have Web-based search interfaces. On the face of it this seems necessary: how can you search the Web if you don't use a Web browser to do it? It turns out, however, that you don't need to use a Web browser to search the Web at all, and in fact you can search the Web more easily and effectively using specialized search applications, only using the Web browser to fetch and display the actual Web documents–which is what Web browsers are meant to do and what they are best at doing. Perhaps the best way to illustrate this is to download a really useful Web search application such as Copernic.[3] Copernic works as a Web meta-search tool: it accepts a single query typed by the user, posts it to multiple search sites such as AltaVista and HotBot, consolidates the results (it parses the HTML pages returned by the servers and extracts the document titles and URLs), and displays the short records all in one very easy-to-use application window. Only when you click on a document URL in the Copernic application window does your Web browser come into play, downloading and displaying the actual document. You can then navigate the Web without losing the page containing the query results, because they reside in a window outside the Web browser. Copernic also persistently displays and stores multiple queries and their result sets outside of the Web browser, making them available during subsequent sessions. This is, partially, what a really useful Web search tool ought to do–but Web browsers do not and cannot provide it. Copernic provides a beautiful illustration of balanced use of Web browsers and specialized applications: use the Web browser only to fetch and display documents, and a specialized search application to support the user interaction appropriate to the retrieval task.

Web-based applications for email and information retrieval provide "lowest common denominator" services that can only crudely ape the interaction provided by applications specifically designed for these purposes and implemented with full use of the GUI widgets supported by the operating system. Web-based applications are supported by advertising because no user would pay for services that are so difficult and irksome to use.

If special applications do better than Web browsers at email and information retrieval, it should come as no surprise that a specialized thesaurus browser application can provide better thesaurus browsing than can a Web browser. A thesaurus browser application, accessing a coordinated network of thesaurus protocol servers, and used with a bibliographic retrieval application and a Web browser to display documents, can provide a semantically coherent and highly usable Web and digital library environment.

Specialized applications that automatically download and install themselves, despite security concerns, are beginning to make inroads into distributed computing and for good reason: the productive and enjoyable use of the Internet for anything other than downloading and displaying documents and clicking on hypertext links requires specialized applications.

ONLINE THESAURUS SERVICES

An online thesaurus Web service would deliver thesaurus data by responding to requests for records from a client program. While a thesaurus browser would be the first type of client program we would think of, and is the focus of the discussion here, other applications can use thesaurus Web services as well and will be described later, though they are no less important and potentially much more so.

An online thesaurus browsing application would fetch thesaurus records from online thesaurus services and, after processing and formatting them, display them to the user. A particular thesaurus service would contain one complete thesaurus such as MeSH or ERIC, for example, and the front end would respond to browser queries with responses in a standardized format. At the back end, offline processes would convert thesauri into forms suitable for delivery by the Web service and store them in an online database.

Displaying and navigating a single thesaurus is a comparatively simple task, regardless of its size or particular structure, and it can typically be presented in a browser window consisting of a term description display and a hierarchy display. Figure 1 illustrates an example of how a thesaurus browser application might look. The display shows the MeSH term *Environmental Microbiology*, with the left-hand pane displaying the scope note and other term information and the right-hand pane displaying the hierarchies in which the term occurs. The icons next to some

FIGURE 1. An example thesaurus browser window.

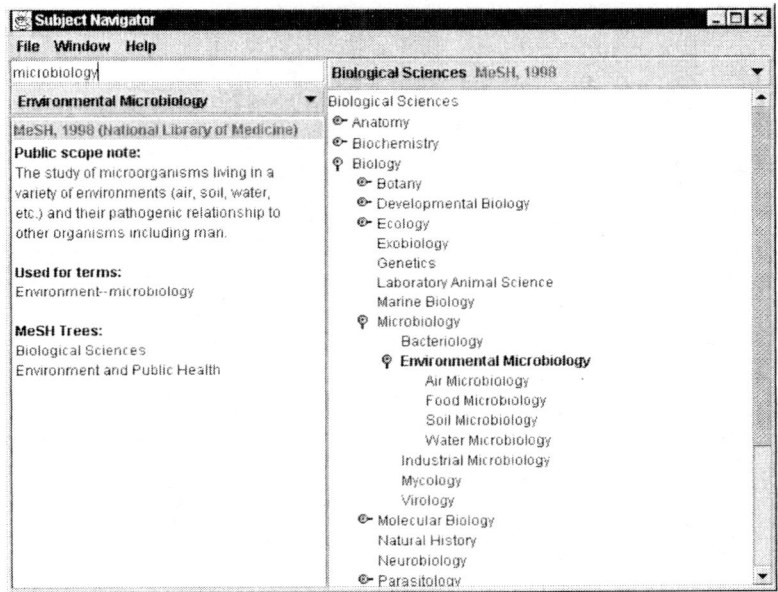

of the terms in the hierarchy display indicate, by their orientation, whether their narrower terms are visible or not.

A thesaurus browser can have a number of features that enhance thesaurus navigation, such as hypertext, a KWIC display (described later), and book marking and history lists analogous to those found in Web browsers. The browser should support thesauri as simple as term lists (which, admittedly, wouldn't provide a very interesting display) or as large and complex as full production vocabularies such as MeSH or LCSH, or even large classification schema such as LCC or UDC, with full support of class numbers, and should provide common ways of navigating them. It should also support the display of other kinds of term-suggestion services, such as automatically generated concept spaces, which contain lists of statistically weighted co-occurring terms but no hierarchies or semantically identified relationships. These would be useful for reasons described later.

XML-based thesaurus protocols have already been proposed and show promise of providing a basis for widespread use. The Alexandria Digital Library Project has published its design for an XML-based thesaurus protocol that provides the minimum required functionality for an online thesaurus service.[4] Briefly, the ADL Thesaurus Protocol provides XML-based markup of thesaurus records and has services that return thesaurus properties, top terms, results of term queries, and hierarchies. It also provides the means for the lexicographer to define extended services for each thesaurus that reflect the particularities of its structure or other special features. As of this writing, the ADL Thesaurus Protocol is in version 1.0.

XML and its related standards provide the flexible infrastructure that allows a service to define its own tags, and for later addition of new tags without modifying the underlying software. At the client end, tools such as eXtensible Stylesheet Language (XSL) and eXtensible Stylesheet Language Transformations (XSLT) allow the client software to modify the structure of server responses and display them by using configuration files (themselves XML documents) downloadable from the thesaurus service server or from the thesaurus client software vendor, who would provide configuration files for at least the most widely used thesauri. Many thesauri could be represented using the same XML Schema (or DTD), and could thus use the same configuration file. Thesaurus browsing is only one type of service that a thesaurus protocol could deliver. Any number of different vocabulary-related client applications could use a single type of standardized thesaurus service for a wide range of uses.

The ADL Thesaurus Protocol provides a useful model for understanding how to apply XML to a thesaurus structure. Consider the following thesaurus record, as it might appear in a printed thesaurus or an online display:

beaches
UF   seashores
BT   coastlines
NT   barrier beaches
        pocket beaches
        shingle beaches
RT   foreshore
        sand dunes
        sandbars
        shoals

This record would have the following XML structure, as defined by the ADL Thesaurus Protocol:

```
<term-description>
    <term>beaches</term>
    <used-for>
        <term>seashores</term>
    </used-for>
    <broader>
        <term>coastlines</term>
    </broader>
    <narrower>
        <term>barrier beaches</term>
        <term>pocket beaches</term>
        <term>shingle beaches</term>
    </narrower>
    <related>
        <term>foreshore</term>
        <term>sand dunes</term>
        <term>sandbars</term>
        <term>shoals</term>
    </related>
</term-description>
```

Note the correspondence between the elements of the displayed thesaurus entry and the XML. XML documents have a tree structure, manifested by the nesting of XML tags. (Actual XML documents have additional tags and headers that define some of the technical details of the XML document. More information about XML can be found at http://www.xml.org/.)

XML restores the information-carrying capacity that HTML took away in the rush to allow the Web to grow as quickly as possible during the 1990s. Like most technologies that enable rapid growth, HTML was the quick-and-dirty solution that hobbled any attempt to provide truly sophisticated information services. Because HTML requires that all intelligence reside in the server, it reduces powerful desktop computers to dumb terminals with nice displays. XML allows us to get back to the original intent of the client-server paradigm, where the server delivers the raw information and the client can control its presentation and may also use it for purposes not anticipated by server administrators. Widespread use of XML will reduce server loads, conserve bandwidth, and improve client intelligence and performance.

Web services provide the means to build special computing services that can accept and deliver XML-encoded information over the Internet, allowing computer software to engage in far more sophisticated kinds of interaction than can Web browsers and HTTP servers. By extension, XML will allow for far more sophisticated Internet applications than are currently feasible without the use of specially designed protocols and a great deal of software development effort.

XML allows document authors to define their own tags, preserving the meaning of each element in an XML document. HTML only defines how each element on a page appears, with no regard for what it means. Therefore, a Web browser can display an HTML page but do nothing else with it. If a Website delivers its HTML pages in a known, consistent layout, a programmer can write a program to parse the HTML and by exploiting knowledge about tag sequences and the location of desired content, can extract the information. Such programs, however, are difficult to write, more difficult to debug, and seldom reliable over long periods of use because they are susceptible to changes in format by the Web site, and therefore must be continually maintained and updated by a highly-paid programming staff. This considerably reduces the extensibility of HTML-based resources, increases their expense, and, most significantly, impedes client-based coordination of information resources. By preserving information for the client side, XML allows client machines to do the kind of results analysis that with HTML can only be done on the server.

An XML document by itself, as in the example shown earlier, contains no display or style information. In other words, XML tags have no inherent fonts, typestyles, or point sizes associated with them as HTML tags do. Therefore, XML documents require an external style sheet to indicate which display styles to apply to the content of each tag in the document. In this way, XML separates content from its presentation. There are currently several XML-related standards that can be used for client-side manipulation and display of data. XSLT running on a client machine could, for example, transform the above XML record into the following:

```
<thesaurus-entry>
     <term>beaches</term>
     <UF>seashores</UF>
     <BT>coastlines</BT>
     <NT>barrier beaches</NT>
     <NT>pocket beaches</NT>
     <NT>shingle beaches</NT>
     <RT>foreshore</RT>
     <RT>sand dunes</RT>
     <RT>sandbars</RT>
     <RT>shoals</RT>
</thesaurus-entry>
```

Or, by using XSL or XML Formatting Objects, directly convert the original XML into displayable form. XSLT can also generate HTML, which it can then pass to a conventional Web browser for display. This would allow for development of software that could run on the client machine and allow for localized manipulation of thesaurus data but still use a Web browser for display.

An XSLT file can also specify more detailed kinds of transformations to allow a client to tailor the data received from the server for uses not anticipated by the designers of the thesaurus protocol. It can, for example, add attributes to particular tags:

```
<thesaurus-entry thesaurus-id="sampleGeo" allow-stem="no">
    <term qualifier="SU.sampleGeo">beaches</term>
    <UFs>
        <term allow-stem="yes">seashores</term>
    </UFs>
    <BTs>
        <term qualifier="SU.sampleGeo">coastlines</term>
    </BTs>
    <NTs>
        <term qualifier="SU.sampleGeo">
            barrier beaches
        </term>
        <term qualifier="SU.sampleGeo">
            pocket beaches
        </term>
        <term qualifier="SU.sampleGeo">
            shingle beaches
        </term>
    </NTs>
    <RTs>
        <term qualifier="SU.sampleGeo">foreshore</term>
        <term qualifier="SU.sampleGeo">sand dunes</term>
        <term qualifier="SU.sampleGeo">sandbars</term>
        <term qualifier="SU.sampleGeo">shoals</term>
    </RTs>
</thesaurus-entry>
```

For a thesaurus display application that worked with a search application, term qualifiers would allow the system to transfer attributes when the user transfers terms from the thesaurus display to the search interface, as shown in Figure 2.

The operating systems now found on desktop and laptop computers allow applications to communicate and interact with each other, so the thesaurus browser could send search terms selected by the user to an information retrieval application. Operating systems also allow for objects, such as search terms, to carry attributes between applications. A search term transferred from a thesaurus browser to a search application could therefore carry with it information about which vocabulary it came from as well as specific information about how that term might be used in the target application. This of course assumes that the search application supports such interaction. The thesaurus browser would therefore be one application in a suite of software applications designed for online indexing, searching, and retrieval. This would bring to the client desktop capabilities

FIGURE 2. Transferring a search term from a thesaurus browser to a search application. The qualifier "SU" used by the search application is an attribute provided by the thesaurus browser.

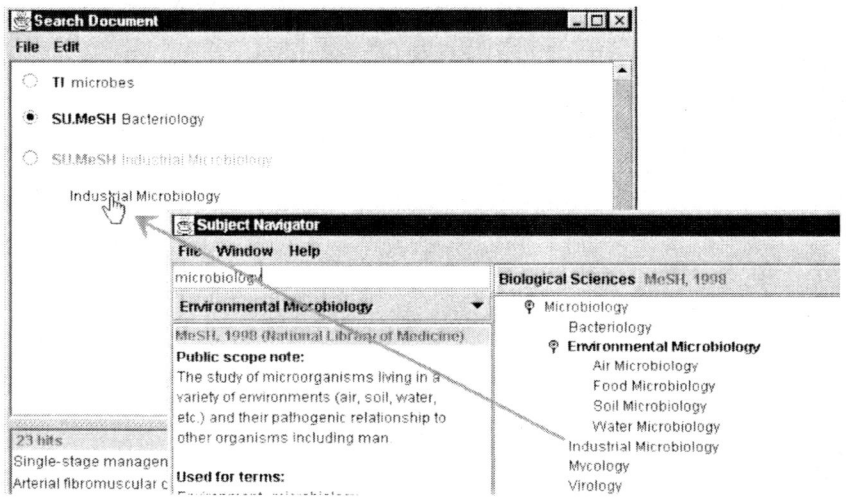

that currently, with HTML and Web browser-based thin clients, can only be coordinated within a single Web server and only between bibliographic and vocabulary sources selected by the server administrator.

EXTENDING THE FUNCTIONALITY OF THESAURUS BROWSING

The retrieval of a single, basic thesaurus record isn't a very impressive feat for a thesaurus service. While basic thesaurus records are an important part of thesaurus displays, a useful electronic thesaurus display must also display the semantic context within which a term occurs, allow the user to navigate among terms shown in a display, and provide the means for accessing terms not shown on a given display.

To provide effective access and navigation for a single thesaurus, a thesaurus browser application must:

- retrieve, cache, process, and display term description records
- retrieve, cache, process, and display large term hierarchies

- transform and/or translate terms and their attributes for use in localized environments and in other applications
- provide keyword-in-context (KWIC) access to preferred and entry vocabulary terms
- support thesaurus browsing using a number of display paradigms (tree, digraph, simple thesaurus record), with special extensions definable for each thesaurus.

Except for individual term strings themselves, a term description record is the smallest unit of granularity in a thesaurus database, containing a term and its relationships to other terms (e.g., BTs, NTs, RTs, UFs) as well as other information such as its entry date and its scope and usage notes. As illustrated earlier, the ADL Thesaurus Protocol manifests a term description record as a `term-description` tag and its contents. A term description record exists as a keyed unit of the thesaurus server database that the client can cache for later use.

Hierarchies are built by starting at a top term and recursively traversing NT relations in a depth-first manner until the entire hierarchy has been built. Understood as a "tree" in computer science, the top term is the "root" and terms at the deepest hierarchical level (having no NTs themselves) are "leaves." Unlike the classically understood tree, however, thesaurus hierarchies can be polyhierarchical, manifested by terms that have more than one broader term. This technically makes a thesaurus polyhierarchy a *lattice,* meaning that there may be more than one path from the top term to a given term some n levels below it if any of the intermediate terms have more than one BT. However, the resulting graph is still acyclic, allowing for convenient methods of validating the hierarchical structure of the thesaurus. Polyhierarchy in a thesaurus manifests itself as repeated subtrees in the thesaurus display, rooted at the term having the multiple BTs; the term with all of its descendants appears as many times as the number of BTs it has.

The particular method by which a thesaurus server delivers a hierarchy to a thesaurus browser client makes a great deal of difference in the performance of the browser and therefore its responsiveness to the user. If a hierarchy is small, containing less than a total of one hundred distinct terms, then the server can deliver the entire hierarchy and its structural information to the client in a single response, and the client can process it for display. This technique, however, does not scale. The download and processing time increase in direct proportion to the size of the hierarchy, and a large hierarchy would take a disproportionately large amount of time to download and display, even when only a small number of the terms from it would end up as part of the final display.

At the other extreme, downloading individual description records to build a hierarchy on the client side would be even slower, due to the great number of individual records downloaded and the excess information contained in each record that may never be used. It would also be highly redundant, as thousands of clients would repeat work that could be done just once on the server.

Dynamically generated HTML displays of thesaurus hierarchies that only show the relevant expansion for a term provide the best example of efficient bandwidth use for a given hierarchy display.[5] However, the Web server must generate a new display and send it to the client every time the user selects a different term, even if it only amounts to a minor change in the display. For efficient, scalable client-server hierarchy navigation, some compromise is required between transferring the whole hierarchy, the part of the hierarchy only needed for display, and transferring individual term description records.

By generating the complete hierarchy, and then breaking it up into manageable-sized chunks, an offline process can produce a hierarchy of medium granularity that it can deliver to a client in an efficient yet flexible manner. A typical hierarchy chunk might contain a subtree several levels deep that would contain perhaps one hundred terms. If a given term within a hierarchy chunk is not a leaf node, it would contain a pointer to a corresponding node at the root of another chunk that would contain its NTs. The particular depth and breadth of a chunk would depend on the structure of the hierarchy it came from. The root node of each chunk would be indexed by an internal tree number generated by the chunking algorithm, which would be stored in each term description record as a foreign key. A term description record would contain as many tree numbers as necessary to specify its locations throughout the hierarchies of the thesaurus. This also allows for hierarchy caching, with the client knowing which hierarchy chunks it already has for any given tree number, and only requesting from the server hierarchy chunks it does not already have. This makes for efficient server use and allows for scalable hierarchy transport, display, and navigation.

Morphological transformation of terms applies to conversion of plural to singular forms of noun phrases, and other uses such as automatic spelling conversion (between American and British thesauri, for example) and language translation. When transferring thesaurus terms to other applications that may perform searches based on keyword matching rather than descriptor searching, the thesaurus browser could provide singular or even stemmed forms of terms to improve retrieval.

Spelling conversion and language translation could allow for such adaptations as using the British INSPEC Thesaurus to organize and access a collection of American documents covering the same domain. The spelling conversion rules would be stored in an XML file with its own particular schema, and used by the thesaurus browser software to perform spelling conversions as it displayed terms.

This idea could be extended to emulate multilingual thesauri by providing XML files containing translations of terms between different languages, as well as general translation rules to apply to multiword terms not specifically provided in the translation tables. When used by the browser, it would allow, for example, the display of an English-language thesaurus in French, Russian, or Japanese, assuming that the appropriate character encodings and fonts were available. The general idea here is that if you find a thesaurus with a useful structure but want it in a different language, you could replicate the thesaurus structure in the target language by combining the thesaurus service protocol with a translation table of the terms in the language you want.

As an example, take a simple English-French term translation table, represented by the XML structure:

```
<term>
     <en>beaches</en><fr>plages</fr>
</term>
<term>
     <en>seashores</en><fr>bords de la mer</fr>
</term>
<term>
     <en>coastlines</en><fr>littoraux</fr>
</term>
<term>
     <en>barrier beaches</en><fr>plages de barrière</fr>
</term>
<term>
     <en>pocket beaches</en><fr>plages de poche</fr>
</term>
<term>
     <en>shingle beaches</en><fr>plages de bardeau</fr>
</term>
<term>
     <en>foreshore</en><fr>lais</fr>
</term>
<term>
     <en>sand dunes</en><fr>dunes</fr>
</term>
<term>
     <en>sandbars</en><fr>bancs de sable</fr>
</term>
<term>
     <en>shoals</en><fr>bas-fonds</fr>
</term>
```

(This is a fragment of a much larger database of term translations that would probably have a more sophisticated XML structure. But it will suffice for this example. Also, someone fluent in both English and French might disagree with the choice of French equivalencies here; they are used only for the sake of example.) By applying these equivalencies to term description records, an equivalent thesaurus in another language can be produced, having the same structure as the original thesaurus. The sample translation table applied to the earlier example XML term description record for "beaches" would yield:

```
<term-description language="français">
    <term>plages</term>
    <used-for>
        <term>bords de la mer</term>
    </used-for>
    <broader>
        <term>littoraux</term>
    </broader>
    <narrower>
        <term>plages de barrière</term>
        <term>plages de poche</term>
        <term>plages de bardeau</term>
    </narrower>
    <related>
        <term>lais</term>
        <term>dunes</term>
        <term>bancs de sable</term>
        <term>bas-fonds</term>
    </related>
</term-description>
```

The same transformation could be applied to any XML record containing thesaurus terms, including hierarchy records. A thesaurus browser client could translate terms without the knowledge of the thesaurus server, and could thereby present the thesaurus to the searcher in ways not foreseen by the lexicographer of the original thesaurus.

KeyWord-In-Context (KWIC) access allows users to enter the thesaurus using keyword matches to its terms and entry vocabulary. The structure of the KWIC index determines how easily the user can find thesaurus terms by typing keyword stems and combinations of partial and whole words to match to the vocabulary index. In response to what the user types, the KWIC display presents a sequence of either single keywords or thesaurus terms from which the user can choose; clicking on a term in the KWIC display causes the thesaurus browser to fetch and display the description and the hierarchy for that term.

The KWIC window presents a lexically ordered, dynamic set of thesaurus terms that changes in response to the user entering a character expression (a "string") in the term entry field (see Figure 3). Burke (1998)

FIGURE 3. Sequence of KWIC displays in response to user input.

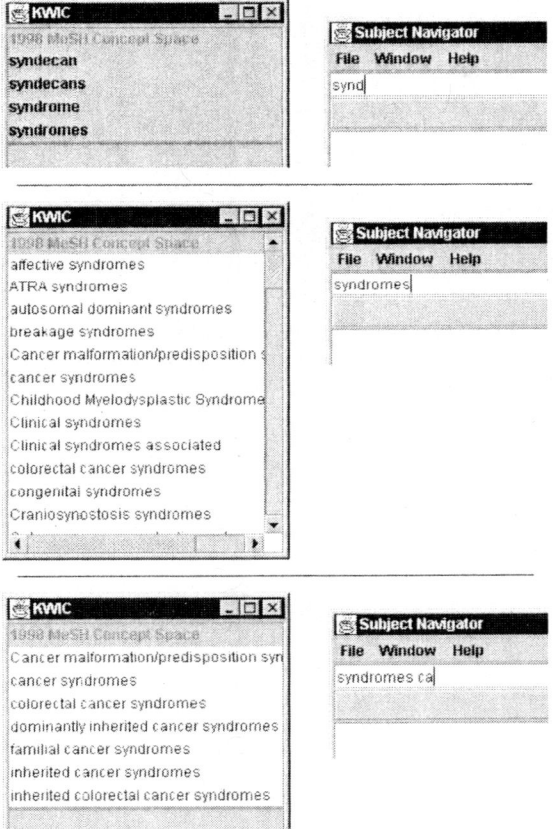

lists some of the ways in which vocabularies could be searched in order to produce sequences of terms in an online lexicon.[6] The ones most readily applicable to subject thesauri are:

- Headword matching, where the string is matched to the beginning of keywords in the vocabulary. This is often applied to all words in each multi-word vocabulary term (yielding a rotated keyword display, sometimes called a "permuterm" display), not just the first word. Headword matching would be the most commonly applied, default setting for a KWIC display, as shown in Figure 3. The

- server processing for headword matching can get somewhat complicated when the user enters multiple keyword stems.
- Free string matching, where the string is matched to any part of the words. This nearly always returns a greater number of matched terms than does headword matching.
- Soundex or fuzzy matching, which relaxes the exact string matching criteria employed by the first two methods. This is more complex than exact string matching and would require the server to process records matched to the key string before returning them to the client.
- Regular expression matching, with which the searcher can enter strings containing metacharacters that are used to perform sophisticated string matching.[7] Users of awk and Perl should be familiar with regular expressions.

To provide dynamic response to the user, a KWIC index must be generated offline and be highly redundant, so that the server can quickly send KWIC index records directly to the client, as the user types, without having to process them in any way. While this can be done for headword and free string matching, it cannot really be done for fuzzy or regular expression matching. As with the chunked hierarchy records described above, KWIC index records are of moderate size and contain a superset of the terms needed so they can be scanned by the client to adjust the particular selection of terms before displaying them in the KWIC window.

The use of KWIC indexes can be a problem for thesaurus browser clients that perform dynamic translation of vocabularies. KWIC indexes, keyed with word stems and matched using fragments of words, would not work for key strings from languages other than the one from which they were generated. A searcher would therefore have to use the native language of the thesaurus to access the KWIC index. To provide multilingual KWIC access, a translation of the entire thesaurus into the target language would have to be generated, and then a new KWIC index generated from that.

Hierarchy chunk records, KWIC index records, and language translation records would each have their own XML schema. The research and development I did with the IODyne multiple view information retrieval client for the Digital Library Initiative at the University of Illinois at Urbana-Champaign demonstrated the practicality and scalability of the hierarchy chunking and KWIC indexing schemes, and were implemented using XML records delivered over a network.[8] Common offline processes can generate hierarchy chunk records and KWIC index records for any given thesaurus, and would be part of the standard back-end of any thesaurus service.

STANDARD THESAURUS USE AND DISCOVERY

To preserve the independence of each thesaurus and its respective community of practice, a thesaurus may have variations in attributes and layout, just as HTML documents may. Despite variations in layout and design, they can still all share a common means of access and a common means of navigation both within a single thesaurus and between multiple thesauri. The ADL Thesaurus Protocol is an example of a thesaurus protocol that supports basic thesaurus records and hierarchies, and supports extensions to the protocol to handle the special requirements of any particular thesaurus. It can therefore handle common features such as hierarchies and relational links, and special features of particular thesauri with extensions provided by their vendors. XML provides the basis for implementing these extensions.

A particular thesaurus, such as MeSH or INSPEC, for example, would be only one of any number of thesauri available for access on the Internet through an agreed-upon thesaurus protocol such as ADL. This would provide, for the first time, a common way to access online thesauri, in much the same way that Z39.50 provided a common way to access library catalogs. Once I have an ADL Thesaurus Protocol browser and there are several dozen thesauri residing on ADL Thesaurus Protocol servers, I can connect to any one of them and query and browse them in exactly the same way. The remaining problem is discovery: how do I know which thesauri are out there and where they are located?

One solution could be institutional: a professional organization could agree to maintain a Web page listing all of the online thesauri it knows about that are served by standard protocol thesaurus services. Searchers could then go to that Web page, find a link to the thesaurus they want to browse, click on it (which would launch the thesaurus browser if it was not already running) and the thesaurus browser would connect to the thesaurus service, possibly load the top terms, and then wait for the user to submit a query. This kind of arrangement is what we have become accustomed to in an Internet ruled by the Web. However, it would be an ad hoc arrangement and would make thesaurus service access dependent on the thesaurus list Web page author updating the list every time a new thesaurus comes online or an existing thesaurus service changes its location.

Universal Description, Discovery and Integration (UDDI[9]) provides an open, global, Internet-based, platform-independent registry for describing any kind of Web service and locating servers that provide those services. UDDI provides automatic methods for the author of a service to register it with a UDDI server and for that registration to become globally accessible nearly instantaneously, in much the same way that Internet server addresses use DNS for global accessibility. A searcher could then access a nearby UDDI server to discover thesaurus services anywhere in the world.

Further, UDDI allows for taxonomies of services. If "Thesaurus" were a top-level service, subdivisions for "Education," "Medicine," "Engineering," etc., would make access more manageable and not require the user to scroll through long lists of thesaurus names to locate the one of interest. After the user (or possibly the client application automatically) selects a thesaurus, the UDDI returns the Internet address of the thesaurus service to the client software, which then accesses the service itself. UDDI can be thought of as a Yellow Pages for Web services, where your client software looks up a service by category and then uses the contact information for the service it finds to connect to and use the service. UDDI is widely supported by major industry players such as Microsoft and IBM, and will attain wide usage within the next few years. The use of UDDI would not preclude using Web pages as additional pointers to thesaurus services.

ACCESSING MULTIPLE THESAURI

A Web browser that did not support hypertext links would not be very useful for navigating the Web, though it could still display individual HTML documents. A thesaurus browser that displays just one thesaurus at a time, and provides no way of linking thesauri, can still navigate one vocabulary. However, to comprehensively cover the subject area of a discipline or a number of related disciplines, we really need to have interlinked thesauri and a browser and Web services that support linking thesauri and can correctly process and display the semantics of such links.

A thesaurus browser could access multiple thesauri in two distinct ways: keyword level and semantic level.

Keyword level multiple thesaurus access would be comparatively simple. A KWIC display could show keyword matches from multiple thesauri without much more effort than from a single thesaurus; it would merely require serially accessing the KWIC database services of each thesaurus and appending the results to the display. In this way a thesaurus browser that supported the display of only one thesaurus could switch between thesauri through the KWIC display or, once terms from each thesaurus have been displayed, through the term history list.

This would be similar to how you can switch between previously viewed pages in a Web browser. This herky-jerky way of navigating is perceptually disruptive, but can still help the searcher and be accomplished without having to add much functionality to the thesaurus browser per se. Multiple thesauri could also be displayed by opening multiple instances of a thesaurus browser, just as you can display multiple Web pages simultaneously by opening multiple Web browsers. With computer screens getting progressively larger, this is not as awkward a prospect as it would have been even a few years ago.

But displaying two or more thesauri side by side, provided they are somehow semantically related, yields only a fragmented view of the context within which a topic may occur. There would be many potential term tracings between the two thesauri that would lie dormant, and the searcher would have to try to mentally trace them while performing related tasks, such as constructing queries and examining retrieved item records. Such a fragmented view of a subject domain would make it unnecessarily difficult for the user to systematically cover the concepts within it.

Linking thesauri on a semantic level would provide a more coherent subject display, but would require extending the thesaurus markup language as well as the services provided by the thesaurus Web service. It would also, of course, require intellectual effort on the part of lexicographers and others with lexigraphic privileges to provide semantic links between thesauri, and these could become very elaborate. Lexicographers would use the extended thesaurus markup language to encode links between terms and substructures in related thesauri as well as to encode general rules that might be applied between them.

This immediately raises the issue of thesaurus independence and how lexicographers would go about creating links between thesauri. The World Wide Web has a standard type of hypertext link, defined in HTML, that Web authors use to create links between documents, even though those same documents may have very different content and structure. HTML links are very simple, consisting of a standard Web address with an optional reference to a designated document fragment. As opposed to links between HTML documents, links between thesauri will have to be semantically sophisticated in order to provide useful navigation between terms and substructures of multiple thesauri.

Unlike documents, thesauri do not have a linear structure, and are randomly accessed rather than read from beginning to end. They also have a very fine granularity, where links would refer to individual records rather than entire documents or to designated document fragments. For a monolingual thesaurus, the term string itself provides the identifier for a term record. UDDI, as described above, can provide the infrastructure required to provide access to a thesaurus with a unique identifier. So the simplest possible link to a term in an external thesaurus would have the form

```
<link thesaurus="thesaurus-id" term="term-id">
```

To illustrate the use of such a link, consider the use of the INSPEC thesaurus entry for "fluid mechanics" by a distributed thesaurus of physical phenomena. Instead of replicating the entire INSPEC term description record, it could merely include the term as a link in the descriptor record for the term:

```
<term-description>
    <term>fluid mechanics</term>
    <broader><term>dynamics</term></broader>
    <link thesaurus="INSPEC" term="fluid mechanics"/>
</term-description>
```

A client thesaurus browser, when it downloads the above term description record, would use UDDI to locate the INSPEC Thesaurus, then use the INSPEC Thesaurus Web service to retrieve the corresponding term description record for "fluid mechanics," with its scope notes, UF, BT, NT, and RT tracings, etc.

The potential for specifying links between thesaurus terms goes beyond mere term description record substitution. It may also specify how much of the structure surrounding the thesaurus term to include. To continue the present example, the INSPEC term "fluid mechanics" has the following NTs:

```
capillarity
cavitation
fluid dynamics
hydrostatics
Mach number
```

Of these narrower terms, "fluid dynamics" itself has a dozen NTs, and half of those terms have NTs of their own, altogether constituting a rather nice little microthesaurus of fluid mechanics. How much of this structure is included in a distributed thesaurus depends on the attributes and additional tags included in the link to "fluid mechanics," the top term of this microthesaurus.

The default behavior, as illustrated in the above example, would only include the immediate NTs of the INSPEC term "fluid mechanics," yielding the hierarchy:

```
fluid mechanics
    capillarity
    cavitation
    fluid dynamics
    hydrostatics
    Mach number
```

An attribute to the link tag indicating the number of NT levels to include would specify how deep the link should recursively follow the NTs encountered in the linked record. (The default behavior shown above would indicate an NT level inclusion of "1." An NT level inclusion of "0" would indicate that no NTs be included.) An NT level of "all" includes the entire subtree, thereby recursively following all of the NT tracings under "fluid mechanics":

```
<term-description>
    <term>fluid mechanics</term>
    <broader><term>dynamics</term></broader>
    <link thesaurus="INSPEC" term="fluid mechanics"
        ntlevel="all"/>
</term-description>
```

The resulting hierarchy is too large to reproduce here.

Once linked to a hierarchy, specific terms may be excluded from an imported subtree. The following example excludes the INSPEC term "Mach number" from the fluid mechanics hierarchy:

```
<term-description>
    <term>fluid mechanics</term>
    <broader><term>dynamics</term></broader>
    <link thesaurus="INSPEC" term="fluid mechanics"
        ntlevel="all">
        <exclude term="Mach number"/>
    </link>
</term-description>
```

This would cause the link to not import the term "Mach number." If "Mach number" had NTs of its own, these would be excluded as well, as would the entire subtree under "Mach number." It does not affect the INSPEC thesaurus itself, only the thesaurus defined by the links.

Terms can also be excluded that are not immediate NTs of the linked term. The term "relativistic fluid dynamics" is an NT of "fluid dynamics," which in turn is an NT of "fluid mechanics." Adding an exclude tag for "relativistic fluid dynamics" to the link still excludes that term, even though it is not an immediate NT of the linked term:

```
<term-description>
    <term>fluid mechanics</term>
    <broader><term>dynamics</term></broader>
    <link thesaurus="INSPEC" term="fluid mechanics"
        ntlevel="all">
        <exclude term="Mach number"/>
        <exclude term="relativistic fluid dynamics"/>
    </link>
</term-description>
```

In this way links can exclude terms from whatever level it finds them.

Links can also add new terms to an imported hierarchy, again without affecting the source thesaurus. To add the admittedly contrived term "bovine hydrodynamics" as a NT of "hydrodynamics," which itself is a NT of "fluid dynamics," the link would be:

```
<term-description>
    <term>fluid mechanics</term>
    <broader><term>dynamics</term></broader>
    <link thesaurus="INSPEC" term="fluid mechanics"
        ntlevel="all">
        <exclude term="Mach number"/>
        <exclude term="relativistic fluid dynamics"/>
        <include term="bovine hydrodynamics"
            bt="hydrodynamics">
    </link>
</term-description>
```

By specifying "hydrodynamics" as a BT of "bovine hydrodynamics," the link should be able to infer the correct placement of the term in the hierarchy even though it is not a direct NT of "fluid mechanics." This also assumes that the thesaurus can access a term description record for "bovine hydrodynamics" that contains complete relationship information, including

```
<broader><term thesaurus="INSPEC">hydrodynamics</term></broader>
```

to validate the relationship stated in the link.

When processing these term description records, the thesaurus service back-end would import the relevant INSPEC term description records from the INSPEC thesaurus service to build the hierarchy chunk records and the KWIC index records. The client thesaurus browser would therefore initially display the hierarchy with the terms included and excluded as specified in the link. However, the user would also be able to select any hierarchies from INSPEC itself, thereby entering the INSPEC thesaurus and having access to its canonical structure without the additions or deletions specified in the links (see Figure 4).

FIGURE 4. Hierarchical context of the term "fluid mechanics" as shown in a thesaurus browser.

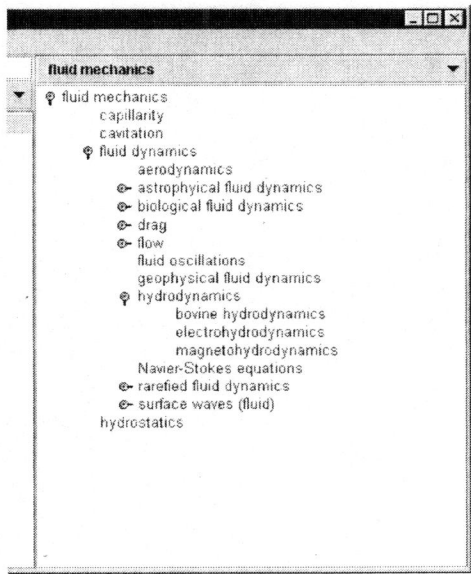

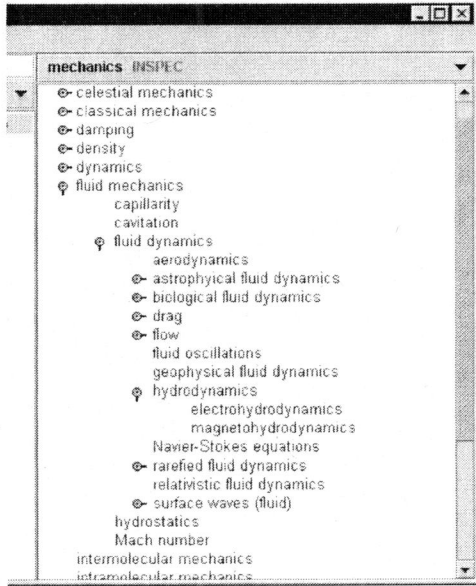

When the user selects the "INSPEC: mechanics" hierarchy, for example, the thesaurus browser retrieves all information for the current term from the INSPEC thesaurus Web service, and the user can continue to browse the INSPEC thesaurus just as if s/he had accessed it directly at the beginning of the section. Because the user at this point would view the hierarchies directly from INSPEC, the subtree under "fluid mechanics" would be restored to its canonical INSPEC form with the terms "Mach number" and "relativistic fluid dynamics" restored and the term "bovine hydrodynamics" removed. The browser would maintain a history list of thesauri and terms viewed, so the user could later return to the altered hierarchy and the complete navigational context of prior thesauri visited, bovine hydrodynamics and all.

This illustrates the kinds of semantic linking that could be provided by the Thesauro-Web, and a tiny glimpse of how users might access and navigate it through an XML-based, Web service-enabled, hypertextual thesaurus browser. As stated previously, the particular XML schema illustrated here is contrived for the sake of example and explanation of concept. Actual schemas to support a Thesauro-Web standard would require a thorough design and review process as well as implementation experience before they could be deployed. A workable scheme would probably resemble that used by UMLS, using several related XML schemas and distributed among several dozen Web services.

Given the amount of semantic information held by the thesaurus browser when it has accessed related terms among multiple thesauri, it may be possible to have the browser itself suggest relationships among terms based on string comparison and recurring patterns of terms with specific relationships. It may also be possible for a thesaurus browser to merge two or more thesauri into compound hierarchies based on term equivalence or other heuristic rules. This type of functionality might be used more by lexicographers than by searchers and could lead to more powerful thesaurus construction and maintenance software.

The full functionality of the Thesauro-Web would go well beyond the simple linking and localized inference suggested here. A network of interlinked thesauri would support the following:

- provide each thesaurus with a unique identifier and provide the means to locate a thesaurus, given its name, anywhere on the Internet (UDDI would provide this);
- refer to any thesaurus by name within another thesaurus, and refer to any given term within that thesaurus (the basis for thesaurus linking described above);

- discovery of thesauri using either keyword searching or references from related thesauri, yielding identifiers of previously unknown thesauri;
- refer to any substructure of a thesaurus, typically a subtree rooted in a particular term, but may also refer to, for example, a neighborhood of RTs surrounding a given term;
- metathesaurus links between individual terms, hierarchies, and other substructures within different thesauri;
- integrated and simultaneous KWIC-based access to multiple thesauri;
- metathesaurus structures that express equivalence between terms in different thesauri;
- conventional hypertext links from scope notes (or other textual elements of term description records) to Web pages;
- links between thesauri and other types of term suggestion services such as concept spaces;
- history of a term across mutliple thesauri and other term suggestion services, including a chronology of the use of the term, any prior terms, and any subsequent terms;
- multiple external metathesaural views, allowing different communities of practice to build their own topical maps of the world from pieces of other thesauri and vocabularies;
- user-defined general rules, based, for example, on regular expressions describing terms, for the meta-linking of newly discovered thesauri;
- a thesaurus query language, allowing for retrieval of terms as well as other terms related in particular ways to the term or terms specified in the query (example: list all terms within 2 RT levels of a given term).

A Thesauro-Web with all of these capabilities would significantly increase the value of the individual thesauri comprising it. This would be a consequence of the "network effect" (also known as the "FAX effect"), where the value of each component of the network grows as more components are added to it. Just as a single computer in isolation has limited utility, but becomes far more useful when connected to a network, the utility and therefore the value of online thesauri will increase when they can be coherently related to other thesauri and vocabulary sources. It is not enough to merely put them online behind a wall of HTML, where they may be viewed but not actually used.

Augmenting the Thesauro-Web with access to concept spaces and other automatic methods would be well worth the effort as well, and would further increase the utility of online thesauri. Adding co-occurrence and subject expert information derived from a concept space computation is one such way to augment a thesaurus, and could be made a regular part of ongoing thesaurus production for a given community of practice. It could also aid lexicographers in updating thesauri, thereby both reducing their cost and improving their quality. Automatically generated components of the Thesauro-Web could be updated far more frequently than can thesauri. Expertly maintained thesauri could provide the semantic core of the Thesauro-Web, which could filter and organize the results of a host of very cheap automatic methods that could, in turn, provide a resource to lexicographers for augmenting the core thesauri. The result would have a synergistic effect that would accelerate the value accrued to the whole enterprise.

OTHER THESAURUS-ENHANCED APPLICATIONS

With consistent and well-defined requests and responses, a thesaurus service can provide information to all kinds of Internet-based software. Software agents that search for specific topical information could use thesaurus services to automatically expand search terms for persistent queries, or as part of interactive processes to suggest additional terms to searchers without the need for them to consult a specialized thesaurus application such as a thesaurus browser.

Lexicographers, who already have thesaurus construction software, would not initially use a Web service to change the vocabulary or the structure of the thesaurus, but would use offline tools to convert and then upload the canonical thesaurus files generated by conventional thesaurus construction software to update the service during planned downtime. At some later point thesaurus construction and management software should be integrated into thesaurus Web services, so that users with lexicographic privileges can change the vocabulary and/or the thesaurus structure without taking the service offline, making thesaurus construction and maintenance distributed, thus realizing the long sought-after vision of a living online vocabulary that changes at pace with the global collection of online documents.

Having a thesaurus served by a powerful computer allows for Web service applications other than thesaurus browsing and maintenance. Two applications readily adaptable to Web services include automatic extraction of vocabulary terms from documents and automatic generation of Boolean queries from documents. Brief examples of the use of each follow.

In the vocabulary extractor Web service application, the user sends a text document of any size to the Web service, which responds with a list of thesaurus terms that it found in the text. The user would select the appropriate Web service vocabulary depending on the subject domain of the document, or a generalized service could compare the text to multiple thesauri and suggest which is most applicable depending on the number of matches in each. Suppose an indexer received the following abstract:

> The association of ventricular arrhythmias with left ventricular (LV) hypertrophy was examined in 6,218 participants. Electrocardiographic (ECG) LV hypertrophy was present in 171 subjects and echocardiographic hypertrophy was detected in 869. Because of low prevalence ECG LV hypertrophy was not associated with arrhythmia in women. After adjustment for age, sex, systolic blood pressure, valvular heart disease, angina pectoris and acute myocardial infarction, the association of echocardiographic but not ECG LV hypertrophy with ventricular arrhythmia remained significant (p less than 0.001).

By sending this abstract to a MeSH-based vocabulary-extraction Web service, the indexer would receive the following MeSH terms:

left ventricular hypertrophy
association
electrocardiography
blood pressure
heart diseases
angina pectoris
mycardial infarction
arrhythmia

This would significantly augment the effort of an indexer looking for vocabulary terms as subject identifiers for a document or abstract. This would not necessarily be the final set of terms, as the indexer would still make the final selection and could use the automatically selected terms as starting points for navigating the vocabulary to search for more relevant terms.

The Boolean query generator Web service would generate a Boolean query using terms extracted from a document and the hierarchical structure of the thesaurus. The idea would be to generate from a document a sophisticated Boolean query that would retrieve other documents in the collection similar to that document. It would use the vocabulary extraction Web service to extract the terms from the document and then use their places in the thesaurus hierarchies to select the terms and group them by semantic distance. The selection algorithm would favor terms at deeper levels of hierarchies and that occur in one or very few distinct hierarchies, implying that they have the most specificity. Effective Boolean query generation therefore requires that a thesaurus have well-developed hierarchies which include most, if not all, of the terms in the thesaurus.

Boolean queries used by professional searchers tend to be in conjunctive normal form. The structure of the thesaurus hierarchies determine the grouping of terms into specific disjunctive clauses, with terms from tightly related parts of hierarchies going into the same disjunctive clause. So the above example terms would generate the query

>   (angina pectoris **or** myocardial infarction **or** left ventricular hypertrophy) **and** electrocardiography **and** blood pressure

For searching collections not indexed with MeSH, further references made into Use-UF relations to automatically include entry terms to hedge the singular conjunctive terms "electrocardiography" and "blood pressure" yield the query

>   (angina pectoris **or** myocardial infarction **or** left ventricular hypertrophy) **and** (electrocardiography **or** ECG **or** EKG **or** electrocardiogram) **and** blood pressure

(The MeSH term "blood pressure" has no entry terms. Depending on how specific the result sets are for the query, such singular conjunctive terms might be eliminated.)

These are two examples of possible uses of Web services other than thesaurus browsing and search term selection. The network effect of multiple interacting thesauri and other vocabulary sources described in the previous section could lead to many more as-yet-unforeseen vocabulary services that would significantly augment the search, retrieval, and information management capabilities of Internet-based researchers. Web services can provide enhanced functionality for all information sources, including bibliographic databases, and in ways that go far beyond the basic kinds of access that we have now.

REFERENCES

1. For more information on Web services, see the Web Services Journal website: http://sys-con.com/webservices/.
2. http://www.google.com/technology/index.html.
3. http://www.copernic.com/.
4. http://alexandria.sdc.ucsb.edu/~gjanee/thesaurus/specification.html.
5. See the MeSH Thesaurus browser: http://www.nlm.nih.gov/mesh/MBrowser.html.
6. Burke, Sean Michael. *The Design of Online Lexicons*. Master's thesis: Northwestern University, Evanston, IL, 1998. http://www.speech.cs.cmu.edu/~sburke/ma/all.html.
7. Friedl, Jeffrey E. F. *Mastering Regular Expressions*. Sebastopol, CA: O'Reilly & Associates, 1997.
8. Johnson, Eric H. "Using IODyne," *Nordic Journal of Documentation* 55, 1 (2000): 9-17.
9. http://uddi.org/.

Tools of the Trade: Vocabulary Management Software

Melissa A. Riesland

SUMMARY. This article defines basic concepts relevant to controlled vocabularies and outlines criteria for evaluating vocabulary management software. A comparison of four representative vocabulary management products is provided in an accompanying appendix. *[Article copies available for a fee from The Haworth Document Delivery Service: 1-800-HAWORTH. E-mail address: <docdelivery@haworthpress.com> Website: <http://www.HaworthPress.com> © 2004 by The Haworth Press, Inc. All rights reserved.]*

KEYWORDS. Thesaurus management software, vocabulary maintenance, product reviews, controlled vocabularies, taxonomies, subject headings, classification, indexing, thesauri, information retrieval

INTRODUCTION

Librarians have known for a long time what the business world is only beginning to discover: Information demands organization. Modern infor-

---

Melissa A. Riesland, MLIS, is a consulting taxonomist for S&T Consulting, Seattle, WA, where she is developing corporate taxonomies for external clients. She is chapter treasurer of the Pacific Northwest Chapter of the American Society for Information Science and Technology (ASIS&T), co-founder of the chapter's Reading Group, and has presented at the past two regional meetings. At the time this article was written, she was developing taxonomies for Singingfish, a multimedia search service.

[Haworth co-indexing entry note]: "Tools of the Trade: Vocabulary Management Software." Riesland, Melissa A. Co-published simultaneously in *Cataloging & Classification Quarterly* (The Haworth Information Press, an imprint of The Haworth Press, Inc.) Vol. 37, No. 3/4, 2004, pp. 155-176; and: *The Thesaurus: Review, Renaissance, and Revision* (ed: Sandra K. Roe, and Alan R. Thomas) The Haworth Information Press, an imprint of The Haworth Press, Inc., 2004, pp. 155-176. Single or multiple copies of this article are available for a fee from The Haworth Document Delivery Service [1-800-HAWORTH, 9:00 a.m. - 5:00 p.m. (EST). E-mail address: docdelivery@haworthpress.com].

http://www.haworthpress.com/web/CCQ
© 2004 by The Haworth Press, Inc. All rights reserved.
Digital Object Identifier: 10.1300/J104v37n03_10

mation technology, especially the Web, allows greater access to information than we could have ever imagined. On the Web, anyone can be a publisher, resulting in an explosion of unorganized information.

Anyone can access this information using the nifty trick of full-text search, which for a short while appeared to render document surrogates obsolete. No longer would the searcher be limited to subject headings, abstracts, titles, and whatever else the indexer or cataloger felt was worthy of recording. No longer would the searcher be unable find a certain short story because it exists within a collection of works and therefore is not individually cataloged. No longer would the searcher have to rely on a librarian to navigate the arcane search technologies of electronic databases. The birth of a shiny new world was proclaimed, relegating librarians to the dustbin. Or so we feared.

But almost immediately queries began returning thousands to millions of results. Search engines were increasingly unable to keep their indexes complete or up to date. And full-text search was nearly powerless when it came to non-text materials such as images or audio/video materials. Users were increasingly frustrated by the rat's nest that is the World Wide Web.

Hearing this frustration, many software companies began developing software for managing the glut. Looking to information science for inspiration, they discovered a technique that would improve end-user searching and navigation: controlled vocabularies. As a result, many developers started offering vocabulary management modules or stand-alone tools.[1]

What this means is that after years of technological neglect, librarians are finally getting some attention. Traditionally there was little interest in developing library software because of the limited market size. Simply put, there was no big money to be made. The Web changed all that, and librarians can benefit from some of this state of-the-art technology.

In my case, this was a timely development. In 2000 I began looking for vocabulary management software. I develop vocabularies for an audio/video search service. In order to prepare a purchase request, I created a spreadsheet comparing the features of candidate products. This article is an outgrowth of that research.

At the end of this article, the Appendix compares what I consider to be a representative sample of available software. In selecting software to compare, I made some assumptions about your needs. I assumed that you are not interested in an automated tool, that you need a stand-alone module only (as opposed to a suite of tools), and that you will have more than one worker using this tool at one time.

Before we get started, a caveat: this is not a buying guide. I will define some terminology, discuss software configurations and suggest some questions to ask before you go shopping.

TERMINOLOGY

The language of our discipline is convoluted. The same terms are used in different ways, and a single concept can have multiple names, causing continual confusion. I do not assume that I can clarify this once and for all, but I hope to shed some light on concepts key to this article. We will start at the top.

Classification

By classification I mean all methods for organizing documents via controlled schemes, whether these are controlled vocabularies or traditional systems used with a notation to hold the order. Chan[2] supports this broad characterization. She defines classification as "A logical system for the arrangement of knowledge." A more verbose definition is available from the Online Dictionary of Library and Information Science (ODLIS).[3]

> *Classification: The process of dividing objects or concepts into classes, subclasses, and sub-subclasses based on the characteristics they have in common and those that distinguish them . . . Classification System: A list of classes arranged in order according to pre-established principles, for the purpose of organizing items in a collection, or entries in an index, bibliography, or catalog, in groups according to their similarities and differences, to facilitate access and retrieval.*

This definition is by no means the universal standard. Some prefer "vocabularies" as the umbrella term.[4] However, I find this gets confused with "controlled vocabularies." I have also heard them called taxonomic or semantic structures. In this article, I will use classification as the umbrella. Under this umbrella there traditionally have been two ways to represent classes: symbolic and controlled natural language. You may be more familiar with these as notation and controlled vocabularies.

Notation and Controlled Vocabularies

Information science traditionally represents classes in one of two ways. The first method is the symbolic language of notation, which represents classes and subclasses of concepts using letters, numbers, or a combination of the two. A familiar use of notation is call letters (also known as call signs, or class marks[5]). Classic examples are the Library of Congress[6] (LCC), Dewey Decimal[7] (DDC), and Universal Decimal[8] (UDC) classification systems.

The second method is controlled vocabularies, known variously as taxonomies, thesauri, subject headings, and so on. Controlled vocabularies traditionally represent concepts using nouns and noun phrases. The key here is "controlled" as the opposite of free, as in controlled vs. free text. In free text, the author or indexer uses whichever words they want to describe an item. It does not matter that I call it soda and you call it pop.

In a controlled vocabulary, the taxonomist selects a preferred term and attaches to it non-preferred synonyms. Preferred terms are then interrelated using one or all of the traditional relationship types: hierarchical, equivalent, and associative.

Relationship Types

The power of controlled vocabularies is relationships. Some vocabularies model only one relationship type. Newer developments such as Topic Maps (ISO 13250[9]) explode the associative relationship to encompass an unlimited number of semantic relationships. But first, the basics.

Hierarchical relationships are like family trees for preferred terms: there are parents, children, and siblings. A relationship is hierarchical when a child is entirely encompassed by the parent. The parent is called the Broader Term (BT), and the children are Narrower Terms (NT). To test hierarchical relationships, try "X is a part of (or type of, and so on) Y." For example, a tornado is a type of thunderstorm or mosques are a type of religious facility.

Controlled vocabularies are either monohierarchical or polyhierarchical, which means that any term has only one (mono) or more than one (poly) parent. In a monohierarchical thesaurus, a dog is only a pet. In a polyhierarchy, a dog is a pet and also a rescue animal, a hunting animal, a racing animal, a carnivore, a drug agent, an assistant for visually disabled persons, and so on.

Hierarchies are flat and fairly rigid. Polyhierarchies allow some dimensionality, but they are still very restrictive when it comes to representing more complex relationships. Later I will discuss how Topic Maps address this problem.

Because human language is so diverse, indexers and searchers need synonymous relationships. Even if we live in the same region or were raised in the same family, each person uses their own personalized mental dictionary. For example, I call sugary carbonated beverages "coke." Others call it "pop," "soda," "cola," "tonic," and so on.[10] No wonder information retrieval is so difficult.

In controlled vocabularies there are many synonymous names or indicators for "equivalence": nonpreferred terms, entry terms, See, Use, Use For, and so on. What qualifies as a synonym depends on the vocabulary's intended use or, in other words, its context. For example, to the Country music fan, the difference between Alt Country, Outlaw Country, Country and Western, Bluegrass, Bakersfield Country, and Young Country is critical. However, these distinctions would be lost on an Opera buff, who might qualify all these as synonyms of Country music.

Synonyms are derived in a variety of ways, such as collapsing child terms under a parent (specific to general). Synonyms can also be exact (cat and feline), near or similar (amortize and liquidate), opposites (transparent and opaque), symbolic (crown for monarchy), and so on. Again, it all depends on context.

In my experience, the associative relationship is the most difficult for people to grasp. ODLIS[3] defines it as "A semantic relation in which two words or phrases are conceptually connected, sometimes within a specific context, but are not related hierarchically . . ." Think of cross-references in a back-of-book index. Associative relationships are usually labeled See Also or Related Term.

Comparing associative with hierarchical, a poodle is a type (child) of dog, but a dog is not a type of kennel. However, most people would associate dogs with dog kennels. Another way is to think in reference-librarian mode: A library patron wants birthday cake recipes, so you suggest that they also check out party planning.

Structural Types

Controlled vocabularies can take the form of simple lists, traditional trees, or more complex, nonhierarchical networks. The common element is relationships.

There are many kinds of lists: glossaries, gazetteers, dictionaries, and authorities, to name a few. Lists often have little to no explicit relational structure. For example, the U.S. Census Bureau's U.S. Gazetteer[11] lists country and place names, but does not explicitly state equivalent (such as Syria and Syrian Arab Republic), hierarchical (such as country to state to city), or associative relationships (Latin America and Spain). Glossaries usually list associative and equivalent relationships. For example, ODLIS[3] uses See and See Also references. Authorities typically are lists of authorized people, place, and organization names, but can also list subjects. There are exceptions, but in general, lists do not explicitly state hierarchy or association. This does not preclude them from development and maintenance with vocabulary management software.

Thesauri and taxonomies are controlled vocabularies with more complex structures. Their structures are traditionally built as hierarchical trees. It can be difficult to distinguish a taxonomy from a thesaurus. Both are hierarchical and usually also contain associative and equivalent relationships. Both have applications for indexing, navigation, and search. Both typically are built with a specific topic area or collection in mind. With so much in common, it is obvious why people confuse the two.

Milstead[13] says the difference is scope: "Most thesauri are designed to facilitate access to the information contained within one database or a group of specific databases, rather than to cover a discipline as a whole." Hodge's[14] definition is similar, but she says the difference is more about specificity: ". . . in general [taxonomies] provide ways to separate entities into 'buckets' or relatively broad topic levels . . . [Taxonomies] lack the explicit relationships presented in a thesaurus."

In short, taxonomies are useful for navigation and browsing because they direct users to a general area. In a library, a taxonomy would get the library user to the Mystery book section, but would not distinguish between books with nuns as detectives and books with firemen as detectives. Thesauri, on the other hand, have the potential to facilitate this type of fine-grained search. In an electronic environment, thesauri are powerful tools for query refinement and expansion, and have three standards devoted to their development.[15,16,17]

Two popular sites illustrate the differences between the two styles. The advanced search at epicurious.com[18] features a thesaurus which allows you to refine your search by meal/course, ingredients, special events, preparation, cuisines, and so on. In contrast, eddiebauer.com[19] provides broad buckets for drilling down to a more specific, but still relatively general, product category, such as Men, then Accessories, then Watches, Belts, Wallets, Socks, and Hats. There is no subcategory offered for leather belts, canvas web belts, elastic belts, woven belts, and so on.

Although "taxonomy" and "thesaurus" are sometimes used as synonyms, both by degreed information scientists and self-trained information architects, the distinction is critical when it comes to networks and Topic Maps because these structures allow relationships not always accommodated by vocabulary management software. Networks are an artificial-intelligence (AI) device for representing knowledge so that humans and machines can communicate. Networks are also known as graphs, ontologies, semantic networks, associative nets, partitioned nets, conceptual graphs or maps, knowledge maps, and so on.[20] Gruber,[21] in his definition of ontologies, says they ". . . associate the names of entities in the universe of discourse . . . with human-readable text describing what the names mean, and formal axioms that constrain the interpretation and well-formed use of these terms."

In contrast to trees, which are fairly rigid and flat, networks are extremely flexible and multidimensional. They also are not limited to nouns and noun phrases or to traditional relationships. This means a network would be able to indicate that George H. W. Bush hates broccoli, and Bill Clinton plays the saxophone, and that these two were both United States presidents.

An emerging model, which many believe is the future of electronic search, merges the best of trees and networks. Topic Maps[9] are based on traditional indexing concepts with knowledge structures (topics and associations or relations) that point to information resources (occurrences, similar to references in an index).[20]

Topic Map associations expand the concept of associative relationships. Here is an example demonstrating the kinds of associations and interconnections that Topic Maps can model:

Virginia Woolf **wrote** *To the Lighthouse*
↓
Virginia Woolf **was married to** Leonard Woolf
↓
Leonard Woolf **founded** the Hogart Press
↓
The Hogart Press **published** T. S. Eliot's *The Wasteland*
↓
Eliot **was influenced by** Ezra Pound

Steve Pepper, editor of the XML Topic Map specification (XTM),[22] compares Topic Maps to Global Positioning Systems (GPS):

> *Topic maps provide an approach that marries the best of several worlds, including those of traditional indexing, library science and knowledge representation, with advanced techniques of linking and addressing. It is our firm conviction that they will become as indispensable for tomorrow's information providers as maps for the traveler. And once topic maps have become ubiquitous, they will indeed constitute the GPS of the information universe.*[20]

With today's powerful computers and increasingly sophisticated search systems, Topic Maps are a real consideration. They model real-world relationships in a way that thesauri cannot. Because of users' frustration with current search technology, Topic Maps are one attempt to manage information and produce a satisfactory search experience.

SOFTWARE

Now that the terminology has been clarified, it is time to look at the tools we can use to build controlled vocabularies. There are a variety of reasons to invest in vocabulary management software. In my current position, I began developing taxonomies using a text editor and my own semi-reliable memory. This obviously had its problems. Thesaurus creation and maintenance is cumbersome, with opportunity rife for errors such as orphans (terms connected to nowhere), inversions and inconsistencies (Government and Politics vs. Politics and Government), and other bloopers.

Dedicated software saves time and money by eliminating extensive, time-consuming crosschecking and proofreading. With products on the market for less than $500, an out-of-box application is well within the reach of small budgets and significantly cheaper than designing a solution in-house.

Currently available software comes with three different areas in which to make choices: automated or manual; bundled or stand-alone; and single or multi-user. Knowing which of these fits your needs will help you narrow the candidate pool.

Automated vs. Manual

There are automated and semi-automated classification tools,[23] some of which claim to be entirely machine run, but the reality is that most require some human interaction.[1] These tools cluster information using statistical or rule-based clustering or training sets.

Statistical clustering creates a classification based on language patterns in the target document collection. For example, terms which are found in close proximity to one another are said to "co-occur." Statistical clustering might detect a relationship between "Dewey" and "classification" if those terms frequently co-occurred within the documents collected. Rule-based clustering creates a classification, not based on the specific needs of any one collection, but from an understanding of the topics. The *Dewey Decimal Classification* is an example of this type; Dewey divided the world of knowledge into ten main classes, each class into ten divisions, and so forth. It was created a priori to library collections. Training introduces a human touch. A classification expert would assign vocabulary terms to a document set. An unclassified set would then be machine-compared to the classified set, and similarities would be clustered. The TREC (Text Retrieval Conference)[24] trials pursue perfection of this concept.

A big problem with automated tools is that they attempt to mechanize an inherently human process. As discussed previously, human language and cognition is inexact. Automated tools have some potential to supplement the taxonomy development process. For example, they can be used to analyze a collection for topic clusters. However, they have problems distinguishing what is important, implied themes, the difference between homonyms (words with multiple meanings), and so on. Peter Morville[25] puts it this way:

> *Information retrieval is inherently messy. Authors struggle to convey complex concepts by stringing together words and phrases into documents. Users try to articulate their information needs with a keyword or two. Attempts to connect the right users with the right content are frustrated by the ambiguity of language and organization and the subjective nature of relevance.*
>
> *If you take a mess and stuff it into a bunch of little blue folders, you still have a mess... People who fall for the auto-magical claims of these search engine vendors are sure to learn the same lesson.*

On the other end of the spectrum are manual tools, which require you to do most of the thinking and data entry. These tools typically offer automatic relationship verification, global updates and deletes, batch importing, and so on. In my opinion, these basic cross-checking tasks save much time and effort and are what make the tools worth licensing.

Bundled vs. Stand-Alone

Bundled tools usually include a thesaurus management module that often is automated or semi-automated. Some include a pre-installed, general-purpose thesaurus; however, these often are extremely broad and difficult to customize. When my company began operation, we licensed Oracle's interMedia Text,[26] which included a pre-fabricated universal taxonomy. We could not view the relationships–only the terms. It essentially was a black box, and its generality made it too broad for our needs.

If all you need is a thesaurus management application, then stand-alone software is a better choice. Stand-alone applications may or may not integrate easily with existing operating systems, database software, or even platforms. Some are built with commercially available configurations, such as Sybase or SQL Server database software. However, small organizations may not be able to afford these heavy-duty applications. Other tools that accommodate small business-sized databases, such as FilemakerPro or Microsoft Access, are more affordable and require less administrative support but are also less robust.

Some vendors, such as Synapse,[27] will host your database on their remote servers. This is a great alternative for small organizations that need more robust database software and administration but cannot afford them.

Single vs. Multiuser

This is probably the easiest decision you will make. Single-user software means that there is only one workstation (or client), and the data generally is stored on that workstation (although it can be stored on a server). It also means that only one user at a time can use the tool.

Multiuser applications accommodate multiple users working at multiple workstations with a variety of administrative privileges (read only, delete, write). Since there are many users usually working concurrently, the software typically will automatically resolve conflicts when edits by different users clash.

YOUR SHOPPING LIST

Every organization has a different set of needs, requirements, and budgetary or technical considerations, and each product offers its own features and configurations. Just like buying a house, it is better to figure out what you absolutely require and what you are willing to sacrifice before walking out the door.

I strongly suggest that you think through what tasks you need this software to perform. Once you have that settled, you can work up a list of feature requirements.

Tasks

The most obvious tasks are selecting terms, building relationships, and maintaining the vocabulary's currency. Vocabularies can be built from scratch or from parts or all of an existing vocabulary. Building from scratch involves gathering terms and building relationships through direct or indirect interactions with users.[28] Examples include literary or user warrant that involve the use of print resources, direct user interviews, and query logs. Alternatively, an existing vocabulary can be customized by supplementing it with "scratch" research. Other tasks fall under administrative record keeping and include documenting term sources, significant dates, disambiguation decisions, internal and external use notes, and so on.

The software you license has the potential to serve other users. If you want to make the taxonomies available to indexers, many products have navigator or display modes, which means indexers can use this same tool for term location and assignment. Some also offer a navigator mode for searchers to select terms and refine or expand queries.

Some software offers easy-to-use report generators for tracking term use, such as which terms indexers assign or searchers select from the vocabularies. You can also find out if those terms are in heavy use or not in use, which can indicate future expansions or deletions.

Once you know what you want to do with the software, you need to figure out your system and environmental requirements. Ganzmann[29] wrote an excellent article and checklist on this subject. Because I found it to be the most-comprehensive source available, I will summarize and expand upon it here in the form of thought-provoking questions.

Technical Specifications

- What is your hardware configuration and operating system? Mac or PC? Windows, Mac, or UNIX?
- How much RAM (random access memory) is required to run the program? How much hard-disk space?
- What programming languages are used? Open source or proprietary? Platform-independent languages and scripts?

- What database software is supported? Oracle, SQL Server, others? Are the data stored in a database application unique to this software or a commercially available database product?
- Is the source code viewable or locked away?
- Is remote (off-site) data storage available?
- Is a data dictionary provided? A data dictionary is a handbook of sorts that shows you the tables in the database and the fields in each table. You would need this information if you plan to tap into the database directly.
- Who is the developer and what is their background? Are there vocabulary specialists or other information-science professionals on the development staff?
- Does the software accommodate multilingual vocabularies?
- For multi-user applications, does the software provide conflict resolution when user edits do not agree?

Versioning and Updates

- How many versions of the software have been released? Is it a mature product or new enough to make you a guinea pig (sometimes called a beta tester)?
- When was the most recent version released?
- When was the last round of bug fixes? What is the response and turn-around time after you report a bug?

Pricing and Licensing

- What is the cost of the basic package, add-ons, support, training, and so on?
- What comes free? Free support for the first 90 days? Free minor upgrades?
- Are major new releases offered at a discount after the initial licensing and installation, or do you have to purchase the software again with each new release?
- Is the software backward compatible–can it successfully use interfaces and data from earlier versions of the system or with other systems?
- Are discounts available for multiple licenses?
- How much does customization cost?
- Is there a charge to format and load your pre-existing taxonomies?

Support and Customer Service

- What forms of support are available? Toll-free hotline, e-mail, or on-site training? Is round-the-clock (24/7) support available?
- Can support personnel communicate with and explain things to non-technical customers?

Acceptance

- Who are this software's major customers? Other libraries? Businesses? Government organizations?
- Is the software widely accepted in the information science community?
- How do licensees feel about the product and its vendor?
- What do professional product reviewers have to say about the product?

Documentation

- Is there a printed manual or on-line help?
- How complete and coherent is the documentation? Can a non-technician understand it? Can a second-language speaker understand it?
- How well indexed is the documentation?
- Does the on-line help have a free-text search engine?

User Experience

- What is the user interface like? Is it easy to read, navigate, and understand? Is it something you can look at for long periods? Are colors, fonts, screen arrangement, and other features customizable?
- Is the interface efficient or are there extra, unnecessary actions (extra clicks)?
- How easy or cumbersome is it to capture relationships?
- What is onscreen interaction like? Scrolling? Navigation? Term selection? Are the control keys common to other software environments, such as *CTL + A* to select all?
- What is the input style? Command driven? Drop-down menus? Mouse-intensive? Drag-and-drop?
- Is the software accessible to disabled persons?
- How is the messaging for errors, alerts, and other feedback? Self-explanatory or cryptic?
- Is there an undo function? Are there confirmation messages for deleting or other major, irreversible actions?

Data Integrity

- Are different user levels available, such as read-only or administrative privileges? Is password protection available?
- What is the back-up procedure?

Structural Criteria

- What are the predefined fields and relationship types?
- What are the field character limits and data types? Can you change the data types and field limits?
- Are additional, user-defined fields available?
- Is notation possible?
- Are there a limited number of relationships between terms, such as a nonpreferred term belonging to more than one preferred term or a child having more than one parent (polyhierarchy)?
- Can the depth be restricted to enforce a shallow thesaurus?

Editing

- How are data modified?
- Are global changes enabled?
- How easy or cumbersome is it to change the status of a term, such as from preferred to non-preferred?
- How difficult or easy is it to move a term to an entirely different branch of the hierarchy?
- What is the procedure for deletion? Is global deletion available? What happens to a deleted term? Does it still exist, but in a disconnected state, or is it gone from the database without a trace?
- Are term relationships automatically controlled and verified? Can controls be user-defined? Does the software check for duplicates, illogical relationships, or spelling errors?

Importing, Exporting, and Reporting

- How is an existing vocabulary input? Is batch loading available? Is special tagging required? Will the vendor convert and load your existing thesaurus?
- Are there mapping features available for integrating heterogeneous vocabularies or accommodating multilingual vocabularies? Mapping capabilities are important for multilingual and parallel

vocabularies. For example, a medical library that serves medical professionals as well as patients might want to map MeSH to a patient vocabulary, or a Canadian company might map French and English vocabularies.
- What is the printer output? Are there standard and user-definable report formats?
- What report formats are available? KWIC and KWOC? Hierarchical and alphabetical? Sorting by notation? By date added?
- What is the output file format? ASCII only? Proprietary formats? Are those formats readable by commercially available software applications? If you sent a file to someone, could they open and read it?
- Are there capabilities for capturing use statistics, both end-user and internal?

Extensibility

- Can the software accommodate new and expanded relationship types, such as those modeled by Topic Maps?
- Can the software be leveraged for indexing or end-user searching?
- If an indexer enters an unknown term, is it rejected?
- Can indexers submit candidate terms through the tool?

PRODUCT AND FEATURE COMPARISON

It is not possible within the confines of this article to do an in-depth analysis of all available thesaurus management software. For this article, I selected four products–Lexico, TermTree 2000, Synaptica, and TermChoir–which I will compare and contrast in the Appendix. All are manual as opposed to automated, stand-alone, and allow more than one worker to use this tool at one time. I selected these products not because I believe they are superior, but because I believe they represent a cross-section of prices and features. An international list of products and vendors is available at the Willpower Information Web site.[30]

I contacted each of the four vendors and requested information on a specific set of criteria and combed vendor Web sites for details. Although Lexico did not reply to my request, they were included based on the documentation available on their Web site because their major client is the Library of Congress. The Appendix presents three categories of information for these four products: technical, cost and support, and editing and reporting.

CONCLUSION

This discussion and the data in the Appendix are only a starting point. I urge you not to assume the data are current by the time this article is published. Between the times I was shopping and writing this article, most of the vendors added features and changed pricing structures. My vendor releases new versions every couple of months. Do your homework, using this article as a springboard for your research.

NOTES

1. Ramana Venkata, "The Importance of Hierarchy Building in Managing Unstructured Data," *Best Practices in Enterprise Content Management*, a special white paper supplement to *KMWorld* <URL: http://www.kmworld.com/publications/specialpublication/index.cfm?action=readarticle&Article_ID=1204&Publication_ID=66> (March 2002). Seen 7 Feb. 2004.
2. Lois Mai Chan, *Cataloging and Classification: An Introduction*, 2nd ed., (New York: McGraw-Hill, Inc., 1994): p. 482.
3. Joan M. Reitz, *Online Dictionary of Library and Information Science* <http://vax.wcsu.edu/library/odlis.html> (2002). Seen 7 Feb. 2004.
4. Michael Buckland, *Vocabulary as a Central Concept in Library and Information Science* <http://www.sims.berkeley.edu/~buckland/colisvoc.htm>. Seen 7 Feb. 2004.
5. Lois Mai Chan, *Cataloging and Classification: An Introduction*, 2nd ed., (New York: McGraw-Hill, Inc., 1994): p. 484.
6. *Library of Congress Classification Outline* <http://www.loc.gov/catdir/cpso/lcco/lcco.html> (6 May 2002). Seen 7 Feb. 2004.
7. *Dewey Decimal Classification* <http://www.oclc.org/dewey/> (2002). Seen 7 Feb. 2004.
8. Outline of the UDC, (The Hague: UDC Consortium) <URL: http://www.udcc.org/outline/outline.htm> Seen 7 Feb. 2004.
9. ISO/IEC 13250, *Topic Maps, Information Technology, Document Description and Processing Languages*, 2nd ed., 19 May 2002. <http://www.y12.doe.gov/sgml/sc34/document/0322_files/iso13250-2nd-ed-v2.pdf>. Seen 7 Feb. 2004.
10. *The Great Pop vs. Soda Controversy* < http://www.popvssoda.com/>. Seen 7 Feb. 2004.
11. *U.S. Gazetteer* <http://www.census.gov/cgi-bin/gazetteer>. Seen 7 Feb. 2004.
12. *Library of Congress Authorities* <http://authorities.loc.gov/> (26 Aug 2002). Seen 7 Feb. 2004.
13. Jessica L. Milstead, *NISO Z39.19: Standard for Structure and Organization of Information Retrieval Thesauri* <http://www.bayside-indexing.com/Milstead/z39.htm> (1998). Seen 7 Feb. 2004.
14. Gail Hodge, *Taxonomy of Knowledge Organization Sources/Systems*. <http://nkos.slis.kent.edu/KOS_taxonomy.htm> (2000). Seen 7 Feb. 2004.
15. *Z39.19* <http://www.niso.org/standards/resources/Z39-19.html> (1 Nov 2001). Seen 7 Feb. 2004.

16. International Organization for Standardization, ISO 5964: 1985. Guidelines for the Establishment and Development of Multilingual Thesauri (Geneva: ISO, 1985).

17. International Organization for Standardization, ISO 2788: 1986. Guidelines for the Establishment and Development of Monolingual Thesauri (Geneva: ISO, 1986).

18. *Epicurious: Enhanced Search* <http://eat.epicurious.com/recipes/enhanced_search/index.ssf/?/recipes/enhanced_search/> (2002). Seen 7 Feb. 2004.

19. Eddie Bauer <http://www.eddiebauer.com> (2002). Seen 7 Feb. 2004.

20. Steve Pepper, *The TAO of Topic Maps: Finding the Way in the Age of Infoglut* <http://www.ontopia.net/topicmaps/materials/tao.html> (April 2002). Seen 7 Feb. 2004.

21. Tom Gruber, *What is an Ontolgy?* <http://www-ksl.stanford.edu/kst/what-is-an-ontology.html>. Seen 7 Feb. 2004.

22. Steve Pepper and Graham Moore, eds., *XML Topic Maps (XTM) 1.0* <http://www.topicmaps.org/xtm/1.0/> (2001). Seen 7 Feb. 2004.

23. Kat Hagedorn, *Extracting Value from Automated Classification Tools* <http://argus-acia.com/white_papers/classification.html> (March 2001). Seen 7 Feb. 2004.

24. Text Retrieval Conference (TREC), <http://trec.nist.gov/>. Seen 7 Feb. 2004.

25. Peter Morville, *Little Blue Folders* <http://argus-acia.com/strange_connections/strange003.html> (10 July 2000). Seen 7 Feb. 2004.

26. *Oracle Text* (formerly *interMedia Text*) <http://technet.oracle.com/products/text/content.html> (2002). Seen 7 Feb. 2004.

27. *Synapse: Knowledge Management, Thesaurus Software, Indexing & Classification* <http://www.synaptica.com> (2002). Seen 7 Feb. 2004.

28. Sinha, Rashmi. "Beyond Cardsorting: Free-Listing Methods to Explore User Categorization," Boxes and Arrows <http://www.boxesandarrows.com/archives/beyond_cardsorting_freelisting_methods_to_explore_user_categorizations.php> 24 Feb. 2003. Seen 7 Feb. 2004.

29. Jochen Ganzmann, *Criteria for the Evaluation of Thesaurus Software* <http://www.willpower.demon.co.uk/ganzmann.htm> (1990). Seen 7 Feb. 2004.

30. Leonard Will, *Software for Building and Editing Thesauri* <http://www.willpower.demon.co.uk/thessoft.htm> (2002). Seen 7 Feb. 2004.

APPENDIX. Selective Comparison of Thesaurus Management Software

Criteria	Lexico	TermTree 2000	Synaptica	TermChoir
Web Site	http://www.pmei.com/lexico.html	http://www.termtree.com.au/	http://www.synaptica.com/	www.webchoir.com
Clients	Library of Congress, Airbus, National Institute for Literacy, US Nuclear Regulatory Commission, US General Accounting Office.	Telstra, New South Wales State Records Office, Australian Intellectual Property and Patents office, Boeing, McKinsey & Company.	Gale Group, Ziff Davis Media Inc., US West, Micromedex, Microsoft, OCLC.	AT&T, Bellcore, BIOSIS, Boeing, Burroughs Wellcome, Centers for Disease Control.
Technical				
Configurations	Manual, Standalone, Multi-user.	Manual, Standalone, Multi-user.	Manual, Standalone, Single or Multi-user.	Manual, Standalone or Bundled, Multi-User.
Platform	Platform independent.	PC. Developed using Delphi and can be ported to Linux via Borland's Kylix product.	PC or UNIX.	PC or Macintosh.
Operating Systems	Microsoft Windows or Windows NT, Sun Solaris, SGI IRIX, or IBM AIX (UNIX).	Microsoft Windows and Windows NT.	Microsoft Windows NT Server, UNIX.	Microsoft Windows NT Server or UNIX.
Minimum System Requirements	Pentium 166 (or equivalent). 32 MB RAM.	Pentium 233 or equivalent. 32 MB RAM.	Depends on the size of the database. Since it is Web-based, it also can be stored on the Synapse server.	Pentium III. 128 MB RAM.
Programming Languages & Other Technologies	Java.	Microsoft ADO 2.1 or later. Requires TCP/IP protocol, but not a Web server facility.	Microsoft Internet Information Server (IIS).	Web server technology, for example, Apache, Netscape Enterprise Server or Microsoft IIS.
Data Storage		Microsoft Access or SQL Server, or Oracle.	Microsoft SQL Server or Oracle.	Oracle, Microsoft SQL Server, or Sybase.
Interface	Web browser. Displays configurable by each user.	GUI and Web browser.	Web browser based on Microsoft Active Server Pages technology.	Either via client/server or Web browser.

Pricing and Support			
Unit Price & Fees	50-user single site, single thesaurus LAN installation is $5950. Quotes available for other configurations, customization, installation, user training, administrator training, and conversion of existing thesauri. Annual fee of $892.50 for software support and upgrades.	Base price $US440.00 and then annual service contract for $US88.00 (or 20% of purchase price) per year.	Range of pricing from $900 for single user/single vocabulary to $50,000 for unlimited enterprise-wide deployment. Includes options for both annual leasing and one-time purchase pricing.	Two products: TermChoir and TCS-8. Various licensing levels. Prices range from $398 for single-user client/server to $15,800 10-user Web based.
Updates	Annual fee includes upgrades.	With the exception of a major upgrade, for which a one-off upgrade fee may be charged, the annual fee covers all released upgrades and bug fixes. Upgrades are posted on the TermTree downloads page.	Updates and patches provided free with annual fee. For one-time purchasers, the first year includes free updates; thereafter you pay for an annual maintenance plan, based on a percentage of the base license fee.	Minor updates free with annual maintenance fee. Major updates free with annual Platinum maintenance fee. Substantial discount to all users with Gold and Silver annual maintenance fees.
Installation & Customization	Two weeks from ordering to operation. Customization available for a fee.	Downloadable executable. Visual Basic or Delphi.	Support available for on-site installation and systems integration. Synapse alternatively offers remote hosting of client systems on servers located in their Denver Technological Center, which means the client needs no special equipment.	For Web-based systems, simply copy files to Web server. For client/server systems, standard set-up programs are provided. The procedure for installations of all WebChoir products is "simple, easy, and mostly automatic." Customization available.

APPENDIX (continued)

Criteria	Lexico	TermTree 2000	Synaptica	TermChoir
Help, Customer Service, Training	Lexico does the initial setup and customization. Training, installation, upload of existing thesauri available. Designed to be operated in a completely interactive mode by non-programmers (may require maintenance by Web administrator). Annual fee includes software support. Online help can be customized.	License fee includes 90-day e-mail or telephone support and updates (usually a one-day turnaround). Continued support then available for $US88.00 (or 20% of purchase price) per year.	Comprehensive support available for on-site installation, user training, technical support, and systems integration. Complete database administration and software support.	On-line/print, telephone and e-mail support.
Editorial and Reports				
Field Size Limits	No limits.	256 characters, with the exception of scope notes, which are effectively unlimited.	Most fields are up to 2,000 characters. Users can specify maximum length for each field, along with other data entry rules.	No character-length limit for scope notes, user-defined notes, and other text fields. Descriptors, UFs, translations, and other string field limited to 240 characters. Other string fields limited to 240 characters.
Multilingual Capabilities	Yes. ISO 8859-1 (Latin1).	No.	Yes. ISO 8859-1 (Latin1). Unicode (UTF-8) version was under development for late 2002.	Yes. UTF-8 for TCS-8, and Unicode for TermChoir. Also translation support.
Polyhierarchical?	Yes.	Yes, but the structure does not appear in this form on the display even though they are stored within the database as polyhierarchical trees.	Yes.	Yes.

Additional Administrative Note Fields	Cataloger, History, Public Notes; date notes, including Creation, Update, Approval. Custom notes. All notes are repeatable.	Reference Class, Date Created, Code, and Date Modified.	User-defined note fields, such as modification dates, approval statuses, administrative tracking.	Customized fields.
Importing Existing Thesauri	Synapse will import existing thesauri for a fee, or you can translate files to approved ASCII formatting and then batch load. By mid-2002, imports via GUI-driven online tools that upload standard source files from the local PC, perform full term and relationship validations, and import with an exception report. Or you can have Synapse do it for a fee.	Three import formats: a. Term Tree 2000 tag format; b. TRIM Record Management System thesaurus export format; and c. Objective Record Management System thesaurus export format. Comma- and tab-delimited import facilities are in development and should be available soon.	Close to completing an automatic import tool for formatted data. Scheduled to be available in late 2002.	Import in ASCII (tag delimited or standard alphabetical), XML, and MARC. Batch loading or data entry.
Editing	Candidate mode, allowing preview before permanent commitment. Validation and error checking. Global updates.	Automatic link validation and reciprocal term creation. Global updates, but within a taxonomy only.	Automatic generation of reciprocal relationships. Global updates. Dynamic validation, such as preventing circular references.	Basic edition or an advanced edition that features advanced searching and reporting, import and export, indexing external databases. Web thesaurus navigator, user-defined relations, class notation generation, log viewer, etc. The user can pick and choose features and pay only for those features.
Searching	Yes. Multiple taxonomies can be cross-linked for searching.	Yes, within a taxonomy only.	Yes. Multiple taxonomies can be cross-linked for searching.	

APPENDIX (continued)

Criteria	Lexico	TermTree 2000	Synaptica	TermChoir
Reports & File Output	Customizable and standardized reports. ASCII, PostScript.	Customizable and standardized reports. Four export formats: a. TermTree 2000 tag format; b. TRIM Record Management System thesaurus export format; c. Objective Record Management System thesaurus export format; d. Comma- or tab-delimited files.	Customizable and standardized reports. Output as HTML or comma-delimited files. Database connections can be made to extract data in relational formats. XML format under development.	Customized and standardized reports. Three export formats: ASCII, XML, or MARC.
Special Features	Hyperlinks to other URLs may be placed in LEXICO screens to allow easy access to databases and search engines.		Supports a comprehensive API, allowing systems-integrators to facilitate real-time communication between the taxonomy system and other systems, such as content management systems, metadata repositories, and publishing systems/portals.	Supports indexing and search of external databases using thesaurus terms.

Multilingual Subject Access: The Linking Approach of MACS

Patrice Landry

SUMMARY. The MACS (Multilingual access to subjects) project is one of the many projects that are currently exploring solutions to multilingual subject access to online catalogs. Its strategy is to develop a Web-based link and search interface through which equivalents between three Subject Heading Languages–SWD/RSWK (Schlagwortnormdatei/Regeln für den Schlagwortkatalog) for German, RAMEAU (Répertoire d'Autorité-Matière Encyclopédique et Alphabétique Unifié) for French, and LCSH (Library of Congress Subject Headings) for English–can be created and maintained, and by which users can access online databases in the language of their choice. Factors that have led to this approach will be examined and the MACS linking strategy will be explained. The trend to using mapping or linking strategies between different controlled vocabularies to create multilingual access challenges the traditional view of the multilingual thesaurus. *[Article copies available for a fee from The Haworth Document Delivery Service: 1-800-HAWORTH. E-mail address: <docdelivery@haworthpress.com> Website: <http://www.HaworthPress.com> © 2004 by The Haworth Press, Inc. All rights reserved.]*

Patrice Landry, MA, MLS, is Head of Subject Indexing, Swiss National Library, Hallwylstrasse 15, 3003 Bern, Switzerland (E-mail: patrice.landry@slb.admin.ch). He was previously at the National Library of Canada.

The author would like to thank Genevieve Clavel-Merrin for her valuable help in reviewing this article.

[Haworth co-indexing entry note]: "Multilingual Subject Access: The Linking Approach of MACS." Landry, Patrice. Co-published simultaneously in *Cataloging & Classification Quarterly* (The Haworth Information Press, an imprint of The Haworth Press, Inc.) Vol. 37, No. 3/4, 2004, pp. 177-191; and: *The Thesaurus: Review, Renaissance, and Revision* (ed: Sandra K. Roe and Alan R. Thomas) The Haworth Information Press, an imprint of The Haworth Press, Inc., 2004, pp. 177-191. Single or multiple copies of this article are available for a fee from The Haworth Document Delivery Service [1-800-HAWORTH, 9:00 a.m. - 5:00 p.m. (EST). E-mail address: docdelivery@haworthpress.com].

http://www.haworthpress.com/web/CCQ
© 2004 by The Haworth Press, Inc. All rights reserved.
Digital Object Identifier: 10.1300/J104v37n03_11

KEYWORDS. MACS (Multilingual access to subjects), multilingual subject access, subject heading languages (SHLs), equivalent headings, Library of Congress Subject Headings (LCSH), Répertoire d'Autorité-Matière Encyclopédique et Alphabétique Unifié (RAMEAU), Schlagwortnormdatei (SWD)/Regeln für den Schlagwortkatalog (RSWK)

INTRODUCTION

Ten years ago, *Cataloging & Classification Quarterly* published a special issue entitled *Languages of the World: Cataloging Issues and Problems* (Vol. 17, No. 1/2). Among the many issues relating to bibliographic control and access to documents published in a variety of languages was that of bilingual subject access. At that time, the principal challenge for some libraries was to ensure bilingual access to collections for language minorities in particular countries including Canada. Two articles dealt with the aspect of subject access and gave different perspectives on bilingual access to collections: the first related to the successful application of the bilingual cataloging policy of the National Library of Canada in using Library of Congress Subject Headings (LCSH) and Canadian Subject Headings (CSH) with the French-Canadian list Répertoire de vedettes-matière (RVM),[1] while the second paper advocated a wider usage of Bilindex, a bilingual Spanish-English subject headings list for providing subject access in Spanish in American libraries.[2]

Looking back at that issue of *CCQ*, it is interesting and also encouraging to note how the issue of bilingual and multilingual subject access has gained importance in the bibliographic access and research environment and is now part of the development agendas of many national libraries and bibliographic utilities. One of the reasons for this change can be attributed largely to the phenomenal technical progress in the field of communication and computer technology. In the early 1990s, as the Internet's impact on libraries was just emerging, some authors were already predicting the creation of a "Global Village Library," the result of interconnectivity between libraries throughout the world. Kenneth E. Dowlin, in an article dealing with the issue of multilingual and multiscript library services, referred to a new goal of the library that should "get the person to the right library immediately" but in the context of linguistic diversity.[3]

The development and impact of the World Wide Web on access to libraries' catalogs have opened up different possibilities and solutions to multilingualism. There has been a real shift in bilingual/multilingual access, where traditionally access was assured through multiple subject headings coded in the authority records. Today, many research initiatives have looked at providing that access through Internet-based linking processes. Concepts such as language cross-linking, or interoperability in subject headings languages, which are common in today's research in multilingual access, were limited ten years ago to language specialists. The MACS (Multilingual access to subjects) Project which will be described is a good example of the progress made in the field of multilingual subject research and development. In this area, MACS is but one of the many solutions that are presently proposed to achieve this goal. It is a good example of the shift in multilingual access, where the solution to multilingual subject access through one's own language can be found in the linking process stage as an alternative to bilingual or multilingual subject cataloging policies and practices.

The MACS project has been well documented though its Web site[4] and through articles and presentations published since 1999. Among these contributions, Clavel-Merrin[5] and MacEwan[6] have presented a synthesis of the pilot study and methodology while Landry[7] presented the development of the MACS prototype. Freyre and Naudi[8] provided an overall summary of work accomplished in the first five years of the project with an emphasis on the MACS management system. At IFLA 2002, Kunz[9] looked at recent developments in multilingual subject retrieval.

This article will present the project in a slightly different way in order to explain the factors that lead to the approach taken. It will show how the technical and bibliographic developments and shift in cooperation strategies that have occurred in the last ten years have impacted subject access to European libraries' databases. The aspects of library cooperation and the development of subject heading languages and subject authority control will first be raised as underlying principles of MACS. The second part of this paper will be devoted to the MACS linking strategy and Web access solution.

THEN AND NOW

MACS was created in 1997 in response to a request by the Conference of European National Librarians (CENL) to find a solution to the problem of multilingual subject access to bibliographic databases. A working group, under the Cobra+ (Computerised Bibliographic Record Actions), a programme partly funded by the European Commission, was set up in order to discuss this issue with regard to national libraries. Among many approaches discussed, the idea of establishing links between different subject heading languages (SHLs) was, for four of the participating libraries, a promising solution. These four libraries, the Swiss National Library (SNL), the Bibliothèque nationale de France (BnF), the British Library (BL) and the Deutsche Bibliothek (DDB) accepted the task of defining a concept and conducting a study to determine the feasibility of such a concept. The MACS project was then set up with its main goal "to provide the means by which library databases can be accessed on a multilingual basis by the use of equivalent headings from subject authority files." The approach taken was to create broad multilingual access that could be used as widely as possible by using indexing languages that are commonly used in most libraries in any given country.

The aim of MACS is to enable users to simultaneously search with a single query in the language of their choice (English, French, or German) for all relevant documents indexed by the project's partner libraries in their own language. This multilingual search is made possible thanks to the equivalence links established between the three Subject Heading Languages used in these libraries: SWD/RSWK for German, RAMEAU for French, and LCSH for English.

EUROPEAN COOPERATION

The fact that four national libraries would undertake such a project shows the importance of multilingualism in the field of bibliographic access. As access to library catalogs gradually increased and improved through advances in network technology, a growing awareness of the needs of local as well as international library users led to discussion on the need to find national or European solutions. In the early 1990s, the subject access to libraries' catalogs in Europe was still mostly provided through monolingual subject access. There were essentially two methods that had been developed in the 1980s. The Royal Library in Brussels and the Swiss Federal Institute of Technology (ETH–Eidgenössische Technische Hochschule) in Zurich and (EPFL–Ecole polytechnique fédérale Lausanne) in Lausanne had adopted the approach of establishing a multilingual authority file based on the translation of a source language. The Royal Library chose to index using the LCSH and to translate the headings used in the indexing into Dutch and French. The multilingual headings were coded in the bibliographic records, and each heading was controlled in an authority record. The ETH libraries used the Universal Decimal Classification (UDC) as the basis for a trilingual subject access system. Each subject notation had a corresponding subject term, originally only in German. In 1982, the ETH libraries instigated a project to translate the German term into English and French.

It is interesting to note that the solutions developed in Brussels and Zurich did not spread to other European libraries looking for a solution to their bibliographic access needs. This can be partly explained by the fact that European libraries and library networks had already developed fairly large databases indexed according to particular indexing systems and were not interested in changing their system to one used in Brussels or Zurich. As many libraries automated their catalogs, attempts were made to investigate both the technical and network approach to multilingual access. At the first European Conference for Library Automation and Networking in 1990, many speakers spoke of the network infrastructures that were put in place in the 1980s and created real possibilities for cooperation. There was a new awareness that technology could increase and expand the levels of cooperation between libraries that had mostly been in the areas of shared cataloguing and interlibrary loan operations. One of the goals of the Conference was to expand cooperation across national boundaries in order to foster the dissemination of information in Europe. Goossens[10] and Clavel-Merrin[11] describe the multilingual subject access experiences in Belgium and Switzerland. These experiences show what had been done so far, and more importantly, what still needed to be accomplished at the European level. At the very least, there was the realisation that certain conditions needed to be achieved in order to find a European solution. Among these was the need for "a clear policy towards data and the development of library networks" that would include as few systems and as few indexing systems as possible, and more importantly, that multilingual subject access should be seen as a national task. And this impetus should come, as suggested by G. Clavel-Merrin, from national libraries.

Shortly after this European Conference, the European Commission launched its Plan of Action for Libraries Programme. This five-year plan (1990-1994) was the third Framework Programme for Research and Technical Development of the European Commission. The specific objectives were to provide better access to library services and resources through library cooperation, and the cost-effective use of information technology with a commitment to standards and compatibility at a national and European level. Calls for proposals yielded over fifty projects, many of which have led to concrete results. More importantly, this programme led to the development of effective collaborative approaches. Strategic alliances between different types of libraries from various countries were created, which have led to long-term cooperative efforts.

The European Commission's 4th Framework Programme contained the Telematics Application Programme, which included the library sector. It is in this context that a proposal from the Deutsche Bibliothek in 1995[12] attempted to bring together several European national libraries to develop a multilingual universal thesaurus by linking equivalents from five national authority files and classification systems. The project called MULIS (Multilingual Subject Authority File) was responding to the demands of German libraries for a system that could assist them in indexing foreign language documents as well as providing multilingual access to their collections. Unfortunately, this project was not retained for funding, but it did show that libraries were now willing to invest resources in a cooperative venture to develop a multilingual solution.

THE GROWTH OF SUBJECT HEADING LANGUAGES AND AUTHORITY CONTROL

This willingness to work together has raised a somewhat diplomatic problem in determining which languages should be considered for global subject access. With several dozen encyclopaedic subject heading languages in several individual European languages, the MACS Project was confronted with limiting its scope for the feasibility study to only a few subject heading languages. This was an indication that many subject heading languages had reached a high level of development, both quantitative and qualitative in the last ten to fifteen years. This evolution was partly based on general adherence to communication format standards–UNIMARC, MARC, MAB–and through well-developed subject indexing manuals.

The decision to use LCSH for English, RAMEAU for French, and SWD for German reflects the level of development and the use of these SHLs in Europe. LCSH needs very little introduction to the readers of *CCQ*. Its evolution has been widely described[13] and its structure is understood by most North American librarians. It is still worth mentioning that LCSH was reintroduced[14] as a subject headings standard at the British Library (BL) in 1995. The BL made this decision based on a survey that indicated that many of the university and research libraries in the United Kingdom favoured LCSH. This resulted in the dropping of the COMPASS system, which itself had replaced the PRECIS system. Currently, the six legal deposit libraries in the UK and Ireland are all using LCSH and making their records available to other British libraries. There are also a number of libraries in Europe that use LCSH as an indexing policy.

RAMEAU[15] is an encyclopaedic list that was constituted in 1980 as an adaptation from the Répertoire de vedettes-matière (RVM) of the Universté Laval in Québec. RVM is a French adaptation and translation of LCSH and used as the French indexing standard in Canada. RAMEAU has evolved as an autonomous subject heading list, initially developed by the BnF, and starting in 1986, in collaboration with university libraries which had adopted the use of RAMEAU as their indexing standard. In the 1990s as the distribution of BnF bibliographic and authority records improved, the use of RAMEAU expanded to municipal and public libraries. Today, RAMEAU is the national indexing standard in France and is used in other francophone countries.[16]

The development of a national indexing standard in Germany followed a similar path.[17] In 1980, the Deutsche Bibliotheksinstitut established a working group of subject experts from national, university and public libraries to define an indexing standard that could be widely used in Germany. Between 1980 and 1986, a group of six experts developed a series of indexing rules entitled *Regeln für den Schlagwortkatalog* (RSWK), inspired from existing rules from the Erlangen University Library and the library of the Frei Universität Berlin. The RSWK, first published in 1986, established rules for the creation of new subject headings and for indexing practices. At the same time, a subject authority file called *Schlagwortnormdatei* (SWD) was created that included the terms created by the libraries that used the Erlangen rules. Originally developed in cooperation with the Deutsche Bibliothek and two German regional networks, the creation of new headings and development of RSWK is now assured through the cooperation of all German regional networks as well as Austrian and Swiss networks. As with RAMEAU, SWD/RSWK has seen a rapid growth in the quantity of new headings and its evolution as a national indexing standard.

Another characteristic of these indexing languages has been their adherence to authority control. RAMEAU and SWD have followed the same practice of authority control in their automated system as LCSH. The RAMEAU, SWD, and LCSH networks have profited from the development of their respective communication format, namely MARC 21 for LCSH, INTERMARC for RAMEAU, and MAB/PICA for SWD. All of the three SHLs have built strong centralised authority control systems with a diversified communication and distribution network.

These three SHLs all refer, either implicitly or explicitly, to existing international standards. The work of subject indexing and thesaurus construction is still based on standards developed or revised in the 1980s. Language-based indexing practices have also referred to national standards. In Germany, the RSWK was constructed on the basis of the DIN-Normen 1463, 2330, 31623, 36631 while in France, RAMEAU is based on the NF-Z44 060, 061, 070 and 079. According to Cordeiro,[18] new specific international standard development in the field of subject indexing has been rather slow in the 1990s. The different SHLs have followed similar construction principles and application principles. The IFLA document, *Principles underlying subject heading languages (SHLs)*,[19] provided evidence of common structural features underlying subject heading languages regardless of cultural and linguistic diversities. In its study of eleven indexing systems, in nine different languages, it concluded that most followed similar semantic and syntax principles as well as mechanisms for efficient subject document retrieval. This efficiency of SHLs still, of course, needs to be tested, as suggested by Hoermann and Furnis.[20] For our purpose, the *Principles* did provide a benchmark from which we could judge the development of each of the SHLs involved in the project and will certainly be used when considering extension of the project to other SHLs.

MACS LINKING APPROACH

By 1997, it appeared that conditions were optimal for further discussions on multilingual subject access to libraries' catalogs. During that year, seven national libraries accepted an invitation to discuss multilingual subject access issues. At a meeting in Frankfurt, a proposal from the Swiss National Library to study the feasibility of establishing links between headings from the LCSH, RAMEAU, and SWD subject headings lists was accepted. The MACS project was then set up between the four national libraries and work started on the feasibility study.

The decision to use the linking approach took into account the fact that the libraries–French, German, English–have invested considerable time and effort in the creation and maintenance of each SHL–LCSH, RAMEAU and SWD–and that they have been used extensively to provide subject access to millions of documents. Creating a new multilingual vocabulary, based on translation, would have been unrealistic and uneconomical. The MACS group also recognized the fact that each SHL offers the library user the optimal tool for subject retrieval. Most library users will use the indexing system in their own language and culture to search online catalogs. In North America, most users have a basic knowledge of LCSH and can conduct successful subject searches by locating the appropriate headings through the richness of the semantic structure of LCSH as coded in the authority record.

The MACS group also acknowledged the fact that each partner library will provide subject access to its collection through a standard subject heading language. At the Swiss National Library, the access is provided though the SWD/RSWK system, even though four national languages exist in Switzerland. Indexing the collections using more than one SHL would be far too expensive and laborious. Maintaining one subject authority file is already an important task in any national library.

By acknowledging the importance of monolingual indexing in its multilingual access solution, MACS aims at what Freyre and Naudi[21] refer to as "disconnecting the language of the search from the language of the catalog." By allowing the library user to search in the language of their choice, MACS restores a linguistic "proximity" between the library user and the document in the language of the user, regardless of the language in which that document was indexed.

The pilot study, which was conducted from 1997 to early 1999, looked at the feasibility of linking headings of the three SHLs. The linking methodology was developed by delimiting subject fields (e.g., Theatre and Sports) from which headings from the different SHLs could be analysed and matched. By working in this closed subject context, the links were established based on an analysis at the terminological level (subject heading), at the semantic level (authority record), and at the syntactic level (application). A match or link is considered successful when a concept, represented by similar headings in the different SHLs which are matched manually (intellectually), return the most closely equivalent results in subject retrieval.

In order to test how the links could be managed and used in a search interface, a Web-based prototype was developed. The basic requirement specified was that the prototype should exist independently of the partners' own library systems and that it should incorporate the different communication formats used–MARC21, INTERMARC, MAB/PICA. The prototype is meant to be used by the partners to add and maintain the links between the different SHLs and by the users to search different library catalogs. The prototype was designed with mechanisms for the management of different types of equivalences, including multiple links, when a subject heading is equivalent to two headings in another language ("**Jumping**" = "**Hochsprung**" OR "**Sprung**" = "**Sauts (athlétisme)**" OR "**Saut en hauteur**") or when it is equivalent to a combination of two headings ("**Child actors**" = "**Kind**" AND "**Schauspieler**"). A search interface was also developed in order to provide any user with the possibility to choose a source language and one or more target catalogues. The user should have the possibility to choose and select subject headings in one SHL and find equivalents to the selected headings. In order to test the methodological approach for linking headings, about 15,000 bibliographic records from each of the partners' databases and 1,000 headings linked to the bibliographic records were loaded into the prototype. Tests were conducted to check the validation of the links against retrieval results and in certain cases modifications were made to the links.

The linking approach was loosely based on the ISO5964 multilingual thesauri guidelines published in 1985.[22] The Guidelines propose several methods for the development of multilingual thesauri, one method being the reconciliation and merging of existing thesauri in two or more working languages. The MACS project referred to it for validation of the linking approach, and in part for methodological considerations, but did not adopt its definition of a multilingual thesaurus. The aim of MACS was not to develop, as Hudon[23] proposes, "a true multilingual thesaurus [that] offers full conceptual and terminological inventories for each language represented." Without a full semantic structure in all languages of a multilingual thesaurus, language equality cannot be achieved. For MACS, this notion of "equal status" is assured through the creation of clusters of linked terms that all refer to a particular concept. Equality of languages is thus assured through the autonomy of each SHL (semantic), and more importantly, the MACS system only contains, as Freyre and Naudi[24] note, "mappings considered as conceptual clusters, identified by a numeric identifier only and nameless." It is clear that the notion of "equality of languages" is problematic in the context of this new environment of mapping, and as Riesthuis[25] suggests, rules will need to be revised completely.

MACS has made searching and a read-only access to the Link Management Interface (LMI) available since 2001. During that time, over 400 people from all over the world have signed up to test the MACS prototype. With comments received and tests conducted by the MACS partners, refinement of the organisation model has resulted in the design of a new version of the MACS system. Scheduled to be operational in

March 2004, this final release of the LMI should improve the tasks of creating and managing links in a decentralized work environment.

Despite improvements in the linking mechanisms, the basic task of establishing links will remain very time-consuming. Luckily the partners can build on existing bilingual links in the RAMEAU authority files managed at the Bibliothèque nationale de France and loaded in the MACS system. Approximately 70,000 RAMEAU authorities contain a proposed LCSH heading and have been assigned a subject domain number. Work on adding the SWD headings to these links will proceed in 2004 by targeting an initial 30,000 links. Work will be divided between partners in Germany and Switzerland according to domains. One of the partners involved will be the École de traduction et d'interprétation, Université de Genève, where a linking method at the semantic level will continue to be tested in order to facilitate link creation.

The search results have shown that pertinent documents can be retrieved using links across subject headings, and a move from using subsets of data to the partners' own databases is planned. In April 2002 tests began with the catalogue of the Deutsche Bibliothek, and in 2003 the Swiss National Library successfully carried out tests and is ready to open its database once sufficient links are available to offer meaningful searches. Changes in the search interface will probably be necessary to ensure that users can obtain manageable queries and search sets.

The MACS solution to the problem of multilingual subject access has been received favorably by the research and library communities in Europe. The positive responses from users who have signed up to test the MACS prototype confirmed the choices and the decision to link headings from the three SHLs that have been used to index millions of documents. Users viewed the MACS prototype as a good base for a functional search tool that could be upgraded to provide efficient searches.

The immediate value for users of the Swiss National Library (SNL) is the real possibility that, in the near future, subject searches will be conducted in more than one language. As a federal institution, the Swiss National Library is committed to serving its users in the three official languages of Switzerland (German, French, and Italian). The SNL's decision in 1998 to adopt the SWD as its indexing standard came with the assurance that the French and Italian users would also profit from that indexing though a multilingual search tool. Going beyond national boundaries, other users of the SNL and of other national libraries will also find their searches facilitated by a multilingual gateway to their catalogs. The Deutsche Bibliothek views the project as a way to foster the value of the SWD and will make the MACS results available to its partners in Germany and Austria. The Bibliothèque nationale de France has already undertaken a survey to look into ways of extending the MACS linking work at a national level.

CONCLUSION

As mentioned in the introduction, the MACS project is but one of the many projects involved in the development of multilingual subject access. Chan,[26] Chan and Zeng,[27] and Doerr[28] present very thorough surveys and analysis of recent mapping efforts involving controlled vocabularies and classification systems. The major projects in the field of multiple subject vocabularies mentioned are the UMLS (Unified Medical Language System),[29] a metathesaurus which merges concepts from about fifty sources; CARMEN,[30] the German project that links different German thesauri; and the AQUARELLE/HEREIN[31] projects. These projects have conducted their mapping similarly to MACS, essentially through an intellectual effort and using computer technology for the management of links and data. Projects such as CARMEN have created "cross-concordances" by using both an intellectual-based method and statistical methods. Researchers such as Doerr[32] seem convinced that the future lies in the coordinated combination of intellectual and statistical methods. The technology and present research in the field of mapping and network-based subject access solutions have progressed rapidly and will certainly impact on methodological applications. Further development will certainly be fuelled by the numerous mapping projects involved in terminology and classification systems.

Multilingual subject access is now an international issue. It has progressed from being a national or a minority language issue that needed to be solved in a particular online system to efforts to create seamless global access to libraries' collections. This "Global Village Library" access philosophy has raised the profile of multilingualism in libraries' project and research agendas. It has also created synergies between the library world and language and computer specialists who had for many years worked in parallel to develop linguistic models for computer applications for multilingual solutions. Many current projects have integrated these specialists, and both have profited from the results achieved through this collaboration. MACS has profited from this new network environment, and it is hoped that it will continue to be part of this quest to improve subject access to library catalogs.

NOTES

1. Virginia Ballance, "Cataloguing in the Official and Heritage Languages at the National Library of Canada," *Cataloging & Classification Quarterly* 17, no. 1/2 (1993): 219-232.
2. Marielena Fina, "The Role of Subject Headings in Access to Information: The Experience of One Spanish-Speaking Patron," *Cataloging & Classification Quarterly* 17, no. 1/2 (1993): 267-274.
3. Kenneth E. Dowlin, "Issues in Offering Multilingual and Multiscript Library Services: The Key to the Global Village Library," in *Automated Systems for Access to Multilingual and Multiscript Library Materials: Proceedings of the Second IFLA Satellite Meeting, Madrid, August 18-19, 1993*, Sally H. McCallum and Monica Ertel, eds. (München: K.G. Saur, 1994): 23-26.
4. Reports and access to MACS prototype are available online at URL: http://infolab.kub.nl/prj/macs.
5. Genevieve Clavel-Merrin, "The Need for Co-Operation in Creating and Maintaining Multilingual Subject Authority Files," 65th IFLA Council and General Conference, Meeting 155. <http://WWW.ifla.org/IV/ifla65/papers/080-155e.htm> (28 July 1999). Seen Feb. 7, 2004.
6. Andrew MacEwan, "Crossing Language Barriers in Europe: Linking LCSH to Other Subject Heading Languages," *Cataloging & Classification Quarterly* 29, no. 1/2 (2000): 199-207.
7. Patrice Landry, "The MACS Project: Multilingual Access to Subject (LCSH, RAMEAU, SWD)," Classification and Indexing Workshop, 66th IFLA and General Conference, Meeting 181. <http://www.ifla.org/IV/ifla66/papers/165-181e.pdf> (15 July 2000). Seen Feb. 7, 2004. Also Published in *International Cataloguing and Bibliographic Control* 30, no. 3 (2001): 46-49.
8. Elisabeth Freyre and Max Naudi, "MACS: Subject Access Across Languages and Networks," in *Subject Retrieval in a Networked Environment: Papers Presented at an IFLA Satellite Meeting Sponsored by the IFLA Section on Classification and Indexing & IFLA Section on Information Technology, OCLC, Dublin, Ohio, USA, 14-16 August 2001.* Dublin, OH: OCLC, 2001.
9. Martin Kunz, "Subject Retrieval in Distributed Resources: A Review of Recent Developments," 68th IFLA Council and General Conference, Meeting 122. <http://www.ifla.org/IV/ifla68/papers/007-122e.pdf> (July 2002). Seen Feb. 7, 2004.
10. Paula Gossens, "Multilingual Bibliographic Access via Subject in Europe," in *Library Automation and Networking: New Tools for a New Identity*, Herman Liebaers and Marc Walckiers, eds. (München: K.G. Saur, 1991): 206-214.
11. Genevieve Clavel-Merrin, "Multilingual Subject Access in Switzerland," in *Library Automation and Networking: New Tools for a New Identity*, Herman Liebaers and Marc Walckiers, eds. (München: K.G. Saur, 1991): 215-228.
12. The MULIS proposal was never published. Many aspects of the MULIS proposal had already been developed as early as 1991 in the following article: Marin Kunz, "Einige grunsätzliche Überlegungen zur Erarbeitung einer mehrsprachigen Schlagwortnormdatei," *Dialog mit Bibliotheken* 3, no. 3 (1991): 26-33.
13. A special issue on LCSH was published in *Cataloging & Classification Quarterly* 29, no. 1/2 (2000).
14. Ia McIlwaine, "Subject Control: The British Viewpoint," in *Subject Indexing: Principles and Practices in the 90's; Proceedings of the IFLA Satellite Meeting*

Held in Lisbon, Portugal, 17-18 August 1993, and Sponsored by the IFLA Section on Classification and Indexing and the Instituto da Biblioteca Nacional e do Livro, Lisbon, Portugal, Robert P. Holley, Dorothy McGarry, Donna Duncan and Elaine Svenonius, eds. (München: K.G. Saur, 1995): 166-180.

15. RAMEAU: Répertoire d'Autorité-Matière Encyclopédique et Alphabétique Unifié. <http://noticesrameau.bnf.fr/> (23 February 2002). Seen Feb. 7, 2004.

16. Suzanne Jouguelet, "Evolution of subject indexing practice in France," in *Subject Indexing: Principles and Practices in the 90's: Proceedings of the IFLA Satellite Meeting Held in Lisbon, Portugal, 17-18 August 1993, and Sponsored by the IFLA Section on Classification and Indexing and the Instituto da Biblioteca Nacional e do Livro, Lisbon, Portugal,* Robert P. Holley, Dorothy McGarry, Donna Duncan and Elaine Svenonius, eds. (München: K.G. Saur, 1995): 64-80.

17. Magda Heiner-Freiling, "Subject Indexing in the Nineties: The Situation in Germany," in *Subject Indexing: Principles and Practices in the 90's: Proceedings of the IFLA Satellite Meeting Held in Lisbon, Portugal, 17-18 August 1993, and Sponsored by the IFLA Section on Classification and Indexing and the Instituto da Biblioteca Nacional e do Livro, Lisbon, Portugal,* Robert P. Holley, Dorothy McGarry, Donna Duncan and Elaine Svenonius, eds. (München: K.G. Saur, 1995): 81-93.

18. Maria Inês Cordeiro, "From Library Authority Control to Network Authoritative Metadata Sources," in *Subject Retrieval in a Networked Environment: Papers Presented at an IFLA Satellite Meeting Sponsored by the IFLA Section on Classification and Indexing & IFLA Section on Information Technology, OCLC, Dublin, Ohio, USA, 14-16 August 2001.* Dublin, OH: OCLC, 2001.

19. Maria Inês Lopes and Julianne Beall, eds., *Principles Underlying Subject Heading Languages (SHLs).* Working Group on Principles Underlying Subject Heading Languages, IFLA Section on Classification and Indexing (München: K.G. Saur, 1999).

20. Heidi Lee Hoerman and Kevin A. Furniss, "Turning Practice into Principles: A Comparison of the IFLA *Principles Underlying Subject Heading Languages (SHLs)* and the Principles Underlying the *Library of Congress Subject Headings* System," *Cataloging & Classification Quarterly* 29, no. 1/2 (2000): 31-52.

21. As 8.

22. International Organization for Standardization, *Documentation–Guidelines for the Establishment and Development of Multilingual Thesauri,* ISO 6964. Geneva: ISO, 1985.

23. Michèle Hudon, "Multilingual Thesaurus Construction: Integration of Views of Different Cultures in One Gateway to Knowledge and Concepts," *Knowledge Organization* 24, no. 2 (1997): 84-91.

24. As 8.

25. Gerhard J.A. Riesthuis, "Information Languages and Multilingual Subject Access," in *Subject Retrieval in a Networked Environment: Papers Presented at an IFLA Satellite Meeting sponsored by the IFLA Section on Classification and Indexing & IFLA Section on Information Technology, OCLC, Dublin, Ohio, USA, 14-16 August 2001.* Dublin, OH: OCLC, 2001.

26. Lois Mai Chan, "Exploiting LCSH, LCC and DDC to Retrieve Networked Resources: Issues and Challenges," in *Bicentennial Conference on Bibliographic Control in the New Millennium, Library of Congress, 2000.* <http://lcweb.loc.gov/catdir/bibcontrol/chan_paper.html> (19 December 2000). Seen Feb. 7, 2004.

27. Lois Mai Chan, and Marcia Lei Zeng, "Ensuring Interoperability Among Subject Vocabularies and Knowledge Organization Schemes: A Methodological

Analysis," 68th IFLA Council and General Conference, Meeting 122. <http://www.ifla.org/IV/ifla68/papers/008-122e.pdf> (July 2002). Seen Feb. 7, 2004.

28. Martin Doerr, "Semantic Problems of Thesaurus Mapping," *Journal of Digital Information* 1, no. 8 (2001) <http://jodi.ecs.soton.ac.uk/Articles/v01/i08/Doerr/> (26 March 2001). Seen Feb. 7, 2004.

29. <http://www.nlm.nih.gov/pubs/factsheets/umlsmeta.html> (7 June 2002). Seen Feb. 7, 2004.

30. <http://www.bibliothek.uni-regensburg.de/projects/carmen12/index.html.en> (18 February 2000). Seen Feb. 7, 2004.

31. <http://www.european-heritage.net/sdx/herein/thesarus/introduction.xsp> Seen Feb. 11, 2004.

32. As 28.

An Interview with Dr. Amy J. Warner (June 2003)

Alan R. Thomas
Sandra K. Roe

SUMMARY. Amy Warner,[1] Project Leader for NISO's Thesaurus Development Team, discusses her involvement in the revision of Z39.19 *Guidelines for the Construction, Format, and Management of Monolingual Thesauri*. *[Article copies available for a fee from The Haworth Document Delivery Service: 1-800-HAWORTH. E-mail address: <docdelivery@haworthpress.com> Website: <http://www.HaworthPress.com> © 2004 by The Haworth Press, Inc. All rights reserved.]*

KEYWORDS. Z39.19, *Guidelines for the Construction, Format, and Management of Monolingual Thesauri*, thesaurus standards, controlled vocabulary standards, National Information Standards Organization, NISO

AT: What is meant by "standard"? Does the National Information Standards Organization (NISO) have a general definition of this term (i.e.,

Alan R. Thomas, MA, FLA, is Visiting Associate Professor, Pratt Institute, New York. Sandra K. Roe, MS, is Serials Librarian, Illinois State University, Normal, IL.

[Haworth co-indexing entry note]: "An Interview with Dr. Amy J. Warner (June 2003)." Thomas, Alan R., and Sandra K. Roe. Co-published simultaneously in *Cataloging & Classification Quarterly* (The Haworth Information Press, an imprint of The Haworth Press, Inc.) Vol. 37, No. 3/4, 2004, pp. 193-198; and: *The Thesaurus: Review, Renaissance, and Revision* (ed: Sandra K. Roe, and Alan R. Thomas) The Haworth Information Press, an imprint of The Haworth Press, Inc., 2004, pp. 193-198. Single or multiple copies of this article are available for a fee from The Haworth Document Delivery Service [1-800-HAWORTH, 9:00 a.m. - 5:00 p.m. (EST). E-mail address: docdelivery@haworthpress.com].

http://www.haworthpress.com/web/CCQ
© 2004 by The Haworth Press, Inc. All rights reserved.
Digital Object Identifier: 10.1300/J104v37n03_12

for ALL of its standards)? Is it simply a set of guidelines, to be interpreted differently by individuals or teams who may choose to utilize it in certain aspects and degrees?

AJW: NISO has many different kinds of 'standards,' from highly technical, specific ones to items that are really more 'guidelines' than 'standards.' A standard gives people specific rules that can be followed unambiguously. Guidelines are less detailed and are more decision-oriented. Z39.19 is really a set of guidelines. Our intent is to give people a set of situations, a set of options in those situations, and then a set of suggestions for what to do in each situation.

AT: Why is there a U.S. standard as such? Could there be an English-language standard (drawing on British, Canadian, Australian, South African and other constituencies in addition to the U.S.)?

AJW: The reason for a U.S. standard is historical. In previous editions, the U.S. and other standards departed from each other. At present there is a U.S. standard and an international (ISO) standard. They are different in some ways but also quite similar in others. Our group working on the revision is in contact with the individuals who are revising the British standard (the British have basically adopted ISO as their standard). We are trying to coordinate our efforts and make sure that where we can agree and be compatible, we will.

AT: Is there any attempt to solicit and take account of criticisms of the existing standard, including the identification of factual, logical, and typographic errors in the text? For example, there are contradictions in the existing standard about the meaning of compound and complex. Sources could include those who teach courses in Thesaurus Design and Construction, practitioners, consultants, and also published reviews.

AJW: Although this is called a revision, it is really a massive overhaul of the last edition. We really are starting from scratch, and therefore the errors and discrepancies in the previous edition won't occur. We will make every attempt to be as consistent as possible in our own work, of course.

AT: How and why have the members of NISO's Thesaurus Development Team[2] been chosen? How far do they represent the information professions?

AJW: The committee was chosen with two basic factors in mind. First, we needed to make sure that agencies funding the project and members of the NISO voting board were represented. Second, we wanted to involve as many constituencies from the information professions as possible. We therefore have people from libraries, the abstracting and indexing industry, government, and industry. We also have people representing the Library and Information Science (LIS) point of view, as well as information architecture and usability.

AT: If someone was interested in becoming involved in the NISO standard-making process in the future, how might they take steps in this direction?

AJW: All they have to do is send me a message at awarner@lexonomy.com. I am very interested in getting as much feedback as I can.

AT: Are the members of the committees of prior standards being consulted in the revision or editing processes?

AJW: There has not been a concerted effort to involve these individuals. However, our effort has been publicized widely, and they are very welcome to provide feedback and advice.

SR: NISO has announced that this committee is its first to introduce "a new model for standards development"–that you have been engaged to draft the revision with support and guidance from an Advisory Team, in part to reduce the revision cycle to eighteen months. How does this model differ from past practice? How is the new model working so far?

AJW: As stated in a previous answer, this is really a massive overhaul of the previous edition of the standard. Substantively, then, it is really going to be very new. However, in order to shorten the time to get it out, we are retaining it as a new edition, which means that we can streamline the process and cut down on the amount of time it takes to get it to the profession. Specifically, we don't have to have approval for a new standard, which takes some time, since this is officially a revision. The process is working very well so far. The advisory group and I have agreed on the scope of the new revision, and we are working through revisions of the entire standard, meeting once a month via teleconference to review drafts and share insights.

SR: We understand that the current project to revise Z39.19 grew out of the recommendations of the Workshop on Electronic Thesauri[3] (Nov. 4-5, 1999). In the summary of the discussions of that workshop, concern was expressed that the term "thesauri" was too constricting. Your "Scope and Discussion Issues" document[4] suggests replacing the word 'thesauri' with 'controlled vocabularies' in the title of the revised standard. What does this change signify?

AJW: The term 'controlled vocabularies' is our working term, and we are prepared to change and/or broaden it if necessary. The important point is that the standard will retain recommendations and guidelines for thesauri in both print and online forms, but will also contain guidelines for other forms of vocabularies, in particular such Web vocabularies as controlled lists and navigations schemes (often called taxonomies).

AT: Will the new standard contain examples of the wide range of gathering techniques, structures, displays that exist or are possible? Or might these be shown in a separate companion work?

AJW: There are plans to incorporate as wide a set of examples as possible. These will come from all of the types of sources just described, not only thesauri, but also things like controlled lists and taxonomies.

AT: Is the standard to be accompanied or followed by some kind of manual, tutorial, or exercises with answers in order to provide a basis for self-instruction, seminars, short courses, or elective courses in LIS?

AJW: I have had some discussion with NISO about offering tutorials and workshops associated with the new revision, and I'm very interested in pursuing this idea. We have only just begun our discussion on this.

AT: Is an inexpensive shorter version to be prepared, which might serve for basic, introductory courses in Organization of Knowledge, Search Techniques (cf. concise AACR, abridged DDC, etc.)?

AJW: I have not been asked to provide a shorter version of the standard. However, this might be a useful component to include in a tutorial or workshop.

SR: In several places, the documentation alludes to this standard's changing audience and the need to revise this standard in order to make

it more accessible to communities beyond libraries and abstracting and indexing services. How is this being accomplished? Once completed, what plans are being made to reach this broader audience?

AJW: We are intending to continue to provide guidance that is relevant to libraries and abstracting and indexing services. We are also committed to providing guidance to all sorts of organizations working in the Web environment. This certainly includes private sector organizations, but we believe that these guidelines will also benefit libraries and abstracting and indexing industries because they are now working in the Web environment as well. To do this, we have representatives from the information architecture community in the Advisory Group. I also believe that one of the reasons I was selected as editor is because my original background is in LIS, and I am now working as an information architecture consultant.

AT: If the new standard is to be aimed at several categories of user, will there be specialized versions to suit each particular group? Or will there be alternative sections within the one publication?

AJW: The way the standard will work is to begin with a statement of scope, indicating what is covered and what is not. It will then address guidelines that are fundamental to all vocabulary types. Specific types of tools (e.g., taxonomies, thesauri) will be addressed in separate chapters.

AT: How are the various categories of user to be canvassed and consulted? Represented?

AJW: Near the beginning of our work, we posted a survey on the Web and got about 70 responses from people who represent a wide variety of information professions. Again, we also have representatives from all user groups on our advisory group.

AT: Will the standard and any dependent documents be issued in various forms? Be available online? Free?

AJW: The previous standard was in both electronic (Web downloadable) and print format. It was also freely downloadable in PDF. I haven't had specific conversations with NISO on formats and availability. We have agreed, however, that our intent is to make this as available to the information professions as possible, and that would suggest that as few barriers to obtaining it will be in place as possible.

NOTES

1. A brief biography for Dr. Warner is available at http://www.lexonomy.com/biography/.
2. A description of the project and a list of the team members are available at http://www.niso.org/committees/MT-info.html.
3. http://www.niso.org/news/events_workshops/thes99rprt.html.
4. http://www.niso.org/committees/TRAG/TRAG_Scopedisc19.pdf.

Index

AAT (Art & Architecture Thesaurus), 5-6, 91-92,95-96
Acceptance criteria, 167
Addition and gap closure determinations, 41-42
ADL Thesaurus Protocol, 130-133, 135-142
AI (artificial intelligence) devices, 161
Aitchison, J., 5-21
Alphabetic index creation, 43-44
Alphabetical presentation development, 9-10,44-45
Amendments (draft), 82
American Institute of Chemical Engineers, 7,90
ANSI/NISO standards
    Z39.19, 9,17,90-91,104
    Z39.50, 141
Approaches (construction), 64-67
AQUARELLE/HEREIN project, 188
ARIST (Annual Review of Information Science and Technology), 92-93
ASI (American Society of Indexers), 25,31
ASIS Thesaurus of Information Science and Librarianship, 104
Assessment- and evaluation-related issues
    evaluation methods, 93-99
        AAT (Art & Architecture Thesaurus) and, 91-92,95-96
        comparative methods, 95-99
        formative methods, 94-95
        forms for, 97-99
        LCTGM (Library of Congress Thesaurus for Graphic Materials) and, 95-96
        mapping methods, 97-99
        observational reports, 95-98
        overviews of, 93-95
        Ruan, L. and, 97-99
        task outlines for, 96
        Thesaurus of ERIC Descriptors and, 88-89,91-92,94
        usability studies and, 94-95
    future perspectives of, 99
    historical perspectives of, 88-93
        ARIST (Annual Review of Information Science and Technology) and, 92-93
        Chemical Engineering Thesaurus (American Institute of Chemical Engineers) and, 90
        DDC (Dewey Decimal Classification) and, 91-92
        E.I. DuPont de Nemours (Engineering Information Center) and, 89-90
        Guidelines for the Construction, Format, and Management of Monolingual Thesauri, 90-91
        LCC (Library of Congress Classification) and, 91-92
        LCSH (Library of Congress Subject Headings) and, 91-94
        MeSH (Medical Subject Headings) and, 91-92
        MultiTes (software program) and, 92
        overviews of, 88-93
        PRECIS (Preferred Context Information System) and, 94
        Report on the Workshop on Electronic Thesauri (NISO) and, 91
        TEST (Thesaurus of Engineering and Scientific Terms) and, 89

Thesaurus of ASTIA Descriptors
(Department of Defense) and,
88-89
TRT (Transportation Research Thesaurus) and, 91-92
Vocabulary Control for Information Retrieval
(Lancaster, F. W.) and, 90
Willpower Information and, 91
overviews of, 87-89,103
reference resources for, 99-102
Authority control issues, 182-184
Automated software, 162-163
Automatic construction, 72-74

Batty, J., 13
Bibliographic essays. *See also* Reference resources
concept-related issues, 58-62,67-72
formation and definition, 68-69
goals, objectives, and focus, 58-62
organization, 70-72
term and concept collections, 67-68
construction-related issues, 62-67, 72-74
approaches, 64-67
automatic construction, 72-74
processes, 62-64
future perspectives of, 74
IR (information retrieval) issues, 58-62
overviews of, 1-3,57-58
Bliss Bibliographic Classification, 12,29
BnF (Bibliothèque nationale de France), 180
Boolean query generators, 151-153
Broad term/facet grouping, 39-40
Browsing functionality extensions, 134-140
BS (British Standard) guidelines
5723, 9,17
6723, 9,17
BSI (British Standards Institute), 17
BSI ROOT Thesaurus, 11-12
Bundled software, 164

CARMEN project, 188
CENL (Conference of European Libraries), 179-180
Chemical Engineering Thesaurus (American Institute of Chemical Engineers), 7,90
Chompsky, N., 27
Clarke, S. D., 5-21
Classification system-thesaurus connections, 27-29
Classified and systematic approaches, 10-12
Coates, E., 11
Collections (terms and concepts), 67-68
Comparative evaluation methods, 95-99
Compilation work, 80-82
Computer-aided construction, 12-13
Concept-related issues
concept formations and definitions, 68-69
formation and definition, 68-69
goals, objectives, and focus, 58-62
organization, 70-72
term and concept collections, 67-68
Construction Industry Thesaurus, 12
Construction-related issues
approaches, 64-67
automatic construction, 72-74
processes, 62-64
Consultant roles
compilation work, 80-82
development, 82
draft amendments, 82
maintenance, 82
overviews of, 80
reviews, 82
scope definitions, 81
starting point determinations, 81
style definitions, 81
thesaurus building, 81-82
contracts and, 80
cost-related issues of, 82-83
decision-making issues of, 78
definition of, 76
future perspectives of, 84

overviews of, 1-3, 75-76
positive aspects of, 77-78
project scopes and, 79
Ranganathan, S. R. and, 76
reference resources for, 84-85
selection-related issues of, 78-79
software and, 83-84
   Flamenco, 84
   overviews of, 83-84
   Waypoint, 84
Contract-related issues, 80
Copernic search applications, 127-128
Cost-related issues, 82-83
Craven, T., 25,32
CRG (Classification Research Group), 11
CSH (Canadian Subject Headings), 178-179

DARPA Unfamiliar Metadata, 107
Data integrity criteria, 168
DDB (Deutsche Bibliothek), 180
DDC (Dewey Decimal Classification), 29,91-92,163
Decision-making issues, 78
Dedicated software, 162
Department of Defense, 7,88-89
Development work, 82
Discovery-related issues, 141-142
Distributed web services
   DNS (Domain Name Service) and, 122-123
   future perspectives of, 152
   historical perspectives of, 122-126
   HTML-based services, 121-153
   online thesaurus services and, 128-150
      ADL Thesaurus Protocol and, 130-133,135-142
      browsing functionality extensions for, 134-140
      INSPEC Thesaurus and, 137-138,141-142,144-150
      KWIC (keyword-in-context) functions and, 129-130, 135-140,142-143

LCC (Library of Congress Classification) and, 129-130
LCSH (Library of Congress Subject Headings) and, 129-130
MeSH (Medical Subject Headings) and, 129-130, 141-142
multiple thesaurus access and, 142-150
overviews of, 128-129
standard uses and discovery, 141-142
UDC (Universal Decimal Classification) and, 129-130
UDDI (Universal Description, Discovery and Integration) and, 141-142,144-150
XSL (eXtensible Stylesheet Language) and, 130-134
XSLT (eXtensible Stylesheet Language Transformations) and, 130-134
Z39.50 and, 141
overviews of, 1-3,121-122
reference resources for, 153
Thesauro-Web concept, 121-153
thesaurus-enhanced applications and, 150-153
   Boolean query generators, 151-153
   overviews of, 150-151
   vocabulary extractors, 151-153
Web portals and, 122-128
   Copernic search applications, 127-128
   Google, 122
   GUI (graphical user interface) elements, 127-128
   overviews of, 122-126
   PageRank algorithm (Page, L.), 122
   problems of, 123-126
   user interaction issues of, 126-128
   Yahoo!, 123,126
XML (eXtensible Mark-up Language)-based services, 121-153

DNS (Domain Name Service), 122-123
Draft amendments, 82

E.I. DuPont de Nemours (Engineering Information Center), 89-90
Empirical query-expansion studies, 103-120
End-user access, 13-14
End-user warrant, 106-107
Engineers Joint Council, 5-10
Enhanced applications, 150-153
ERIC (Thesaurus of ERIC Descriptors), 88-89,91-92,94,104
Evaluations, 87-102. *See also* Assessment- and evaluation-related issues
Extensibility criteria, 169
Extractors (vocabulary), 151-153

Facet analyses, 10-12
Facet grouping, 39-40
Flamenco (software), 84
Focus (concepts), 58-62
Formation and definition (concepts), 68-69
Formative evaluation methods, 94-95
Forms (evaluations), 97-99
Foskett, D. J., 11
Functionality extensions (browsing), 134-140
Future perspectives
    of assessment- and evaluation-related issues, 99
    of bibliographic essays, 74
    of consultant roles, 84
    of distributed web services, 152
    of information retrieval thesauri, 117-118
    of key issues, 74
    of multilingual subject access, 188
    of nine-stage procedures, 46
    of NISO (National Information Standards Organization), 197
    of self-instruction procedures, 32-33
    of user comprehension and search techniques, 117-118
    of vocabulary management software, 170

Gap closure determinations, 41-42
Generators (Boolean query), 151-153
Gilchrist, A., 6
Global Village Library concept, 178-179,188-189
Goals, objectives, and focus (concepts), 58-62
Google, 122
Greenberg, J., 103-120
Grouping (broad term/facet), 39-40
GUI (graphical user interface) elements, 127-128
Guidelines for the Construction, Format, and Management of Monolingual Thesauri, 90-91,104
Guidelines for the Establishment of Multilingual Thesauri, 8-9,17

Heading language growth, 182-184
Historical perspectives
    AAT (Art & Architecture Thesaurus), 5-6
    of alphabetical approaches, 9-10
    Macrothesaurus (Viet, J.), 9-10
    MeSH (Medical Subject Headings), 10
    overviews of, 9-10
    of assessment- and evaluation-related issues, 88-93
    bibliographic essays about, 54-74. *See also* Bibliographic essays
    of classified and systematic approaches, 10-12
    Bliss Bibliographic Classification, 12
    BSI ROOT Thesaurus, 11-12

Coates, E. and, 11
Construction Industry Thesaurus, 12
CRG (Classification Research Group) and, 11
facet analyses, 10-12
Foskett, D. J. and, 11
International Thesaurus of Refugee Terms, 11-12
Mills, J. and, 11
overviews of, 10-12
Ranganathan, S. R. and, 10-11
Thesaurofacet, 5-6,11-12
Thesaurus Construction and Use, 12
UNESCO Thesaurus, 11-12
Vickery, B. C. and, 11
of computer-aided construction, 12-13
overviews of, 12-13
Transportation Research Thesaurus (Batty, J.), 13
of distributed web services, 122-126
early history, 6-8
Chemical Engineering Thesaurus (American Institute of Chemical Engineers) and, 7
overviews of, 6-8
Shorter Oxford Dictionary and, 6
TEST (Thesaurus of Engineering and Scientific Terms) and, 5-10
Thesaurus in Retrieval (Gilchrist, A.) and, 6
Thesaurus of ASTIA Descriptors (Department of Defense) and, 7
Thesaurus of Engineering Terms (Engineers Joint Council), 7-8
Thesaurus of English Words and Phrases (Roget, P. M.) and, 6
Uniterm System and, 7
of end-user access, 13-14
future perspectives and, 18
of information retrieval thesauri, 106-107
of interoperability-related issues, 16-17

of intuitive vocabularies, 14-16
ontology, 16
overviews of, 14
Semantic Web and, 15-17
synonym sets and preferred terms, 15-16
taxonomies, 14-15
Yahoo! and, 14
of multilingual subject access, 179-180
overviews of, 1-3,5-6
reference resources for, 18-21
of standards, 8-9,17
BS (British Standard) 5723, 9,17
BS (British Standard) 6723, 9,17
BSI (British Standards Institute) and, 17
ISO 2788, 6,8-9,17
ISO 5964, 8-9,17
PRECIS (Preferred Context Information System) and, 8-9
UNESCO Guidelines for the Establishment and Development of Monolingual Thesauri, 8
Z39.19, 9,17
of user comprehension and search techniques, 106-107
Homograph determinations, 37-39
HTML-based services, 121-153

Information retrieval thesauri
empirical query-expansion studies of, 103-120
data analyses for, 109-116
methods for, 108
overviews of, 103-107
procedures for, 108-109
research questions for, 108
future perspectives of, 117-118
historical perspectives of, 106-107
overviews of, 103-105
ProQuest Controlled Vocabulary and, 103-120
reference resources for, 118-119
user comprehension and searching strategies for, 103-120

INSPEC Thesaurus, 137-138,141-142,
    144-150
Interaction issues, 126-128
Interface design research, 106
INTERMARC, 183-184
International Thesaurus of Refugee
    Terms, 11-12
Interoperability-related issues, 16-17
Introductory-related materials, 24-26
Intuitive vocabularies, 14-16
IR (information retrieval), 58-62
ISO standards
    2788, 6,8-9,17
    5964, 8-9,17,186
ISPEC Thesaurus, 137-138,141-142,
    144-150

Johnson, E. H., 121-153

Key issues
    concept-related issues, 58-62,67-72
        concept formations and
            definitions, 68-69
        concept organization, 70-72
        goals, objectives, and focus, 58-62
        term and concept collections,
            67-68
    construction-related issues, 62-67,
        72-74
        approaches, 64-67
        automatic construction, 72-74
        processes, 62-64
    future perspectives of, 74
    IR (information retrieval) issues, 58-62
    overviews of, 1-3,57-58
    reference resources for, 57-74. *See*
        also Reference resources
KWIC (keyword-in-context) functions,
    129-130,135-140,142-143

Lancaster, F. W., 90
Landry, P., 177-191

Language growth, 182-184
LCC (Library of Congress Classification),
    29,91-92,129-130
LCSH (Library of Congress Subject
    Headings), 29,91-94,129-130,
    177-191
LCTGM (Library of Congress Thesaurus
    for Graphic Materials), 95-96
Least effort principle, 106-107
Lexico (software), 172-176
Library warrant concept, 104-105
Linking approaches, 184-188

Macrothesaurus (Viet, J.), 9-10
MACS (Multilingual access to subjects)
    project, 177-191
Mapping methods, 97-99
MARC, 182-183
MARC 21, 183-186
MeSH (Medical Subject Headings), 10,
    91-92,129-130,141-142
Metadata, 107
Mills, J., 11
MULIS (Multilingual Subject Authority
    File) project, 182
Multilingual subject access
    BnF (Bibliothèque nationale de
        France) and, 180
    CENL (Conference of European
        Libraries) and, 179-180
    DDB (Deutsche Bibliothek) and,
        180
    future perspectives of, 188
    Global Village Library concept and,
        178-179,188-189
    MACS (Multilingual access to
        subjects) project, 177-191
    AQUARELLE/HEREIN project,
        188
    authority control and, 182-184
    CARMEN project and, 188
    CSH (Canadian Subject
        Headings) and, 178-179
    European cooperation, 180-182

historical perspectives of, 179-180
INTERMARC and, 183-186
ISO 5964 and, 186
LCSH (Library of Congress Subject Headings) and, 177-191
linking approach of, 184-188
MARC 21 and, 183-186
MARC and, 182-183
overviews of, 177-179
RAMEAU (Répertoire d'Autorité-Matière Encyclopédique et Alphabertique Unifié) and, 177-191
RVM (Répertoire de vedettes-matière) and, 178-179, 183
subject heading language growth and, 182-184
SWD/RSWK *(Schlagwortnormdatei/Regeln für den Schlagwortkatalog)* and, 177-191
UDC (Universal Decimal Classification) and, 181-182
UNIMARC and, 182-183
MULIS (Multilingual Subject Authority File) project and, 182
overviews of, 1-3,177-179
reference resources for, 189-191
SNL (Swiss National Library) and, 180
Multiple thesaurus access, 142-150
MultiTes (software), 25-26,32,92
Multiuser software, 164

Nielsen, M. L., 57-74
Nine-stage procedures
diagrams of, 36
exercises for, 37,39-45,47-56
descriptions, 37,39-45
solutions, 47-56
future perspectives of, 46

overviews of, 1-3,35-36
reference resources for, 46
stages, 37-45
stage 1 (raw term collection), 37
stage 2 (synonym linkages and homograph determinations), 37-39
stage 3 (broad term/facet grouping), 39-40
stage 4 (facet and sub-facet ordering), 40-41
stage 5 (term addition and gap closure determinations), 41-42
stage 6 (notation determinations), 42-43
stage 7 (relationship identification), 43
stage 8 (alphabetic index creation), 43-44
stage 9 (alphabetical presentation development), 44-45
NISO (National Information Standards Organization) standards
definitions of, 193-194
future perspectives of, 197
overviews of, 103,193
reference resources for, 198
Report on the Workshop of Electronic Thesauri, 91
revision processes, 195-198
Warner, A. J. (interviews), 193-198
Z39.19, 9,17,90-91,104
Z39.50, 141
Notation determinations, 42-43

Observational evaluation reports, 95-98
ODLIS (Online Dictionary of Library and Information Science), 159-162
Online thesaurus services, 128-140
Ontology concept, 16
Organization (concepts), 70-72
Owens, L. A., 87-102

Page, L., 122
PageRank algorithm, 122
Portals (Web), 122-128
PRECIS (Preferred Context Information System), 8-9,26-27,29-30,94
Preferred terms and synonym sets, 15-16
Presentation development, 44-45
Processes (construction), 62-64
ProQuest Controlled Vocabulary, 103-120

Query-expansion studies, 103-120
Query generators (Boolean), 151-153

RAMEAU (Répertoire d'Autorité-Matière Encyclopédique et Alphabertique Unifié), 177-191
Ranganathan, S. R., 10-11,76
Raw term collection, 37
Reference resources
   for assessment- and evaluation-related issues, 99-102
   for consultant roles, 84-85
   for distributed web services, 153
   for historical perspectives, 18-21
   for information retrieval thesauri, 118-119
   for key issues, 57-74
   for multilingual subject access, 189-191
   for nine-stage procedures, 46
   NISO (National Information Standards Organization) standards, 198
   for self-instruction procedures, 33
   thesaurus construction (general), 3
   for user comprehension and search techniques, 118-119
   for vocabulary management software, 170-171
Report on the Workshop on Electronic Thesauri (NISO), 91
Review-related issues, 30-31
Riesland, M. A., 155-176
Roe, S. K., 1-3,193-198
Roget, P. M., 6,104-105
Ruan, L., 97-99

Scope definitions, 81
Selection-related issues, 78-79
Self-instruction procedures
   ASI (American Society of Indexers) and, 25,31
   Chompsky, N. and, 27
   classification system-thesaurus connections, 27-29
      Bliss Bibliographic Classification and, 29
      DDC (Dewey Decimal Classification) and, 29
      LCC (Library of Congress Classification) and, 29
      LCSH (Library of Congress Subject Headings) and, 29
      overviews of, 27-29
      UDC (Universal Decimal Classification) and, 29
   exercises for, 29-30,32-33
   future perspectives of, 32-33
   introductory-related materials, 24-26
   knowledge and skill requirements, 26-27
   overviews of, 1-3,23-24
   PRECIS (Preferred Context Information System) and, 26-27,29-30
   reference resources for, 33
   review-related issues, 30-31
   software and, 25-26,32
      MultiTes, 25-26,32
      STRIDE, 25-26,32
      TermTree 2000, 25-26,32
      W32, 32
   Thesaurus Construction (Craven, T.) and, 25,32

thesaurus definitions, 24-25
    user preference considerations, 31
Semantic Web, 14-17
Semi-automated software, 162-163
Shearer, J. R., 35-56
Shorter Oxford Dictionary, 6
Single-user software, 164
SNL (Swiss National Library), 180
Software
    Flamenco, 84
    Lexico, 172-176
    MultiTes, 25-26,32,92
    overviews of, 83-84
    STRIDE, 25-26,32
    Synaptica, 172-176
    TermChoir, 172-176
    TermTree 2000, 25-26,32,172-176
    vocabulary management software, 155-176. *See also* Vocabulary management software
    W32, 32
    Waypoint, 84
Stand-alone software, 164
Standards, 8-9,17,193-194
Starting point determinations, 81
STRIDE (software), 25-26,32
Style definitions, 81
Subject heading language growth, 182-184
SWD/RSWK
    (Schlagwortnormdatei/Regeln für den Schlagwortkatalog), 177-191
Synaptica (software), 172-176
Synonyms
    linkages and homograph determinations, 37-39
    sets and preferred terms, 15-16
Systematic and classified approaches, 10-12

Task outlines (evaluations), 96
Taxonomies, 14-15
Term addition and gap closure determinations, 41-42

Term and concept collections, 67-68
TermChoir (software), 172-176
TermTree 2000 (software), 25-26,32, 172-176
TEST *(Thesaurus of Engineering and Scientific Terms),* 5-10,89
Thesauri-consultants, 75-85. *See also* Consultant roles
Thesauro-Web concept, 121-153
Thesaurofacet, 5-6,11-12
Thesaurus construction. *See also under individual topics*
    assessment- and evaluation-realted issues of, 87-102
    bibliographic essays about, 57-74
    consultant roles for, 75-85
    distributed web services and, 103-120
    historical perspectives of, 5-21
    key issues about, 57-74
    multilingual subject access and, 177-191
    NISO (National Information Standards Organization) standards for, 193-198
    overviews of, 1-3
    procedures for, 23-33,35-56
        nine-stage procedures, 35-56
        self-instruction procedures, 23-33
    reference resources for. *See* Reference resources
    self-instruction procedures for, 23-33
    user comprehension and search techniques for, 103-120
    vocabulary management software for, 155-176
Thesaurus Construction and Use, 12
Thesaurus Construction (Craven, T.), 25,32
Thesaurus-enhanced applications, 150-153
Thesaurus in Retrieval (Gilchrist, A.), 6
Thesaurus of ASTIA Descriptors (Department of Defense), 7,88-89
Thesaurus of Engineering Terms (Engineers Joint Council), 7-8

Thesaurus of English Words and Phrases
(Roget, P. M.), 6,104-105
Thesaurus of ERIC Descriptors, 88-89, 91-92,94,104
Thomas, A. R., 1-3,23-33,193-198
Transportation Research Thesaurus
(Batty, J.), 13
TRT (Transportation Research Thesaurus), 91-92

UDC (Universal Decimal Classification), 29,129-130,181-182
UDDI (Universal Description, Discovery and Integration), 141-142,144-150
UNESCO Guidelines for the Establishment and Development of Monolingual Thesauri, 8
UNESCO Thesaurus, 11-12
UNIMARC, 182-183
Uniterm System, 7
Usability studies, 94-95
User comprehension and search techniques
 ASIS Thesaurus of Information Science and Librarianship and, 104
 empirical query-expansion studies, 103-120
 DARPA Unfamiliar Metadata and, 107
 data analyses for, 109-116
 interface design research and, 106
 least effort principle and, 106-107
 methods for, 108
 overviews of, 103-106
 participant-related data for, 110-113
 preferred processing methods and, 115-116
 procedures for, 108-109
 research questions of, 108
 summary of, 107
 term selection tests for, 120
 user definitions, 105

 end-user warrant and, 106-107
 future perspectives of, 117-118
 historical perspectives of, 106-107
 for information retrieval thesauri, 103-105
 definition of, 104
 overviews of, 103
 standards and, 104-105
 library warrant concept and, 104-105
 overviews of, 1-3,103-105
 ProQuest Controlled Vocabulary and, 103-120
 reference resources for, 118-119
 Thesaurus of English Words and Phrases (Roget, P. M.) and, 104-105
 Thesaurus of ERIC Descriptors and, 104
 Z39.19 and, 104
User interaction issues, 126-128

Vickery, B. C., 11
Viet, J., 9-10
Vocabularies (intuitive), 14-16
Vocabulary Control for Information Retrieval (Lancaster, F. W.), 90
Vocabulary extractors, 151-153
Vocabulary management software
 DDC (Dewey Decimal Classification) and, 163
 future perspectives of, 170
 overviews of, 1-3,155-157
 product and feature comparisons of, 169,172-176
  Lexico, 172-176
  listings of, 169
  overviews of, 169
  Synaptica, 172-176
  TermChoir, 172-176
  TermTree 2000, 172-176
 reference resources for, 170-171
 selection criteria for, 164-169
  acceptance, 167
  customer service, 167

data integrity, 168
documentation, 167
editing capabilities, 168
exporting capabilities, 168-169
extensibility, 169
importing capabilities, 168-169
licensing, 166
overviews of, 164-165
pricing, 166
reporting capabilities, 168-169
structural-related criteria, 168
support, 167
task-related requirements, 165
technical specifications, 165-166
user experiences, 167
versioning and updates, 166
terminology for, 157-162
    AI (artificial intelligence) devices, 161
    classification, 157
    controlled vocabularies, 158
    notation, 158
    ODLIS (Online Dictionary of Library and Information Science) and, 159-162
    overviews of, 157
    relationship types, 158-159
    structural types, 159-162
types of, 162-164
    automated software, 162-163
    bundled software, 164
    dedicated software, 162
    multiuser software, 164
    overviews of, 162
    semi-automated software, 162-163
    single-user software, 164
    stand-alone software, 164

W32 (Craven, T.), 32
Warner, A. J. (interviews), 193-198
Waypoint (software), 84
Web portals, 122-128
Web services (distributed), 121-153. *See also* Distributed web services
Will, L., 75-85

XML (eXtensible Mark-up Language)-based services, 121-153
XSL (eXtensible Stylesheet Language), 130-134
XSLT (eXtensible Stylesheet Language Transformations), 130-134

Yahoo!, 14,123,126

Z39.19, 9,17,90-91,104,196
Z39.50, 141

SPECIAL 25%-OFF DISCOUNT!

Order a copy of this book with this form or online at:
http://www.haworthpress.com/store/product.asp?sku=5134
Use Sale Code BOF25 in the online bookshop to receive 25% off!

The Thesaurus
Review, Renaissance, and Revision

___ in softbound at $14.96 (regularly $19.95) (ISBN: 0-7890-1979-5)
___ in hardbound at $29.96 (regularly $39.95) (ISBN: 0-7890-1978-7)

COST OF BOOKS _____	❏ BILL ME LATER:
Outside USA/ Canada/ Mexico: Add 20%. _____	Bill-me option is good on US/Canada/ Mexico orders only; not good to jobbers, wholesalers, or subscription agencies.
POSTAGE & HANDLING _____	
US: $4.00 for first book & $1.50 for each additional book	❏ Signature _____
Outside US: $5.00 for first book & $2.00 for each additional book.	❏ Payment Enclosed: $ _____
	❏ PLEASE CHARGE TO MY CREDIT CARD:
SUBTOTAL _____	❏ Visa ❏ MasterCard ❏ AmEx ❏ Discover
In Canada: add 7% GST. _____	❏ Diner's Club ❏ Eurocard ❏ JCB
STATE TAX _____	Account # _____
CA, IL, IN, MN, NY, OH, & SD residents please add appropriate local sales tax.	Exp Date _____
FINAL TOTAL _____	Signature _____
If paying in Canadian funds, convert using the current exchange rate. UNESCO coupons welcome.	*(Prices in US dollars and subject to change without notice.)*

PLEASE PRINT ALL INFORMATION OR ATTACH YOUR BUSINESS CARD

Name

Address

City   State/Province   Zip/Postal Code

Country

Tel   Fax

E-Mail

May we use your e-mail address for confirmations and other types of information? ❏Yes ❏No We appreciate receiving your e-mail address. Haworth would like to e-mail special discount offers to you, as a preferred customer. **We will never share, rent, or exchange your e-mail address.** We regard such actions as an invasion of your privacy.

Order From Your Local Bookstore or Directly From
The Haworth Press, Inc.
10 Alice Street, Binghamton, New York 13904-1580 • USA
Call Our toll-free number (1-800-429-6784) / Outside US/Canada: (607) 722-5857
Fax: 1-800-895-0582 / Outside US/Canada: (607) 771-0012
E-Mail your order to us: Orders@haworthpress.com

Please Photocopy this form for your personal use.
www.HaworthPress.com

BOF04